Japanese War Crimes during World War II

Atrocity and the Psychology of Collective Violence

Frank Jacob

An Imprint of ABC-CLIO, LLC
Santa Barbara, California • Denver, Colorado

Copyright © 2018 by Frank Jacob

All rights reserved. No part of this publication may be reproduced, stored in a retrieval system, or transmitted, in any form or by any means, electronic, mechanical, photocopying, recording, or otherwise, except for the inclusion of brief quotations in a review, without prior permission in writing from the publisher.

Library of Congress Cataloging-in-Publication Data

Names: Jacob, Frank, author.
Title: Japanese war crimes during World War II : atrocity and the psychology of collective violence / Frank Jacob.
Description: Santa Barbara, California : Praeger, 2018. | Includes bibliographical references and index.
Identifiers: LCCN 2018005505 (print) | LCCN 2018019849 (ebook) | ISBN 9781440844508 (ebook) | ISBN 9781440844492 (hardcopy)
Subjects: LCSH: War crimes—Japan—History—20th century. | World War, 1939–1945—Atrocities—Asia. | Sino-Japanese War, 1937–1945—Atrocities. | Japan—Armed Forces—History—20th century. | Collective behavior—Case studies. | War—Moral and ethical aspects—Case studies.
Classification: LCC D804.J3 (ebook) | LCC D804.J3 J33 2018 (print) | DDC 940.54/050952—dc23
LC record available at https://lccn.loc.gov/2018005505

ISBN: 978-1-4408-4449-2 (print)
    978-1-4408-4450-8 (ebook)

22 21 20 19 18   1 2 3 4 5

This book is also available as an eBook.

Praeger
An Imprint of ABC-CLIO, LLC

ABC-CLIO, LLC
130 Cremona Drive, P.O. Box 1911
Santa Barbara, California 93116-1911
www.abc-clio.com

This book is printed on acid-free paper ∞

Manufactured in the United States of America

Contents

	Introduction	1
Chapter 1	On Violence and Perpetrators	14
Chapter 2	The Rape of Nanjing	38
Chapter 3	Rape: A Theoretical Analysis	56
Chapter 4	The Comfort Women System	67
Chapter 5	The Bataan Death March	94
Chapter 6	POWs of the Japanese	109
Chapter 7	Unit 731	132
	Conclusion	145
Notes		149
Works Cited		189
Index		211

Introduction

The late Iris Chang (1968–2004) wrote an important book, yet not a good one.[1] Like others who followed her example, she used the term "Asian Holocaust"[2] and thereby tried to highlight the events related to the so-called "Rape of Nanjing" or "Nanjing Massacre" in which soldiers of the Japanese Imperial Army raped, tortured, and murdered Chinese civilians in the Chinese city of Nanjing in 1937 and 1938. The history and knowledge of these events, as Gayle K. Sato correctly remarked, "did not figure prominently in Asian American war memory."[3] Although a comparison with the historical dimensions of the Holocaust is rather inappropriate,[4] Chang and later authors chose to bring greater attention to the topic. However, in pursuit of gaining this attention, Chang delivered what can be called a "controversial international bestseller"[5] that was more Japan bashing than a provision of profound discussion about why violence erupted in Nanjing.[6] The narrative served the victims and their families, who still directed their anger toward Japan as the enemy, but it did not allow readers to understand why the event occurred[7]; why these people became victims of the Japanese soldiers' violence was not explained. The Japanese were claimed to be evil by nature, incapable of sympathy toward their victims and therefore deemed not as equals, but rather as dangerous enemies. Chang was correct when she claimed that "even by the standards of history's most destructive war, the Rape of Nanking represents one of the worst instances of mass extermination."[8] On the other hand, however, she would "condemn all Japanese people for not acknowledging the facts, even if there are parts of the modern Japanese society that do understand the meaning of the Rape of Nanking and recognize it as a Japanese war crime."[9]

Nanjing was not Auschwitz. However, Jürgen Habermas emphasized that "Auschwitz has changed the basis for the continuity of the conditions of life within history,"[10] and this also applies to the victims of Nanjing who endured rape and torture in China under Japanese rule. Regardless of this fact, it would not serve the Chinese survivors well to compare their own history with that of the Holocaust survivors. It does not matter if the lives shattered by war number in the thousands or in the millions—every single one deserves to be remembered, and human deaths should not become meaningless simply because more people had been killed elsewhere. Although Saul Friedländer argued that the Holocaust must be understood in its contemporary and geographical context,[11] the same should be done with the atrocities against the Chinese, the Koreans, and many others in East and Southeast Asia under Japanese rule.[12] The events of Nanjing had nearly been forgotten (especially when civil war struck China), but it is now the basis of the antipathy between the People's Republic of China and Japan, who are incapable of "fruitful or even civil dialogue" but instead possess "venom now flow[ing] at peak levels" for one another.[13] While the Nanjing Mausoleum is "for the Chinese what Yad Vashem is for Israelis and Jews worldwide," the Chinese people are particularly angry about the lack of the Japanese people's courtesy to apologize for the Imperial Japanese Army's war crimes, especially because Prince Asaka Yasuhiko (1887–1981), an uncle of the Shōwa Emperor and commander of the Shanghai Expeditionary Force, had been directly involved in the events related to the Rape of Nanjing.[14]

Although Chang was partially right regarding the Japanese denial faction, which continues to doubt the legitimacy of the anti-Japanese claims,[15] other Japanese journalists and scholars have done important work to uncover the crimes of the Imperial Japanese Army during the Second Sino-Japanese War (1937–1945) and the Pacific War (1941–1945).[16] Yet further discussion beyond Asia was definitely stimulated by Iris Chang's work, which is why her impact on the development of research on Japanese war crimes in general and the Rape of Nanjing in particular can be considered crucial. Yamamoto Masahiro's *Nanking: Anatomy of an Atrocity* (2000)[17] answered questions and addressed the need for the discussion that had been initiated by Chang in 1997. Further studies in other parts of Asia added to the history of Japanese war crimes from specific national perspectives.[18] New documents were also found over the years that helped reconstruct some of the atrocities and massacres committed by the Japanese Imperial Army, whose soldiers had, to name just one example, been ordered to execute thousands of unarmed Chinese soldiers during the war.[19]

Naturally, one would argue that such acts are war crimes. However, to quote historian Daqing Yang, "what is considered a war crime—a prosecutable war crime, in particular—is as much a political issue as a legal one."[20] For many years, the American public was not concerned about the crimes committed by Japanese soldiers between 1931 and 1945 in the Pacific theater and in parts of China. Whereas crimes against U.S. prisoners of war (POWs) were widely acknowledged in memoirs and in stories by survivors, the fate of Asian victims was of no interest to the U.S. public. When the 1990s saw a revival of interest in the crimes committed by the Japanese soldiers in the name of the early Shōwa Empire (1926–1945), it became obvious that many war criminals

Introduction 3

had not been punished—instead, they continued to live life uncontested by criminal investigations in postwar Japan.[21] Even three postwar prime ministers, Hatoyama Ichirō (1883–1959), Ikeda Hayato (1899–1965), and Kishi Nobusuke (1896–1987), were guilty of war crimes, and a Class A war criminal who had been convicted during the trials in Tokyo, Shigemitsu Mamoru (1887–1957), regained his position of foreign minister in 1954. The fact that these criminals, as well as Emperor Hirohito (1901–1989), were treated so favorably by the Supreme Commander of the Allied Powers (SCAP), General Douglas MacArthur (1880–1964),[22] explains the anger about the lack of interest that Chang expressed in her book. U.S. military historian Edward J. Drea emphasized that

> Chang's moving testament to the Chinese victims of the sack of Nanjing in 1937 graphically detailed the horror and scope of the crime and indicted the Japanese government and people for their collective amnesia about the wartime army's atrocious conduct. The bestselling book spurred a tremendous amount of renewed interest in Japanese wartime conduct in China, Korea, the Philippines, Southeast Asia, and the Pacific.[23]

It is also important to consider that the U.S. public had been informed about the atrocities in China early on when reports about the rape, killings, and executions of unarmed Chinese soldiers appeared in American newspapers and when returning missionaries and other eyewitnesses reported their experiences in the war zone.

However, the events faded away from public view, and something specific caused Japan's lack of interest in critically dealing with its own past; in contrast to Germany, whose authorities took responsibility to express guilt for its crimes against peace and humanity between 1933 and 1945, the Japanese government rejected and downplayed such a responsibility.[24] An official apology was never granted, and the history textbook controversy[25] and the non-depiction of war crimes at the Yasukuni Shrine museum in Tokyo[26] caused anger in Asia. If there were any official or nonofficial comments about the Japanese military's war crimes, they usually insisted that the numbers stated in the accusations were exaggerated. Deniers continue to have a strong lobby in Japan, and the government seems to have backed such voices thus far. The number of people actually brought to trial in Japan is also rather low; although 28 Class A war criminals had been brought to trial during the Tokyo War Crimes Tribunal between May 1946 and November 1948—to be accused of crimes against peace, war crimes, and crimes against humanity, eventually reaching 25 convictions—the imprisoned war criminals were released in 1956, and most of the Japanese perpetrators never saw the inside of a courtroom and continued their lives as if nothing had happened. There was never a large-scale prosecution of former war criminals in Japan, and too many went on to pursue careers in the political and economic sectors. However, the Allied

Powers held trials in 49 locations in Asia between October 1945 and April 1956. Britain prosecuted the Japanese war criminals who had been involved in planning and constructing the Thai-Burma Railway due to which many British POWs died, and Australian prosecutors tried Japanese war criminals at several locations as well. Dutch judges tried Japanese people who were responsible for war crimes in the Dutch East Indies during the war, and the Soviet Union brought former members of the Biological Warfare Unit 731 to trial at Khabarovsk in 1949.[27] In total, only 5,379 Japanese war criminals were tried, 4,300 of whom were convicted (almost 1,000 with death penalties).[28] Considering the number of atrocities committed by the Japanese Imperial Army between 1931 and 1945, far too few people were tried after the war, and the longer it took to arouse public interest in the crimes, the easier it was for those guilty of murder, rape, and torture to disappear forever to lead a normal life. Additionally, most of them got away because documents that could have proven their guilt were destroyed before U.S. forces could reach Japanese soil.

From when a ceasefire was announced on August 15, 1945, until August 28, 1945—when the first American troops arrived in Japan—the Japanese military and civil authorities invested a large amount of work in destroying compromising archival materials, especially those related to the war years between 1942 and 1945. Field units were ordered to burn materials that would have provided evidence of violence and torture against POWs, among other things. It is estimated that 70 percent of the existing sources were destroyed in these two weeks,[29] leaving behind a gap in history that can never be filled again and providing former war criminals with a chance to lead ordinary lives. Regardless of this intense purge of Japan's official documentation of the war, the U.S. military was still able to collect more than 350,000 documents related to the war and the crimes committed during it.[30] Although most historians today agree that the vast majority of the documents that could have incriminated more Japanese war criminals were destroyed due to orders from the military command during the aforementioned 13-day period,[31] the remaining ones provide a glimpse of the cruelties that dominated the war in the Pacific and Southeast Asia. Once the Allied Powers had concluded the trials, interest in Japanese war crimes faded quickly, as the Cold War demanded new allies in the region against the Soviet Union and the People's Republic of China. Because Japan became important again, the harsh prosecution of war criminals might have complicated the new alliance against communism.

In Japan itself, the situation remained dominated by right-wing powers. When in 1957 a group of returning veterans, who had spent years in a Chinese prison, published their own first-person accounts of war crimes[32] that had been committed in China during the war, it generated great interest. However, a reprint of the book, whose first edition sold out within three weeks,

Introduction

was prevented due to political pressure. It took almost four decades until historians actively began to do research related to the issue when the Japan Center for Research on War Responsibility (Nihon sensō sekinin shiryō senta) was established in 1993 and began to publish the quarterly journal *Research in War Responsibility* (Sensō sekinin kenkyū). In a way, this followed the lead of the Chinese Academy of Social Science, whose members had established a quarterly journal in *Studies of the War of Resistance against Japan* (Kang-Ri zhanzheng yanjiu) in 1991 that also often addressed the issue of Japanese war crimes. In the years that followed, Chinese Americans and Korean Americans played a vital role in arousing public interest in specific issues related to Japanese war crimes (e.g., the so-called comfort women issue).[33] Japan's biological warfare program, usually referred to as Unit 731, also caused interest and further research since the early 1990s when the first document collection related to the work of this unit was published in Japanese.[34]

Works published on Japanese war crimes usually tend to cover four specific areas[35]:

1. Japanese war crimes in general
2. Violence and torture against POWs and civilian work forces
3. The Japanese biological warfare program known as Unit 731
4. Forced prostitution and the so-called comfort women system

Single events, such as the massacre of 100,000 Filipinos during the Battle of Manila in early 1945, have also attracted interest.[36] However, the greatest number of English books was probably written on the treatment of Allied POWs, which were stimulated by the first-person eyewitness accounts by many American soldiers and sailors who had survived mistreatment in such prison camps. The issue naturally aroused public interest, especially since 27 percent of American and British POWs died in Japanese captivity, in contrast to the 4 percent death rate of POWs in German and Italian camps.[37] The event most familiar to American readers related to the mistreatment of U.S. POWs is the Bataan Death March, during which up to 2,000 American and up to 16,500 Filipino prisoners lost their lives after the surrender of Bataan on April 10, 1942.[38] Another POW-related case is the building of the Burma-Thailand Railway, which entered common memory through cinema and remained alive through the images in David Lean's film *The Bridge on the River Kwai* (1957). Thousands of POWs and Asian people who were forced to work on the railway died in the jungles of Burma and Thailand under the yelling and beating of their Japanese supervisors.[39] Many POWs (ca. 30,000) were also transported to Japan, where they were used as workers in mines and factories alike. To reach Japan, they had to cross the ocean on so-called "hell ships," which were unmarked and very often sunk by submarines under

Allied command who were unaware the ships carried their own troops. Ten percent of these POWs—3,526, to be exact—died before the war ended; they drowned at sea, starved, or were beaten to death while being exploited by Japanese companies.[40]

The treatment of POWs by the Japanese soldiers was extreme and surprising to many, because Japan was considered to have set an example of how to treat POWs, especially during the first conflicts of the 20th century such as the Russo-Japanese War (1904–1905) and the First World War (1914–1918).[41] Even harsher, however, was the treatment of Asian civilians who were also regularly exploited by Japanese troops. Estimations list up to half a million Southeast Asian people being mobilized for Japanese construction projects, due to which many of them died a horrible death amidst the whips and insults of the soldiers who supervised and mistreated them in the name of the emperor.[42] To name another example, Chinese laborers were also forced to work in Japan; nearly a quarter of them died by the end of the war.[43] Japanese officials, however, claim that these people were recruits who had voluntarily decided to serve in Japan. The same argument was used in addressing the claims of former sex slaves, the so-called "comfort women" who were forced into prostitution by the Japanese army. Although the list of war crimes could be continued here, the issue of comfort women shall be discussed briefly.[44]

American scholar Ustinia Dolgopol was right when she emphasized that "[t]he history of the comfort women is the story of voices being denied and suppressed,"[45] as for years nobody would follow the leads that would have demanded attention on the issue. When the first survivors testified, the Japanese government ignored the truth of their accounts. While the Japanese Embassy in South Korea has "acknowledged the comfort women issue and extended official apologies on many important occasions," the survivors themselves "reject such statements on the grounds that these gestures were short in both legitimacy and reparations."[46] The matter of a formal Japanese apology to former "comfort women" (*ianfu*) is a "hot-button issue in the Far East,"[47] regularly causing tension between China and Korea on one side and Japan on the other. The problem involves not only the issue of a formal apology, but is also affected by memory policies and nationalism within the three countries involved. When former comfort women testified before the U.S. Congress in 1996 demanding that the American government put pressure on Japan to acknowledge the Japanese army's responsibility in forcing young Korean and Chinese women into prostitution, the issue became global and has remained so ever since.[48] Of course, the fact that up to 200,000 women were forced to be prostitutes—being sexually abused, beaten, and even killed by Japanese soldiers—is an issue that causes tension, especially because Japan tends to neglect the matter without accepting guilt about its military plans to establish the comfort system since the early 1930s. Women and girls were

Introduction

"kidnapped, enslaved, tortured, and brutally raped,"[49] and if they survived, they were simply forgotten. Although Prime Minister Abe Shinzō expressed his sympathies and apologized for the situation these women were in, a formal apology that acknowledged Japan's responsibility is still lacking.[50] The prime minister even denied the coercion by the Japanese military in 2007. In his claims, as Hayashi Hirofumi remarked, he "was supported by more than a few politicians, and his opinion may be viewed as a reflection of the nationalistic atmosphere of Japanese society."[51] In fact, Abe leads a faction in Japanese politics that is interested in reversing the research done so far for the sake of reestablishing Japan's honor, which is why members of the group around the prime minister claim that "the Nanjing Massacre was fabricated, that comfort women were regular prostitutes rather than victims of war crimes, and that Japan did not act aggressively"[52] during the Second World War. Neo-nationalists like Katō Norihiro argue that the "distortions" that exist within Japan's postwar society make a sincere apology impossible.[53] He claimed that significant problems have been left out of the discussion in postwar Japan, especially the Japanese war dead. In addition to such revisionist arguments, those Japanese who were born after 1945 have to decide "what kind of opinions they should have about the wartime atrocities Japanese committed against other Asians."[54] To achieve such a decision, the research results related to Japanese war crimes would have to be broadly communicated within Japan's society, an approach that is regularly sabotaged by revisionist interest groups, and Japanese scholars who are truly interested in shedding light on the cruelties of the past are sometimes better known outside Japan than in their home country.

The situation is also complicated by the fact that the victim narrative is affected by existing nationalism in countries where survivors tend to be politically instrumentalized.[55] When the prosecution of Nazi crimes took place, the prosecutors were accused of being either too eager or too slack; the penalties were either too harsh or too soft.[56] Although the trials reflect a certain "good will,"[57] this sentiment seems to be lacking in Japan, where a war crime trial was never initiated without pressure from a foreign power. Moreover, the general population detests identifying with the perpetrators, so closely examining the past might cause people inconvenience and lead to unpleasant questions about one's individual or familial roles during those dark times.[58] Regarding such atrocities and war crimes, witnesses cannot adopt a neutral approach lest their accounts lose power; as with the Japanese, if there are no documents to back up their reports, witnesses themselves will be accused as liars.[59] Herein lies another problem: many of the perpetrators remain anonymous and will probably never be brought to justice. It thus seems more important to understand how it became possible for "ordinary men" to be so violent against women forced into sex slavery, POWs, and civilians.

First of all, violence is still present in modern societies even if we tend to believe that so-called postmodern nation-states have been able to overcome violence simply because war has not affected them in the last seven decades.[60] As Steven Pinker highlighted, violence is of interest to anyone who seeks to learn about human nature.[61] Although he also argues that we must take a closer look at the numbers to see if violence is increasing or decreasing, he makes it clear that all suffering, whether it affects one person or many, deserves our sympathy.[62] It consequently seems redundant to discuss numbers and dates; it is far more important to discuss violence itself, especially because the history of war is the history of organized violence meant to kill.[63] War itself is often considered a form of ordered, organized, and collective violence that re-establishes a space-time continuum and creates a struggle for its control.[64] Within a specific space-time continuum, however, violence can also take a form that is no longer bound by existing law and order and thus become indefinite. The possibility of otherwise criminal acts having no punishment in war creates a new space-time continuum that imposes no limitations on the violence used within it. Consequently, war also creates specific group identities: soldiers, men, Japanese people, etc. Such group identities are often dichotomous among existing enemy groups and often seek to violently extinguish each other.

Of course, we must accept that no theoretical approach toward violence can explain its complexity,[65] but it is important to understand the processes that enable the acts of common soldiers and ordinary men within conflict. The question of why they act so violently can then be at least partially answered and help prevent similar violent scenarios in the future. People in general seem to have three options during a violent conflict such as war: they can try to escape, they can suffer, or they can participate.[66] Noncombatants are the victims in such circumstances because they may not be able to escape war and be doomed to suffer; this has been the case in many past wars, and it will most likely be in the future as well. The question that remains, however, is about the atrocities and cruelties that some wars are particularly well known for. The Rape of Nanjing, to name just one example, stands out because its violence was so indefinite that it exceeded all known and usually accepted limits of violence, despite the conflict being part of a war. The German sociologist Trutz von Trotha (1946–2013) connected levels of extreme violence or cruelty to the social preconditions of the perpetrators when he stated that

> [c]ruelty is a mirror of the living conditions and achievements of a society. It appears to be as old as humanity itself and crosses societal and cultural boundaries. No society can say that it does not allow cruelty to exist, even if societies differ to an extreme in the amount of space they give to cruelty and which forms are practiced in these particular spaces.[67]

Introduction

It is therefore society that creates the potential for violent eruptions in a newly established space-time continuum by planting the seeds of cruelty—chauvinism, prejudice, racism, or other ideological beliefs—into its members. In addition to that, acts are usually based on certain emotional conditions, which are usually also dictated by a society's narrative, for example, about its enemies who supposedly only deserve to be hated, degraded, and tortured.[68] The self-identity of the perpetrator, as a member of a specific society that bases its beliefs on the aforementioned negative factors, allows him or her to act violently against nongroup members, particularly in a space-time continuum that is molded by war.

Violence, being an extremely complex phenomenon, is often the expression of all those factors combined.[69] In addition, it can not only lead to danger, but also become a plausible way for human beings to act, which is why regulating violence must be a precondition for the peaceful coexistence of different human identity groups. Democratic states usually prevent violence because it is monopolized and controlled by the state.[70] Particularly in a reshaped space-time continuum in a war zone, limitations disappear, narratives for legitimization are overemphasized, and eventually violence grows to have no purpose beyond its own sake. For the perpetrators, ideologies and cultural factors—including existing military culture—can be decisive for the use of violence.[71] For the war in Asia from 1937 to 1945, historian John W. Dower emphasizes that "considerations of race and power are inseparable" and that "governments on all sides presented the conflict as a holy war for national survival and glory, a mission to defend and propagate the finest values of their state and culture."[72] The participating combatants considered the war to be a "race war," and the level of violence was most likely "fueled by racial pride, arrogance, and rage on many sides."[73] Yet one cannot solely explain the perpetrators' acts with racism, especially because, to quote Alan Kramer, "compliance of perpetrators with orders to carry out genocidal acts was founded in a range of motivations."[74] We should therefore not forget that "sheer pleasure in danger-free killing" might also have played an important role in the cruelties that were committed in the specific war zone.[75] It is always shocking to find out that those who are engaged in such unthinkable acts are quite ordinary,[76] and as such, it is important to understand how violence was made possible in a specific space-time continuum without using the nationality of the perpetrator as an explanatory factor. Violence does not know any nationality, much like the suffering of the victims knows no nationality and should be grieved without national limitations.

Memories of genocidal acts always lie with those who survived war; as Lawrence Langer put it, a "remnant of a ruined past."[77] After the violence ends, a struggle for the power to dictate memory of the events begins and "for the perpetrators and their apologists, the incomplete erasure of their deeds must be followed by a redefinition of their meaning, lest the memory of the victims monopolize the narrative of the past."[78] It is thus difficult for many victims to come forward with their own witness accounts, especially because many of them would rather forget what had happened to them during the war. Holocaust survivor Heda Kovály (1919–2010) described the process of remembering as follows:

> I do not want to write. I do not want to remember. My memories are not simple recollections. They are a return to the bottom of an abyss; I have to gather up the shattered bones that have lain still for so long, climb back over the crags, and tumble in once more. Only this time I have to do it deliberately, in slow motion, noticing and examining each wound, each bruise on the way, most of all the ones of which I was least conscious in my first headlong fall.[79]

Lawrence Langer also further emphasized the problem of the memory of those who perished for those who survived; victims are frustrated by their "efforts to see survival as a simple chronology of returning from an abnormal to a normal world. Without denying the reality or the significance of [a] present life, [they insist] on the discontinuity between it and [the] past, an unresolved and . . . unresolvable stress that nurtures anxiety."[80]

However, there is another problem regarding memories of cruelty and atrocity in war and genocide. Primo Levi (1919–1987) emphasized that "[reality] slides fatally towards simplification and stereotype, a trend against which I would like to erect here a dike. . . . It is the task of the historian to bridge this gap, which widens as we get farther away from the events under examination."[81] Therefore, it must be the historian's task to better understand not only what happened, but how it happened. It is not important to consider the nationalities of the victims or perpetrators beyond the specific national factors that might play a role in the violence involved. However, it is unproductive to establish a ranking of violent nationalities. The Japanese are not inherently more violent than the Germans or the Americans. What must be established is a set of factors that would possibly increase violence in a specific spacetime continuum and then to prove if in such a continuum the predetermined factors existed or not. The memories of the perpetrators and victims alike are of importance, even if I would argue that none of them can provide the truth behind the events.

It is the "historian's very stock in trade"[82] to remember the past, but memories are often far away from the past itself. Although testimonies about the Holocaust, Nanjing, the comfort women system or any other form of genocidal violence are considered "acts of resistance in the face of the systematic destruction of a whole people, tradition and culture,"[83] they must be treated carefully when examined by the historian. As Levi convincingly argued, "We

Introduction

also tend to simplify history; but the pattern within which events are ordered is not always identifiable in a single, unequivocal fashion, and therefore different historians may understand and construe history in ways that are incompatible with one another."[84] Prisoners or victims of a totalitarian and violent system, Levi continued, are forced to very often admit a co-perpetrator status within the system of a POW camp, a concentration camp, or a destruction camp: a *lager* or a camp "on a smaller scale but with amplified characteristics reproduced the hierarchical structure of the totalitarian state, in which all power is invested from above and control from below is almost impossible."[85] The victims are eventually even further victimized upon accepting their statuses as those who existed within a system of torture and violence: "We [the perpetrators, F.J.] have embraced you [the victims, F.J.], corrupted you, dragged you to the bottom with us. You are like us, you proud people: dirtied with your own blood, as we are. You too, like us and Cain, have killed the brother. Come, we can play together."[86] Another thing that is important in the historian's perspective is that we will never be able to reconstruct all the victims' suffering: "There is no proportion between the pity we feel and the extent of the pain by which the pity is aroused: a single Anne Frank excites more emotion than the myriads who suffered as she did but whose image has remained in the shadows. Perhaps it is necessary that it can be so. If we had to and were able to suffer the sufferings of everyone, we could not live."[87] Although Levi eventually emphasized that "one is never in another's place [and e]ach individual is so complex that there is no point in trying to foresee his behavior, all the more so in extreme situations; nor is it possible to foresee one's own behavior,"[88] historians should try to deal with the past to determine the factors that could, but not necessarily coercively, lead to greater eruptions of violence in war.

Even for a substantial number of sadistic perpetrators who enjoyed killing victims in the cruelest ways possible, there were always "unexpected acts of humanity,"[89] although they were rather rare. Those who have survived genocide will usually become part of a "victims' culture,"[90] but how much it is accepted by following generations depends on the society at hand. There is, however, also the danger of abusing such a "victims' culture" for political instrumentalization. The same could be done with a "perpetrator culture" that would be based on a specific nationality and used as a tool of reprimand within an existing political struggle. When China, Korea, and Japan struggle more than 70 years after the Second World War about the interpretation of the past—rather than agree to prevent similar forms of violence—it emphasizes how bad the overemphasis of specific memory-narratives (particularly that of victim vs. the perpetrator) can be in political struggles. That said, many perpetrators choose to remain silent instead of confessing their sins against humanity and are often unknown.[91] Usually, former perpetrators avoid being accountable and instead blame the political system or their own group dynamics for what happened. They may not even discuss guilt per se, which usually leads to conflicts among families if members of the following generations ask about their parents' roles during the war.[92]

As such, it is dangerous to leave out the perpetrators' perspectives when discussing violence. When public memory only focuses on victims of a given tragedy, it detaches the events from the perpetrators; this distance can become solidified in history and create a self-image that is less problematic and morally superior.[93] It is therefore unsurprising that violence committed by one's own identity group is considered legal, whereas that of others is considered cruel and despicable.[94] Hannah Arendt, however, made it clear that intellect does not protect us from crime.[95] She continued her theoretical discussion of pure evil by emphasizing that unlimited and extreme evil is only possible when limitations to such evil are nonexistent.[96] It is particularly the loss of the self within a group identity, which is determined by the society to be violent against another group identity, that is supposed to be a legitimate victim of violence that creates the pure evil. This pure evil eventually becomes so endemic in a specifically created space-time continuum that it is considered normal, even banal.[97] Simply put, "What somebody does relies upon who somebody is."[98] The present book's goal is to find out who the Japanese perpetrators were and what specific space-time continuum allowed them to be as violent as they were. The aim is therefore not to write an apologetic account; what the Japanese soldiers did was horrible, and so, too, is it horrible that the Japanese government cannot express guilt for the past. Yet it would help to understand how such cruelties come into existence and condemn them in the future.

The first chapter will continue the discussion about violence and perpetrators and form a theoretical framework for the discussion about Japanese war crimes related to these categories. Chapter 2 will analyze the space-time continuum of the Rape of Nanjing to find out what triggered the immense eruption of violence in late 1937 and early 1938. After that, another theoretical chapter will deal with sociobiological theories on rape before the fourth chapter discusses the sexual abuse of the "comfort women" to see how victim-perpetrator identities affected the cruel sexual exploitation of so many young women in Asia.

Chapter 5 will analyze the Bataan Death March and the interrelationship between the specific group identities of the Japanese soldiers and the American and Filipino POWs. The subsequent chapter will continue this analysis about the POW camps by the Japanese and the building of the Burma-Thailand Railway. The last chapter will then deal with the war crimes related to Unit 731 and the Japanese Biological Warfare Program that caused several plagues to spread in China, exploiting mostly Chinese human beings as guinea pigs in deadly experiments. All of the named chapters will deal with extremely cruel human behavior, and it is not easy to explain why human beings could

Introduction

act in the ways described. However, it must be emphasized that every one of us, including me and you, would be capable of doing the same under the appropriate circumstances. Nobody possesses an exclusive right to be violent. Every human being can be as violent as the Japanese soldiers tended to be in Nanjing, at Bataan, at the comfort stations, and beyond. We must be extremely careful in understanding how violence works to actively prevent it from spreading again; the present book is just a minor step in achieving that, but it seeks to further explain and elaborate on the "how and why" of extreme violence during the wars in East and Southeast Asia between 1937 and 1945.

CHAPTER ONE

On Violence and Perpetrators

Before dealing with the specific dimensions of Japanese war crimes, it is important to further analyze the theoretical aspects of violence, the perspectives of perpetrators, and how the likelihood of violent behavior in war increases. This analysis will serve as a precondition for a better understanding of violence, a factor of history that Hannah Arendt called a phenomenon of human action.[1] The World Health Organization (WHO) defined violence as "the intentional use of physical force or power, threatened or actual, against oneself, another person, or against a group or community, that either results in or has a high likelihood of resulting in injury, death, psychological harm, maldevelopment or deprivation."[2] However, when discussing violence, we must understand—as American psychologists Robin R. Vallacher and Christopher Brooks have emphasized—that violence "is not considered an end-state or a goal but rather a readily available means by which higher-order concerns can be redressed or goals can be achieved."[3] In human historical records, violence has always been used at the individual, group, or even state levels to achieve specific aims. Consequently, voluntary, planned, or direct violence, as well as involuntary, affective, and indirect violence, has been used as tools for one's own or society's advantage. Arendt highlighted the importance of violence within this historical process when she stated that "no one engaged in thought about history and politics can remain unaware of the enormous role violence has always played in human affairs; and it is at first glance rather surprising that violence has been singled out so seldom for special consideration."[4] Arendt even went a step further and declared violence to be the "midwife of history," but also a force that "creates history as less as the midwife creates the child."[5] Whenever the individual or societal interests lead to a dichotomy, the danger of violent outbreaks increases; much like power, strength, and authority, violence is a tool to dominate others.[6]

On Violence and Perpetrators

German historian Karl Heinz Metz, who wrote *History of Violence* (*Geschichte der Gewalt*), came to a similar evaluation of violence in relation to human existence and its history:

> In history there is always violence—and always the longing for peace. The question about violence is probably the seminal question of the human being. From violence all religion and all politics evolve: Religion as the attempt of a symbolic answer to the question, why humans are not able to abolish violence, politics as the attempt to practically overcome violence by rule, which might tame it. And yet, violence never disappears, neither in the state, which cannot secure inner peace without the threat of violence, and which often uses excessive violence, as war, towards its external, nor in religion, which also becomes violent against heretics and pagans, as soon as religion begins to wish to order society after its own values.[7]

Evidently, violence is always "instrumental by its nature"[8] and usually needs a purpose to be used. Because violence is a tool used to achieve goals, it requires justification.[9]

Furthermore, violence is a form of social action, which can be omnipresent and contingent at the same time. There has never been a society without violence, and it is likely that humanity will never be able to fully abolish violence.[10] Even postmodern societies that often claim to have achieved this status will never exist without it, if one is to believe the Polish-British sociologist Zygmunt Bauman (1925–2017).[11] In any society, violence is usually not an "ontological or pre-social category, but a normative, moral, and ethical one."[12] Violence must also be defined by existing social norms, meaning that what is perceived as violent depends on the "specific chronological, social, and cultural condition and order."[13] What is individually and collectively considered violent depends on developmental processes that determine and reconfigure the social order and its understanding or categorization of violence. Sociologist and director of the Hamburg Institute for Social Research, Wolfgang Knöbl, warned against analyzing violence with "totally new methodological and theoretical approaches," as they are "neither helpful nor necessary."[14] Instead of making violence seem exotic and far-removed, which enables the Western perspective of having "outlived" it, examining violence closely may help people understand its probable endlessness. To analyze violence and its occurrences within specific time periods, its geographical and sociocultural contexts and the number of active players within it can be used to both characterize and comparatively analyze violence.[15]

Forms of violence are usually standardized by social norms; that is, society determines what is allowed and what is not, but these norms are changeable based on redefinitions of socially accepted values or limitations. Violence, however, can never cease to exist, as it provides "an always existing possible course of action for human beings and is therefore always at least present as a menace."[16] As such, violence is a likely expression of specific human emotions—no more, no less. It is "nothing uncommon."[17] Excluding ordered violence or genocide during war, violence is usually not planned in the long term. Instead, everyday perpetrators unthinkingly use violence to achieve ends driven by anger or hate. However, if a perpetrator develops a positive emotional perception of using violence, it becomes self-serving and goes beyond specific emotions, and, as such, becomes purposeless. The use of violence for its own sake becomes something else: cruelty.[18] One must emphasize that in this context, violence is seldom rational and cannot be explained following rational categories and rules.[19]

The desire or impulse to be violent is often contained by existing social norms; as such, motives need not fuel violence, and motive alone cannot fully explain violence. In most cases, violence is not premeditated, as it usually arises from specific interactions between human beings—perpetrators and victims, to be more precise—that determine if and to what extent violence is used.[20] Historians and social scientists refer to assailants' motives to explain violence, but they often realize that motives are frequently constructs to explain acts after the fact and do not explain the true root of the violence in question.[21] For example, murderers might try to legitimize their actions by formulating motives such as self-defense. Because soldiers kill as part of their professions, their jobs can be considered their motives. To name one possible narrative, this form of "work" can be legitimized by war itself or by self-defense against enemies during war. That also means that postact narratives may be fabrications that cannot fully explain acts, and as American sociologist Jack Katz put it, "If research subjects can reliably report why they do the things we want to understand, who would need us?"[22] The "why" of certain acts can therefore only be partially reconstructed; yet if we compare different scenarios of actual violent eruptions (e.g., by soldiers) to develop a palette of factors that reappear whenever violence occurs, we might narrow down possible violence-stimulating parameters to better understand in which situations violence is most likely to manifest. Although motives can be any one of such parameters, they alone do not create perpetrators. To put it simply, those who hate their neighbors are not often violent against them by default, even if they would like to be. To legitimize violence, a space-time continuum must exist that allows people to be violent without fearing legal consequences. War is such a space-time continuum in which law and order are reshaped and the use of violence is sanctioned as a tool to wage and eventually win the conflict at hand.

Violence in War

During a war, violence is legal to kill the enemy; because it is only considered excessive if it is deemed illegitimate, violence is as normal as it can be in the context of war.[23] War itself is based on organized violence and a space-time continuum in which killing and dying are essential. Destruction is the purpose of war, and killing the enemy without being killed is the task. Violence is therefore functional in war, and as discussed earlier, it becomes legitimate for securing victory and/or self-defense.[24] Yet there are two perspectives on this form of violence; soldiers' and society's views on their own cohort's use of violence is often positivistic, whereas the "other's" use of violence is condemned as cruel, excessive, and illegitimate.[25] Especially in colonial armies, the use of violence against an "inferior" enemy (a narrative similar to that used by the Japanese Imperial Army fighting against Chinese troops) caused no conscious issues for soldiers. In expansive or pacifying wars in the colonial era, the use of brute force almost became a military habitus.[26] Guerilla warfare tends to arise in such a circumstance and is chosen to fight a superior force. It blurs the line between civilians and combatants, leading to extreme forms of violence against those who, in the soldier's minds, may or may not be enemies.[27]

If we consider the Japanese army's war in China as a form of colonial conflict, we must take these preconditions into consideration to better understand the violent eruptions in the region (e.g., in Nanjing). The paranoid fear of guerilla fighters, which were unidentifiable to the Japanese, might have led to a preventive form of violence against those whom the soldiers perceived as dangerous enemies. However, the specific space-time continuum involving the Rape of Nanjing will be discussed in detail later. Colonial wars also paint enemies as they are portrayed in stereotypical colonial narratives. Furthermore, if professional translators are unavailable to solve language barriers between soldiers and civilians, then violence may result from miscommunication. Another factor that can stimulate violence is the geographical distance between soldiers and legal jurisdictions; the farther away a war takes place from home, the less control the state seems to have, which is why conflicts in colonial environments tend to follow different rules.[28] German historian Susanne Kuss explains forms of violence in colonial conflicts by analyzing the following aspects:

1. geographical setting;
2. cultural geography;
3. local protagonists;
4. foreign protagonist groups;

5. aims and purpose of the conflict, and
6. the friction between military plans and reality.[29]

In the case of the Japanese Imperial Army and the violence committed in the specific colonial contexts of the Second Sino-Japanese War and the Pacific War, the factors of the specific conflicts are:

1. China and Southeast Asia
2. Non-Japanese civilians
3. Local soldiers and cooperative natives, as well as resistant natives (e.g., guerilla fighters)
4. Japanese soldiers and foreign (American, British, Dutch, etc.) soldiers
5. The extension of the Japanese empire, ideologically to free Asia from white colonialism
6. Japanese expectations of swift victories not correlating with military realities

To better understand the violence that may occur in such conflicts, Susanne Kuss also recommends considering the following aspects related to assailants:

1. the motivation of the soldiers;
2. military training and armament;
3. the image of the enemy and ideological disposition;
4. the space and the existing enemy;
5. the existence of diseases or wounds;
6. the perception of the enemy's reason to resist colonial rule; and
7. the legitimizing narratives for your own acts.[30]

In the case of the Japanese soldiers who committed atrocities in China and other regions of Southeast Asia, these aspects would be:

1. Serving the Japanese empire and the Tennō
2. Violent military training
3. A sense of Japanese superiority
4. Foreign environments and fear of an invisible enemy
5. Venereal diseases and other war-related diseases
6. The Chinese or other enemies' resistance being considered unreasonable
7. Racism, jingoism, and chauvinism as narratives that legitimize Japanese actions

Although war is usually regimented by idealized concepts of honor and glory or by existing conventions such as the Geneva Convention that reflect specific norms expressed by the signing states and the societies the state powers represent, colonial and/or asymmetric conflicts between soldiers and noncombatants cause a higher potential for acts outside these norms.[31] In the time of the Roman Empire, war had to be legitimized as a just war (*ius ad bellum*),[32] and violence was declared legitimate when it was used for defense or to prevent danger for a majority of the people.[33] The same was true for violence and its use by the state—whether against internal or external enemies—and the state used geopolitics, prestige, or defending national honor as narratives to legitimize its use.[34] Although the general belief in war as a legitimate tool to achieve political goals has decreased, especially due to the war in Iraq, the belief in warfare as a tool to achieve national aims was particularly strong in the first half of the 20th century.[35]

On the micro level, violence is always related to interactions between individuals, but these acts must be perceived in a larger context. Simply speaking, limited forms of violence entails limited analyses of how they are used; however, understanding the where and the when of such individual acts of violence must be considered to better understand the phenomenon itself. Solid analyses of violence must be conducted on the micro level to be embedded into the historical macro level. In other words, forms of violence must be related to their contexts; specifically, the how must be compared to the when, where, and why.[36] Special consideration should also be directed toward the conflict's environment, because extreme violence regularly occurs in spaces where states are weak and their control is either damaged or destroyed. Space is a causal unit for the creation of violence and becomes a constituent element of it,[37] and violent excesses are more likely to happen in unrestricted spaces far from political control. Although the role of space in the development of violence has been criticized as a crucial factor,[38] I would argue that it is the interrelationship of space and time that is particularly responsible for creating perpetrators' uncontested use of violence that would not exist in a different space-time continuum. "Ordinary men" are therefore only ordinary in a specific space-time setting and can become violent perpetrators in another. Following Johan Galtung,[39] not considering space and time as eminent factors for the existence of violence would cause us to consider violence as a structural component of all existing situations, a notion I would disagree with.[40] This disagreement is not to use space-time continua to justify assailants' actions, but rather to better understand the factors that trigger violent acts within their specific contexts of time and space.

In our modern narrative, we have mastered the containment of violence to secure human freedom and integrity. The argument of this narrative emphasizes that only societies that have reached modernity, in contrast to those with higher rates of violence, can be considered peaceful (and thereby modern).

Because of this narrative, violence is usually viewed as unnatural, uncivilized, and unacceptable as part of modern society. However, this line of thinking ignores the universality of violence and its existence beyond factors of time and space, and modern societies try to dismiss the possibility of violent behavior, which is depicted as shocking and impossible within the limits of modernity. Instead, violence is suggested as being premodern. The German sociologist Teresa Koloma Beck consequently argues that "the equalization of violence and pre-modernity lacks to see, that the human capability to use violence and the simultaneously existing vulnerability by violence are part of the *conditio humana*, and can neither be overcome by culture nor by progress."[41] To be violent, one does not require specific training or equipment, especially because the human body is not entirely robust against violence. Actions against vulnerable bodies cause asymmetric relationships in which the strong demand control over the weak. Therefore, violence creates a hierarchy between perpetrators and victims by establishing control, domination, and sometimes even political rule.[42] When societies are established, rules about who may use violence often occur because only by limiting violence (usually through law and order) can a society be established as a functional and coexisting order. Although we consider violence an interruption of such an order, we must accept that at the same time, such units often use violence to establish themselves. In this regard, it seems ironic that violence is controlled by the threat of using violence. This dilemma divides humans between those who can use violence as a regulative force that stabilizes society or as a disruptive force that creates chaos.[43]

As Teresa Koloma Beck highlights, the existence of stability in such an order is dependent on the rationality of modern subjects who accept being nonviolent, not just because the state demands it, but because they willingly accept violence as unsuitable in their present orders. In addition to violence securing the integrity and autonomy of the state, philosophical and political values become established and render violence increasingly obsolete.[44] However, a society that comes to this conclusion usually establishes a dichotomy between condemning violence enacted by citizens and increasing the state's potential for violence to control its subjects.[45] Before we can analyze the violence of the Japanese soldiers during the Second World War in its specific space-time continuum, it is important to accept that violence is a possible action or reaction for any human being, regardless of age, sex, nationality, or profession.

Research on violence is often a sociology of cause rather than a sociology of violence, focusing rather on the why than on the how of this "constitutive problem of social order."[46] The aforementioned German sociologist Trutz von Trotha emphasized this lack of study, pointing not only to the fact that classical works by Durkheim, Marx, Simmel, or Weber do not provide a clear

On Violence and Perpetrators

analysis of violence, but also made an argument for studying violence as a social act:

> In the same dimension in which the term violence becomes contourless, the phenomenon itself becomes subordinate and does not demand further analysis, which, however, should be in the center of every analysis of violence and belongs to the most momentous (and most awful) phenomenon: violence as physical harm and especially as killing of other people.[47]

As previously mentioned, the intentional physical harming of others as a demonstration of power creates a violent hierarchy. However, Trotha criticized the reductionist trend of solely studying reasons for violence, which seem to be of interest because they support the idea that violence is like an illness that can be cured. We tend to focus on reasons and causes for violence because they remove focus from the perpetrators, bystanders, and victims alike.[48] Following Trotha's argument, "the key to violence can be found in the forms of violence."[49] It is therefore important to compare forms of violence, particularly in the case of the Japanese Imperial Army, to better understand the acts themselves. It is of particular importance to focus on violent acts, the suffering of the victims, and both the victims' and assailants' perceptions of the situation—their emotions, thoughts, and relationships with one another and with bystanders and observers. Furthermore, we must accept that violence is a dynamic process, meaning that violence can gain momentum as it is being used.[50] Yet once the how of violence is explained, we may also better understand the why, even if the latter is a mere postact construction to fit memorial narratives.

Violence is either consciously or subconsciously remembered by perpetrators and victims alike, and violent people must legitimize their actions with a narrative to accept what they have done.[51] German sociologist Birgitta Nedelmann formulated five points to illustrate a sociology of violence that can help us better understand violent acts in general and those of the Japanese Imperial Army in particular:

1. Developing a conceptual frame of reference with
    a. Actors;
    b. An understanding of physical pain and suffering;
    c. An analysis of the situation and its organizational, institutional, cultural, and political aspects;
    d. A description of violence and its dynamics; and
    e. The consequences for perpetrators, victims, and bystanders

2. Explicitly focusing on physical harm
3. Analyzing reciprocal sensations (e.g., "Why do people hurt others?" = motive question)
4. Employing methodical pluralism (e.g., analyzing both perpetrator-related documents and victims' ego documents and narratives)
5. Developing theories of social subjectivity (e.g., analyzing how violence is perceived)[52]

However, before we can further examine the perpetrator's perspective (the one that is of specific interest in this book), a final element of violence must be dealt with from a theoretical perspective: cruelty.

Trotha described cruelty as "an empirical phenomenon [that] appears unable to avoid the cultural and historical relativity of good and evil, morality and immorality, and right and wrong."[53] In contrast to simple violent acts, which can stem from emotions, cruelty is intentional; it is a specific subset of violence that can be psychological, physiological, social, or spiritual in nature. However, although it can be "a manifestation of human beings, of social behavior, and of rule, specifically political rule,"[54] it tends to follow one purpose: hurting others. Cruel people not only want to establish dominance, but they want victims to suffer. Power is a driving force of cruelty and "the perfection of power is just realized when cruelty is so purposeless and accordingly uncoordinated as possible, when it only relegates to itself."[55] Cruelty indicates might, and when law and order are overcome by cruelty, not even taboos are taken into consideration. If cruelty is understood to establish power, it can become a dangerous tool in the hands of a ruling party, such as soldiers who seek to dominate enemies and break the spirits of those they hold in captivity. However, reasons for cruelty can differ. Some might feel pleasure while being cruel or while devising new ways to be violent; as such, entertainment and pleasure play a key role in cruelty. As Trotha put it, "violence and cruelty are stimulants of the senses."[56] Cruelty, in contrast to pragmatic violence, is excessive.[57] In war, cruelty targets the morale of the enemy, and humiliation plays a decisive role in this.[58] Higher rates of violence are observable in colonial wars where colonizers use brute force against resistance. Consequently, colonialism goes hand in hand with the use of cruelty against indigenous people, and it would be promising to further investigate such interrelationships even beyond a Japanese perspective.[59] The perpetrators in such an environment probably considered their use of violence appropriate in response to claims they considered false and incongruent with their existing hierarchical order.

Although violence is usually anchored onto psychological and physical forces, the initial mobilizers of violence are often factors like hate or racism, which can also be felt as a result of group pressure.[60] In such situations, individuals and collectives alike can eliminate resistance against them by using either direct (physical) or indirect (psychological) means against opponents.[61] They will necessitate violence based on existing narratives of superiority and/or other forms of legitimization based on class, gender, nationality, race, religion, etc. Individual or collective acts are therefore legitimized by narratives that may have been used by the state to sanction violence, which become translated into the perpetrators' existing space-time continua.

Regarding gender, men—even if they do not hold a monopoly on violence—seem more likely to use excessive forms of violence against others. As David M. Buss and Joshua D. Duntley emphasize, men "tend to physically, psychologically, and emotionally abuse their own intimate partners"[62] and also compete with one another using violence, asserting dominance in relationships using continued violence or cruelty.[63] In the same way, Japanese guards of American or British prisoners of war (POWs) reconfirmed the hierarchy within the camp environment to remind prisoners of their subordinate roles as a consequence of their defeat.

To engage in collective violence during war, consensus among the perpetrator group is required.[64] Once a military attack is underway, order can be destroyed and irrational emotional factors can become the determining forces of action. Enjoyment can replace careful planning, and violence can easily exceed rational levels. In a victorious situation, such emotions could lead to an overkill phenomenon, which can also be applied to the Rape of Nanjing. As American archaeologist Steven A. LeBlanc described it, an overkill happens "[w]hen victory is complete and the winners do not have to retreat promptly to avoid retaliation" and "they frequently resort to mutilation of the victims or sometimes they continue to spear, shoot arrows into them or otherwise hack them up far beyond what is needed to kill them."[65] Considering that "violent intergroup conflict is pervasive,"[66] particularly during war, and that men are more likely to risk preemptive violence to destroy a possible but unproven menace, outrageous forms of violence against civilians might be the consequence of paranoid fears of a nonexistent enemy stimulated by the psychological pressure caused by war. It therefore seems fruitful to have a closer look at perpetrators' perspectives on warfare.

Perpetrators

As previously mentioned, those involved in war tend to legitimize their actions in the context of a supposedly just war,[67] and in this sense, moral compasses affect war. However, aggressive acts are not performed individually and are instead embedded in a larger context; in such cases, the collective's members tend to base their acts on learned paradigms.[68] As mentioned earlier, such violent acts are usually used to achieve specific goals and in specific situations where violence is considered appropriate by the perpetrators. Although wars usually entail moral consciousness, whether violence is considered legitimate or not depends on its perception by the acting collective and/or individual.[69] However, there are also different ways to categorize individual (micro) and collective (macro) violence, as proposed by German sociologist Peter Imbusch (see Table 1.1).[70]

Although this book focuses on perpetrators, victims must also be included in its analysis because violent actions can only be fully understood as interactions.[71] However, at this point, we must first discuss some basic theories about perpetrators.

Research on perpetrators, especially with regard to the history of the Holocaust, has increased since the 1990s and has been particularly stimulated by the Goldhagen Controversy, which asked for the motives of the perpetrator group and questioned how far perpetrators could be separated from their respective societies.[72] In the years after the Second World War, it was generally thought that there were few diabolic perpetrators relative to the rest of society.[73] The debate about "little" perpetrators began after the end of the Soviet Union and still leads to the prosecution of former criminals, especially in the context of the Holocaust. Although the Holocaust and its study demanded such acts for

Table 1.1 Individual vs. Collective Violence

	Individual or Micro Violence	Collective or Macro Violence
Phenomenology	Isolated and punctual event: violence against an individual, robbery, rape, or vandalism	Violence as part of a collective organizational context: war, genocide, and other forms of mass destruction
Type of Violence	Individual and usually direct form of violence (physical or psychological) against other individuals or things; apolitical and intentional	Collective and/or state violence, usually a direct and structural form; political and functional
Perpetrator	Individual perpetrator or small group that allows the identification of a single action	Larger groups or collectives, state-related organizations such as armies or other armed units
Victim	Individual victim with or without specifics that categorize him or her as a victim	A designated victim group identified through religion, ethnicity, etc.

On Violence and Perpetrators

the sake of criminal prosecution, the Japanese government seems to lack such efforts, and those demanding investigations into Japanese war crimes seem to remain a minority within the East Asian country's society. Studies in perpetration in the West, however, also went through various stages in which diverse images of perpetrators dominated the discourse:

1. 1940s and 1950s: a demonizing image of perpetrators
2. 1960s to 1990s: a victimizing image of perpetrators (individuals who only followed orders)
3. Since the 1990s: diverse approaches to the image of perpetrators[74]

Society tends to depict perpetrators as abnormal because they "seem to be the evil per se—the inhumane, pathological other in the humane world of the normal and healthy."[75] The Frankfurt Auschwitz Trials (1963–1965) were also often determined by a dichotomy that allowed only two perspectives: demonic perpetrators on one side and suffering victims on the other.[76] A demonizing image of the perpetrators is important, as Thomas Kühne remarks, for the "production of a moral, emotional, and mental distance"[77] between the perpetrator group and the spectators. He continues his evaluation by emphasizing that "the demonization of the perpetrator allows the spectator to fade out questions about their own actual and potential roles in the social and political arrangement of mass violence . . . and to assure oneself of their own moral integrity."[78] As outlined in Hannah Arendt's dictum of the banality of evil, perpetrators were often considered to have been victims of the bureaucratization of killing. Up until today, the "master narratives" to explain the Holocaust are either 1) intentionalist, claiming that Hitler had a long-standing plan to extinguish the Jews, and 2) functionalist, arguing that the events were improvised as a consequence of competition between several authorities who eagerly tried to achieve *weltanschauliche* aims by using their own power in their specific working environments.[79] "Perpetratorship," as Thomas Kühne argues, is usually based on a multitude of cognitive and situational factors (see Table 1.2).[80]

Table 1.2 Cognitive and Situational Factors for the Use of Violence

Cognitive Factors	Situational Factors
Education	Group dynamics and pressure
Propaganda-related dispositions	Military hierarchies
Racism	Availability of supplies
Dehumanization of the enemy	Emotional deprivation
Existing utopian beliefs	Friend-foe image in war
Martial masculinity	

It is difficult to categorize perpetrators; in many instances,[81] a combination of the individual and collective forms of violence exist and might stem from different cognitive and/or situational factors. Analyzing Japanese war crimes means not only focusing on the treatment of POWs—which many English publications on the topic tend to do[82]—but also closely examining different crimes and categorizing them following the discussed categories. This process will allow an understanding of how and why Japanese soldiers committed violent acts.

It was hard to assess the perpetrators' motivations after 1945, particularly because their acts of violence were not related to classical motives for murder; in Nazi Germany and Shōwa Japan alike, assailants were institutionally socialized, educated, and trained to be violent before entering the war.[83] Furthermore, such an environment provided career prospects for people like the members of the German Einsatzgruppen or the Japanese Unit 731, who climbed existing hierarchies that would not have existed without the war. An institutionally determined practice of action—as Frank Bajohr, scientific director of the Center for Holocaust Studies in Munich, calls it—stimulated a helix of violence, provoking or even demanding the excess violence used by the perpetrators.[84] Hannah Arendt emphasized that power and violence are intertwined, especially in the military where group dynamics and power relations can also be accountable for increases in violence. Oftentimes, "sociopsychological group mechanisms" prevented antagonism against extreme forms of violence within specific perpetrator groups.[85] Once these forms of violence had been used by common soldiers, they became habitual; the more that ordinary men were exposed to extremely violent acts, the more they normalized the violence. Because this process was embedded in the social preconditioning of the soldiers, whose socialization and education laid the framework for their actions, they become part of what German historian Christian Gerlach calls "extremely violent societies." Gerlach uses this term to describe

> formations where *various population groups* become victims of massive physical violence, in which, acting together with organs of the state, *diverse social groups participate for a multitude of reasons*. Simply put, the occurrence and the thrust of mass violence depends on broad and diverse support, but this is based on a variety of motives and interests that cause violence to spread in different directions and varying intensities and forms.[86]

As soon as violence is deemed legal or acceptable in a space-time continuum that has prepared for extreme violence, it becomes limitless and excessive. As German social psychologist Amélie Mummendey emphasizes, a particular behavior can be evaluated differently depending on whether the person judging it considers the action legitimate or not, and individuals tend to be even more violent when acting in groups.[87] The reasons for the latter form of violent intensification are likely related to the earlier mentioned dynamics in male groups. Such groups establish their own norms regarding the battlefield and their daily violent environments, which also causes the group to reconfigure its normative orientation from a peaceful context to a violent one.

Thomas Kühne highlights that in a "social culture of hard, aggressive, and unpitying manhood the deniers represent the other, the vestige (*Schwundstufe*) of this manhood" and are forced to participate in criminal acts to prove their loyalty toward and affiliation with the group. What is thereby achieved is "collectivization through crime."[88] This collectivization would later cause trouble when the image of "ordinary" perpetrators was promoted by the Eichmann Process in 1961.[89] Arendt described Adolf Eichmann (1906–1962) as a mechanical part, like a gear-wheel aiding a process of destruction, a "servile, motiveless, and submissive bureaucrat at a desk, who, with few exceptions developed his own initiative, and who lacked a diabolic character as well as a fanatic Antisemitism."[90] Arendt identified Eichmann's wish to have a career and his "slavish obedience" as the determining factors of his actions. However, she failed to consider his performance in his glass booth in front of the world media. Eichmann staged his own interpretation of the Holocaust; he tried to escape judgment by attributing his actions to his obedient acceptance of society and to a space-time continuum that demanded violent actions, which were also considered legal.[91] Although such an image merely helped relieve Germany's early postwar conscience, it is still accepted by many Japanese who believe that past generations of perpetrators are unworthy of individual guilt due to the nature of war. It is easy to accept that perpetrators are "human beings, who execute an act related to guilt"[92] from our perspectives, but the perpetrators themselves, especially those who still defend their acts, must accept this assessment before society can begin to face and deal with its past. This step is still missing in Japan, where only historians, journalists, and interest groups are concerned with disputes about the past. Another problem lies in the fact that a crime—that is, before it is considered a crime by social determination—is a simple act.[93] Although we generally condemn crime, extremely violent societies allowed people to increase their self-esteem with violence based on a specific ideology of destruction.[94]

Furthermore, we have to accept that, regardless of the fact that male perpetrators are quite common, the discussed space-time continuum also provided room for female actors who kept the violent system running.[95] It is important to discard the idea that perpetrators have a specific gender or nationality.[96] Such arguments are nothing more than a narrative to point the finger at others to neglect one's own capacity to use excessive force in a suitable space-time continuum. They did not contribute to analytical research; instead, they were purely political arguments at a time when nationalism increased its hold on political agendas. There is no nationality with a monopoly on violence. Scholars who follow such narratives are not interested in fruitful discussions about war crimes and violence, but are instead interested in establishing accusatory narratives and whitewashing crimes by comparing them with more excessive forms of violence. This is academic nonsense and a shame for victims of any form of violence.

It is important to establish other factors besides soldiers' nationalities to establish a normative frame for their violent actions. Killing was integrated into soldiers' daily working lives such that they did not perceive their crimes as crimes at all.[97] The victims were socially ostracized as fellow human beings based on racist ideologies in Germany and Japan alike. Sometimes, killing became a moral obligation for the greater good of the nation-state (e.g., for those participating in Unit 731's experiments).[98] Two factors particularly stimulated the Japanese potential for violence: military training and obedience. The latter, which German sociologist Harald Welzer considers to be a willing decision, is also related to a frame of reference in which war demands killing as part of soldiers' duties.[99] In a violent situation, perpetrators "use the absolutely one-sided dispositions of power as a structure of chance, to test, how far they can go, and they try to use the arising opportunity on the material, sexual, and emotional level to the maximum."[100]

The military training they received partially sanctioned their actions.[101] Clear hierarchies exist in the military, and life in a military casern resembles prison life. Strict drills, corporal punishment, no personal rights, and obeying superior officers characterize daily routines. In this environment, recruits must "earn any subsequent position" by neglecting their individuality.[102] Violence is directed downward in military structures, and "each [soldier or officer] has the power to command and punish those below and the duty to obey those above."[103] In the meantime, "everything is planned and everything is public,"[104] and a soldier's individual existence is fully integrated into the collective of the army, specifically his unit. There is no security and no escape from violence, as Theweleit puts it, because "each newcomer . . . necessarily repeats the mistakes of his predecessors, who in turn recognize and welcome the apparent opportunity to treat their successors as they themselves have previously been treated."[105] Communication is therefore violent, and each mistake is met with immediate punishment by a superior. This, in turn, causes soldiers to seek opportunities to blow off steam as soon as they encounter somebody with a lower hierarchical ranking. As punishment "always remains the prerogative of [. . .] elders"[106] within the army, the only chance to let this "violent steam" out is to direct it toward somebody who is not part of the military collective (i.e., foreign soldiers or civilians). The steady confrontation with violence as a tool for punishment makes sure that, as Theweleit continues in his analysis, "no feeling or desire remains unclarified, all are transformed into clear perception: the desire for bodily warmth into a perception of the heat of bodily pain; the desire for contact into a perception of the whiplash."[107] In the end, soldiers will live under an impression that is solely based on violence: "what is nice is what hurts."[108] This military space-time continuum eventually places soldiers into war zones for which they have been well prepared by deindividualization and psychological reformation:

> The soldier's limbs are described as if severed from their bodies; they are fused together to form new totalities. The leg of the individual has a closer functional connection to the leg of his neighbor than to his own torso. In the machine, then, new body totalities are formed: bodies no longer identical with the bodies of individual human beings.[109]

War eventually becomes the condition of the soldiers' beings, and it

> offers an opportunity for discharge, for the front to be released from internal pressure. In peacetime, the front presses inward toward its own interior, compressing the individual components of the [military] machine. It produces internal tensions of high intensity that press for discharge.[110]

What is ultimately discharged in the battlefield, especially in the case of the Japanese troops, is a being that has been forcefully accustomed to an order based on brute force that allows low ranks to channel violence toward real or imagined external enemies. However, this does not mean that soldiers do not act as individuals in the war zone, because "in battle the formation dissolves. The macromachine separates into its components. Each component in the soldierly totality-body has been made functional by the drill; battle gives it the opportunity to prove that its own function conforms to the functioning principle of the machine itself."[111] The soldier eventually becomes "a true child of the drill-machine, created without the help of a woman, parentless,"[112] and is finally able to take revenge for his own upbringing within the military machine. On the battlefield, the time for being punished ends and punishment can instead be actively exacted on others; the war provides candidates for such punishment. Soldiers' social bonds, which are based on military structure and male bonding, provide a frame of action in the newly created space-time continuum.[113]

The soldier shares a martial masculinity with his comrades, as proven in battle. Theweleit described it as follows:

> The new man is a man whose physique has been machinized, his psyche eliminated—or in part displaced into his body armor, his "predatory" suppleness. . . . In the moment of action, he is devoid of fear as of any other emotion. His knowledge of being able to do what he does is his only consciousness of self.[114]

Violence can even be a form of self-expression, much like an "orgasm is not so much experienced as suffered."[115] While drills build up a soldier's tolerance to tension, the arrival of the battle eventually "digs out a new demand for the stream of the libido," which is violently directed toward external enemies who are "accessible to the soldier's overwrought body."[116] What keeps the soldier in this violent system is clear: obedience.

Because it is so important, I would like to provide a brief survey of the role of obedience following Stanley Milgram's experiment, as well as how obedience affected soldiers in their specific space-time continuum of war. Following Milgram,

> Obedience is as basic an element in the structure of social life as one can point to. Some system of authority is a requirement of all communal living, and it is only the man dwelling in isolation who is not forced to respond, through defiance or submission, to the commands of others. Obedience, as a determinant of behavior, is of particular relevance to our time.[117]

However, he also points out that many crimes have been committed in the name of obedience. In his experiment,[118] Milgram stated that "to extricate himself from the situation, the subject must make a clear break with authority."[119] For the Japanese soldier in his space-time continuum in China during the Second World War, the end of violence would have meant the end of his existence in the contemporary legal order, and returning to peace would not only do away with military authority but with the existing space-time continuum; soldiers would have then desired common, nonviolent lives in a nonwar environment. Milgram wanted to find out "when and how people would defy authority in the face of a clear moral imperative."[120] His findings were astonishing because they proved that "ordinary" people tended to be more violent than needed to appeal to higher authority. Even those who were not considered to be in "the sadistic fringe of society"[121] were more than willing to inflict extreme violence upon other human beings, and as explained earlier, "collectivization through crime" took place because the responsibility for the actions of the test subjects was shared with the authority that demanded the violence from them. It therefore seems clear that "ordinary people, simply doing their jobs, and without hostility on their part, can become agents in a terrible destructive process."[122] The perpetrators, in their war-defined space-time continuum, like Milgram's test subjects, perceive themselves as fulfilling a requirement that is simply serving a higher aim. They almost believe they are serving society by committing evil actions.[123] However, obedience is not only a psychological category but also established by societies. In this context, modern Japan is an obedience-oriented society in which group dynamics and roles are more of a concern than in more individualistic societies, where break with authority is easier. Milgram considered several factors responsible for "[laying] the groundwork for obedience."[124] These factors are:

1. The family,
2. The institutional setting (meaning an "institutional system of authority," such as a school or the military),

3. The possibility for rewards, such as moving up in a hierarchy, and
4. The immediate antecedent conditions, meaning that the individual expects some authority to exist when he or she enters a new situation.[125]

In each new established space-time continuum, the soldiers would consequently be looking for an authority. If such an authority was missing, like during the Rape of Nanjing, the soldiers naturally established their own new order, which, as described earlier, was highly related to actual and threatened violence against inferior victims.

However, obedience also needs an ideology because "ideological justification is vital in obtaining willing obedience for it permits the person to see his behavior as serving a desirable end. Only when viewed in this light, is compliance easily exacted."[126] Thinking they are obliged to be obedient to the higher authorities and the higher aims they represent, common men become willing executioners, fulfilling the bloody reality of racist dreams and ambitions that were created in the offices of Imperial Japan and Nazi Germany alike. While doing that, the only point of orientation for the soldiers—who were often young men in their first military experiences—was their superior officer, because "the person in authority, by virtue of that position, is in the optimal position to bestow benefits or inflict deprivations."[127] It was the unit leader, the military superior, who was responsible for success or degradation of the soldier, who decided if life would be easy or not. Obedience was also a form of self-protection in situations where soldiers underwent tension. Once soldiers have the chance to relieve anger about their dependency, they would use any sign of weakness to impart their stock of assembled violent experiences within the army and the war to somebody else.

In war, morality is redefined to support violent environments instead of peace. What are morals in war? The answer is easy: "Morality [in war] does not disappear, but acquires a radically different focus: the subordinate person feels shame or pride depending on how adequately he has performed the actions called for by authority."[128] The fact that so many ordinary men become violent perpetrators in war confirms Milgram's final assumption that "culture has failed, almost entirely, in inculcating internal controls on actions that have their origin in authority. For this reason [. . .] [obedience] constitutes a far greater danger to human survival."[129] Milgram leaves us with the crux that although "actions performed under command are, from the subject's viewpoint, virtually guiltless, however inhumane they may be,"[130] it is important to educate people about the possibility of moral control over their obedience. On the other hand, a lack of obedience might endanger the functionality of the military order as such, because obedience seems to be one of its essential elements.

The last point that I would like to examine in this chapter is how memory is remembered before shortly describing the Japanese soldiers' general situation in the Second World War, whose war crimes will then be discussed in further detail in the subsequent chapters. The norms and values of the social context determine what is illegal, violent, or cruel.[131] Modern society considers itself to be civilized because extreme acts of violence do not usually occur publicly, as has been the case in other times. Violent eruptions in modern states are rare, which is why the need for explanations in such cases is particularly high.[132] The public debate about violence is usually influenced by existing stereotypes about perpetrators. Nationalities, ethnicities, gender, etc., end up being highlighted categories, and the perpetrator's sociostructural characteristics are projected onto whole populations—Chang did this in her book when she accused all Japanese people of being guilty for the crimes of a specific group that also happened to be Japanese.[133] Within a mass of perpetrators there also exists social condensations and group dynamics. As such, violent acts are seldom anonymous, but they are executed by individuals whose acts are perceived and sanctioned by the participating members (and to be judged later by nonparticipants). The evaluation of the violence relates to the position of the person judging the act, as well as to his or her own involvement in the matter. The social condensation within the violent space-time continuum provides not only security while committing violent acts, but it also promises to include the perpetrator in a secure environment within the new and probably safer space-time continuum in which group members are bound by their shared guilt.[134]

Once such a group sanctions extreme forms of violence, civilians can and will become victims as well because it is the specific perpetrator group that will redefine what is allowed on the battlefield.[135] In a way, it also indirectly allows the guilt to vanish later, when perpetrators (e.g., those serving in Unit 731) swear to keep their knowledge about the events secret. This makes an evaluation of the events, especially when documents were lost, extremely hard, and very often only a few documents in combination with victim statements can be used to re-create an impression of what must have happened. The individual perpetrator's perspective very often remains in the dark, something that makes it hard to fully understand why and how something happened. Considering that history itself consists of a myriad of extremely violent events, it is important to better understand how it comes into existence. To obtain the answer to this question, one must carefully analyze the human psyche and its reaction to a battlefield environment. Although no perpetrator testimony can be considered to be a truthful description of the how and why, they at least offer an impression of how extreme forms of violence are remembered by those who committed them, which is why it is compelling to deal with them.[136]

Violence and Perpetrator Memory

Karl Heinz Metz makes the argument that "war is war, violence is violence, nothing else, nothing moral or immoral."[137] This may be true of the act itself, but once committed, violence must be embedded in both a legitimizing narrative and in memory. A violent act must often be incorporated into a larger context (e.g., as a necessary expansionist force) or at least be legitimate to the one who committed it.[138] Consequently, the question of war and the violence within it is a question of human beings, their thoughts, and their memorial narratives as well. The conscience requires justification for actions, even if reflective thought about the latter can only begin once the former has been realized.[139] Violence is thus not only a form of action; it is also a form of historical experience, which is why the act itself and experiencing the act are parts of the same coin.[140] Harald Welzer remarks that to inquire about this experience "with investigations, autobiographies, and interviews with historical witnesses" is difficult because "the people concerned know how a period of history has turned out, and that ex post facto knowledge obscures how they experienced and saw things at the time."[141]

Welzer and German military historian Sönke Neitzel analyzed statements of German POWs during the Second World War about their violent acts and came to unexpected conclusions. Whereas a common thought is "that war brutalized, that soldiers are turned into beasts by the experience of violence, by being confronted with mutilated bodies and dead comrades or, in the case of a campaign of annihilation, with masses of murdered men, women and children,"[142] and whereas "[a]utobiographies and war fiction reinforce the impression that over time, soldiers become brutal as they themselves are exposed to increasing brutality,"[143] there is also evidence that leads to another conclusion: "The brutalization hypothesis excludes the possibility that violent behavior can be something attractive for which one 'itches,' and it presumes, with no real proof, that people need to be somehow pre-trained to commit acts of extreme violence."[144] Neitzel and Welzer, in contrast to the brutalization hypothesis but correct in its evaluation, remark that it is adrenaline in the war environment—"the feeling of having power in areas where one normally has none"—combined with a "social framework in which killing is permissible, even desirable"[145] that makes the violent eruption of the perpetrators on the battlefield (i.e., the soldiers) possible.

Although military training usually covers a longer time span, soldiers are often quickly acclimatized to committing extreme forms of violence.[146] However, violence may become like a sport or a hunt for soldiers in which they may prove not only their abilities, but also superiority within the group. Professionalism in killing thus justifies the position of the individual in the collective's hierarchy. Eventually, there will be those who use a form of autotelic violence, that is, violence committed for the sake of it and for no other reason.

This form is usually considered cruel because it "challenges our powers of comprehension since it radically contradicts the civilized self-image maintained by modern societies and their members."[147] However, soldiers might also get used to these forms of violence because they encounter new limits of death and destruction with each day they spend in the military. The illusion of nonviolent human societies that we envision makes an understanding of autotelic violence extremely hard for us because "we consider the use of violence to solve problems normal, whereas using violence for its own sake is pathological."[148] We must also understand that violence was more accepted in Japanese and German societies during the Second World War. It was considered "far more normal, expected, legitimate, and commonplace,"[149] which is why we must also think about the societies in which the soldiers lived before they committed war crimes.

For them, as Neitzel and Welzer highlight, "violence was part of their frame of reference, and killing part of their duty."[150] Considering Theweleit's analysis, which was discussed earlier, the soldier was a functioning part of the war machine, got accustomed to extreme forms of violence, and eventually reproduced violence. Soldiers were not alienated for extreme forms of violence, but were instead integrated into the military order, sharing guilt with other perpetrators. Taking responsibility for these acts may have been "a highly attractive mixture of ability, technological superiority, and thrill."[151] The narratives would not openly admit this, but rather camouflage it with sport- or hunting-related stories. The soldiers did not talk about their duty of killing the enemy directly; instead, they paraphrased it. Violence was like a sport, and as the "soldiers inhabited one and the same world, a world in which hitting targets and having fun went hand in hand,"[152] most of them were able to decipher this code of reference. The battlefield itself, as discussed about the establishment of violence-demanding space-time continua, also provided the essential preconditions for violence because "individually perpetrated violence, such as rape or killing, becomes more possible and likely. In other words, war creates a social space that is more conducive to violence than peace. Force becomes expected, accepted, and normal."[153] However, most important for the soldier was surviving war under continued stress due to paranoia of being killed, and it was common for soldiers to develop tendencies to use violence against civilians, whose roles on the battlefield were re-examined and whose potential for attacking the soldiers became increasingly threatening. Eventually, as Neitzel and Welzer put it, "[F]antastic delusions about what sorts of people might belong to the enemy are by no means unique. . . . This is not a sign of insanity. It marks the shifting of a frame of reference so that group membership is more important than all other defining characteristics, including age [or gender], in determining who the enemy is."[154] Once the first people are killed, "the floodgates of violence are opened, [and] anything can provide an impetus and justification for soldiers to start shooting."[155] Killing is then no longer uncommon, but rather turns into a daily practice that is an essential part of the existing space-time continuum.

Numerous soldiers not only defended themselves or prevented a possible attack against their own by being violent, but, as Thomas Kühne emphasized, they "were even more intoxicated with omnipotence and grandiosity."[156] In the Second World War, in contrast to the Great War, values that had been considered soldierly, like honor, chivalry, or even mercy, no longer played a role. They were considered weaknesses in the fight between racist ideologies that demanded strength and manhood instead of mercy and pardon. Many soldiers instead "embraced military service as the ultimate test of their maleness"[157] and as proof of their spirit. The war created a "moral no man's land" where soldiers could act uncontested by regular laws, which were replaced with ideologically preconditioned value sets. Special comradeship "produced in the machines of destruction and deprivation"[158] was the only moral compass. Once the soldier as an individual gave in to be a permanent and uncontested part of a group, the dynamics ruling this group would affect him; he would become a violent perpetrator who would use autotelic violence and be cruel to his victims based on patterns sanctioned by his group.

Violence, as reported in perpetrator narratives, also became a tool to solve issues that existed on the battlefield and eventually became a banality, something that did not need to be morally discussed among group members. Once sanctioned, it was established as a *sine qua non* for victory and the actions on the battlefield in particular.[159] This must be understood to better grasp the role of low-rank perpetrators, whom Omer Bartov calls the "little people."[160] To get in touch with their specific roles, as they are largely only remembered in a larger context, "the commonly accepted view of the killers as sadistic, inhuman, faceless individuals, who have very little in common with any of us and can therefore not be understood on the same terms"[161] must be abandoned, because only the acceptance of the fact that we ourselves could be assailants will help us understand how and why they became that way. We are in constant danger of becoming parts of the right space-time continuum conducive to such behavior. Primo Levi had already expressed a "growing pessimism and disenchantment with a world that merely uses the horror of the past for its own instant gratification"[162] instead of accepting that we could not only reproduce similar forms of violence in the right social and spatial context, but also the fact that there were grey areas between victims and perpetrators that showed glimpses of humanity in a time of war. We must also realize that many soldiers experienced things during the war they had not been prepared for. Although life in the army or a paramilitary organization like the German SA initially might have "offered not only activity, adventure, novelty . . . , [and] a chance, perhaps the first in their lives, to escape the boredom and isolation of their own homes and communities,"[163] these dreams turned into violent experiences of inhumane acts of destruction, killing, and dehumanization of victims. However, later testimonies related to the events naturally block the latter events and focus on the positive experiences of comradeship and of serving in the army as an honorable act of love for the nation.[164]

Hannah Arendt considered such experiences harder to accept, especially because nobody can master or overcome (*bewältigen*) it.[165] The radical evil that dominated such acts led to self-damnation, an "absurdum morale"[166] that forced perpetrators to lie not only to the public but to themselves. Because sadism is considered to be the "vice of all vices" in a peaceful space-time continuum, the narratives of the perpetrators gained a new momentum far removed from the violent acts of the past.[167] Arendt therefore concludes that "in exceptional times, only those who could say 'I cannot' are the morally reliable humans."[168] Most of the acting soldiers who will be described in the following chapters did not have the desire, the power, or the chance to say so. Such people complied with their contemporary space-time continuum and group rules instead of their own moral code or social standards of a peaceful society. The perpetrators often neglect these facts, but Arendt correctly emphasizes that to repent for past acts, it is essential to remember them.[169] In a society like the Japanese one, where wrongdoings and past crimes were not publicly discussed, an attempt to repent could be made neither by society nor by soldiers. Said soldiers' situations will be elaborated on shortly before their individual war crimes will be analyzed in more detail.

The Japanese Context

John W. Dower correctly highlighted that during the early Shōwa years, Japan "encompassed in its early decades so much repression, aggression, atrocity, misery, and plain dark conflict."[170] A critical debate about the violent and criminal aspects of the Second World War and of the years before it was likely prevented by the Americans' decision to keep the Japanese emperor in power after their occupation, and also because the Supreme Commander of the Allied Powers, Douglas MacArthur, had established his rule over the islands of Japan. However, the U.S. public was fixated on the evil nature of the Japanese during the war, and the common American soldier considered them to be "subhuman and repulsive" as well as a "racial enemy."[171] The Japanese soldiers shared similar racist beliefs and ideas. Consequently, the war "exposed core patterns of racist perception in many forms: formulaic expressions, code words, everyday metaphors, visual stereotypes."[172] U.S. soldiers were dehumanized, and by the time Japanese troops encountered the first POWs, they were already preconditioned to be violent. These victories—"coupled with the spectacle of Japanese brutality and atrocity—set whole new worlds of racial thinking in motion," and the American press "argued that the Japanese as a collectivity were mentally and emotionally unstable—neurotic, schizophrenic, psychotic, or simply hysterical."[173] Similar racism would also legitimize the Japanese soldiers' violence against white POWs in their prison camps as the notion of racial revenge against an "impure" enemy whose army had threatened and suppressed Asia for centuries gained momentum. The soldiers who surrendered in Bataan were seen as "filthy water running from the sewage of a nation which derives from impure origins and has lost its pride of race."[174] The American and British wartime prisoners were considered demons or monsters,[175] and in the end, there was (as Dower coined it) an "obsession with extermination on both sides—a war without mercy."[176] Chinese civilians and American prisoners alike were regarded as subhuman, weak, impure, and unworthy of life. Japanese soldiers would kill them without hesitation, and racism was responsible for much violence. We tend to believe that eliminating racism will reduce violent behavior, but there are far more factors responsible for violence than racism, which is only one facet of violence. Nevertheless, Dower already remarked that "the bayonet was the poor man's counterpart to the samurai sword" and "for the Freudian analyst, the wanton frenzy with which these conscripts plunged this weapon into Allied prisoners as well as defenseless people everywhere in Asia must be of more than passing interest."[177]

Many factors must be considered when analyzing, studying, and teaching about the acts of the Japanese soldiers. First, I will try to describe the specific space-time continuum in which the crimes were committed, which will be discussed in each of the next chapters before discussing the how and why that determined the Japanese violence and war crimes in each example. Eventually, we will possess a better understanding of the perpetrators and their actions. Those who want to continue to use the "Japaneseness" of the perpetrators in a national context as the only argument for their narrative of guilt should stop reading now—indeed, what the Japanese did is horrible, and the Japanese government's actions ever since deserve scorn from anyone interested in historical research. However, I will not discuss these issues in the following chapters, as I am interested in better understanding the how and why of these horrible crimes from a human perspective; as such, I accept that anyone could be capable of the same violent actions, regardless of national identity. I consequently do not blame the soldiers for being Japanese, but for not having had a stronger moral compass in a time of ethical darkness and for neglecting to sympathize with other human beings. How and why the moral compasses of so many people collapsed is the main point of interest, and this, of course, will be discussed in the context of each existing space-time continuum.

CHAPTER TWO

The Rape of Nanjing

In 2002, Japanese historian Kasahara Tokushi provided a reasonable definition for the Rape of Nanjing (or the Nanjing Massacre), detailing the events at Nanjing during December 1937 and February/March 1938:

> The term Nanking Massacre refers to the totality of atrocities committed by Japanese troops against Chinese soldiers and civilians during and after the attack on Nanking. These atrocities were illegal from the perspectives of both international law on combat behavior and international humanitarian law. The geographical scope of this incident applies to all areas under the jurisdiction of the Nanking Special Municipality, which included the city of Nanking as well as six counties in the vicinity. This is the Battle Zone of Nanking as well as the area occupied by the Japanese troops after the fall of the city.[1]

The Japanese army occupied the Chinese capital and did so until the end of the Second World War, but it was during the first few months of that occupation that the Japanese soldiers went rogue and raped, tortured, and murdered at least 200,000 civilians. Most discourse about the Second World War is from a Eurocentric perspective and does not consider Nanjing in a broad perspective.[2] Although the events had been brought to light in two tribunals in Nanjing and Tokyo after the war, only two higher officers were found guilty; Lt. General Tani Hisao (1882–1947) and General Matsui Iwane (1878–1948) were classified as Class B war criminals and executed after the two trials.[3]

Regardless of the well-known facts that had been reported in "testimonies from surviving victims, American Missionaries, a Nazi-businessman, and even Japanese soldiers who committed the crime,"[4] the Japanese government refuses to accept the findings and conclusions of the military tribunals. Many Japanese historians have tried to diminish the number of victims and have even claimed the events did not happen at all. Although "all the evidence presented by the prosecutors was beyond any reasonable doubt,"[5] a stubborn political view persists that denies an understanding between the interest groups involved. Japanese historian Yamamoto Masahiro, whose work *Nanking: Anatomy of an Atrocity* was called "a work that is easily the most objective historical account of Nanjing in the English-language literature,"[6] explains the problems that exist regarding the historical perception of the Rape of Nanjing:

> Among these notorious historical events, the Rape of Nanking is exceptional because of the unusual degree of attention paid to it for an extraordinarily long time. Despite the time and energy of many people who have discussed this subject, however there appears to be no consensus over such crucial questions as how and why the Rape of Nanking happened and how extensive the loss of human life was.[7]

Yamamoto argues that "in [the] case of the Rape of Nanking, historical research should attempt to determine why, how, and to what extent the Japanese committed the alleged atrocities."[8] I agree with his first two demands, which is why I tend to argue that it does not matter if there were 50,000 or 100,000 women raped by Japanese soldiers. The number alone does not change the criminal nature of the act. Every woman who was raped by Japanese soldiers in Nanjing or in "comfort stations" was one too many. The Japanese government should not argue about the numbers but should instead accept responsibility for the crimes, no matter how many suffered from them. Such discourse practically demands a numeric quota of victims to achieve criminal status, and this should not be the line of argument, especially considering the victims.

Yamamoto's arguments, which he calls revisionist instead of repudiating,[9] are also apologetic:

> A close examination of reliable primary materials indicates that a large majority of victims were adult males whom the Japanese troops rounded up and subsequently executed on the pretext of clearing the city of former soldiers disguised in civilian clothes. Apart from such mass executions of soldiers and civilians *misidentified* as soldiers, individual Japanese soldiers committed numerous criminal acts. Yet, there were violent acts that the soldiers engaged in as *individuals outside the supervision of the military command* and did not result in a huge number of deaths.[10]

For Yamamoto, acts by individuals are not the state's responsibility. However, I argue that these individual soldiers acted as professionals ordered to commit violence against an enemy of Japan. Furthermore, if the military command was not able to immediately condemn such forms of individual violence, it deserved all possible punishment because it failed to contain the violence of its personnel, thereby causing unnecessary civilian suffering. Apologetically arguing for those responsible on the Japanese side, Yamamoto emphasizes that "the ways American researchers have approached the Rape of Nanking are seriously flawed, resulting in an incorrect analysis and conclusion. Consequently, many people in this country accept the conclusion of such a flawed research and analysis and develop their own ideas—some of them problematic—about the incident as well as about the Japanese in general."[11]

Such arguments are made possible by the Japan-bashing[12] works of American scholars and journalists like the late Iris Chang, whose work, in which "numerous historical facts are misconstrued,"[13] is more accusatory than it is neutral and historically accurate.[14] As discussed earlier, comparing Nanjing to the Holocaust does not help strengthen Nanjing's historical dimension either, as this approach may lead to a "victim culture" and help deniers and revisionists who can claim that Nanjing was not as bad as the Shoah.[15] However, as American historian Roger B. Jeans correctly argues, "Chang strives to portray it as an unexamined Asian holocaust. Unfortunately, she undermines her argument—she is not a trained historian—by neglecting the wealth of sources in English and Japanese on this event."[16] Her anti-Japanese position was clear, and by arguing that all Japanese neglect to accept the historicity of the events was simply Japan bashing and not an accurate discussion of the reality. Yet there are indeed specific Chinese and Japanese perspectives on the Rape of Nanjing that tend to stimulate such aggressive and senseless reinterpretations of the past.

Narratives of the events have tended to present the Chinese as helpless victims, an image that did not fit the heroic narratives of the fight against the Japanese enemy during the Maoist era.[17] It took until the mid-1980s before the topic—as Sinologist Michael Berry remarked—"began to reenter the Chinese consciousness."[18] In contrast, in the West, the Rape of Nanjing remained a marginal event in the history of the Second World War until Chang's book caused a more intense discussion. For the Chinese perception and memorial conservation of the events, the Memorial Hall of the Victims in Nanjing Massacre by Japanese Invaders (Nanjing Memorial Hall) would become the most important mourning site. Built in 1985, it commemorates the victims of the events in 1937–1938 and was extended 10 years later to preserve knowledge about the events, ensuring that the victims of Nanjing were not forgotten.[19] The events, however, were also used for propaganda purposes, for example, to "stir up Chinese patriotism as well as anti-American and anti-Japanese sentiments" during the Korean War.[20] What stimulated the Chinese interest in preserving documents and oral testimonies related to the events were the Japanese denials. As a response, Nanjing University, in cooperation with the local archives, formed the Committee to Compile Materials on the Japanese

Military's Nanjing Massacre (Qin-Hua Rijun Nanjing datusha shiliao bianji weiyuanhui), which would spend years and invaluable efforts compiling historical materials related to the events, which would also be made available to the public.[21] Testimonies from more than 1,700 survivors, who were interviewed by the committee in 1984, were also given to the Memorial Hall where their important oral histories could be displayed. Due to these developments, as Yuki Miyamoto highlighted, "[T]he Nanjing Massacre was reframed, transformed from a shameful incident in China's past into part of glorious history elevating the Chinese people, who evinced the strength to overcome such atrocities."[22]

Public interest in the events was further stimulated by documentary film productions that took a closer look at the Rape of Nanjing. Luo Guanqun's *Massacre in Nanjing* (Tucheng xuezheng, 1987), T. F. Mou's *Black Sun: The Nanjing Massacre* (Hei taiyang: Nanjing datusha, 1995), and Wu Ziniu's *Don't Cry, Nanking* (Nanjing 1937, 1995) helped revive the memory of the events by gaining the sympathy of millions of movie-goers in China and abroad.[23] Consequently, activists established a movement to create national holidays to commemorate the Rape of Nanjing on December 13 and February 27 that were sanctioned by the National People's Congress (NPC).[24] The People's Republic of China also tried to list documents related to the events and the comfort women system with UNESCO's register for heritage documents, which underlines the Chinese effort to put greater weight on the commemoration of the Rape of Nanjing and the preservation of documents related to it.[25] The Rape of Nanjing was eventually dealt with in a variety of media, including more films and novels.[26]

It is true that "[f]or Chinese worldwide, Nanjing is not only a potent cry for justice, but a channel for national pride—even at the cost of strong anti-Japanese sentiment,"[27] and such sentiments are also fueled by Japanese denials. However, the anti-Japanese sentiments, as they are expressed in the *Chinese American Forum*, are often based on stereotypes. They neither help people overcome their anger about the matter, nor do they pave the way for reconciliation. One of these aggressive statements emphasizes this problem:

> Why did the Nanjing Massacre happen? Japanese people appear to be such courteous, law-abiding and peaceful people. Indeed, [the] majority of them are peace-loving, except they are ignorant of historical facts deliberately covered up by the right wing government. The soldiers who committed such horrible crimes were also normal people before the atrocities. What caused normal Japanese to turn into slaughtering beasts committing crimes of murder, rape, plunder and arson? This has to do with Japan's SAMURAI culture. . . . We must be alert on Japan's ambition to dominate in Asia again. Americans should not forget Pearl Harbor.[28]

As Germany will be remembered for being responsible for the Holocaust, Japan has and will be remembered for its war crimes in many regions of Asia during the Second World War. Japan wishes to "whitewash or understate,"[29] so the Japanese side often argues that "Hiroshima was a crime planned in cold blood. Nanking was the kind of thing that happens in any war"[30] to establish a victim narrative. In contrast to Germany's handling of the past (and where its discussion was mostly dominated by historians), the debate about Nanjing was mostly led by nonhistorians. The Rape of Nanjing became a "symbol of Japanese evil,"[31] but the events were not officially embedded into the national and public narrative of Japan's history of its own role during the Second World War.[32]

Although Japan's official position is disgusting, to say the least, one must emphasize that there is no unified Japanese position toward the events and that "the reality is a struggle in which conservatives and right-wingers duel with moderates and leftists over the 'correct history' of the war."[33] There are three different factions:

1. those who accept the events as historical fact, usually referred to as the Massacre School;
2. those who are moderate, accept the events as facts, but deny the numbers as too high, usually referred to as the Centrist School; and
3. the revisionists, who deny the events at all, usually referred to as the Illusion School.[34]

In contrast to most of their Chinese colleagues who argue with maximal victim numbers, conservative Japanese historians tend to downplay the number of victims. However, the deniers' works are published without a problem in Japan because they serve a conservative lobby that is strong in the circles of ruling politicians throughout the country. Although the centrist school accepts that the events happened, they tend to argue that the number of victims could not have been that high and is made up in unreliable Western and Chinese sources.[35] One could argue that such a discussion is obsolete, as guilt should not require hundreds or thousands of victims but rather individual ones—civilians or prisoners of war (POWs), regardless of nationality, gender, or age—who were killed by Japanese soldiers during the Second World War.

Japan has thus had a long-lasting problem dealing with its own past. In 1972, Honda Katsuichi published a book in which he collected interviews with Chinese survivors of the Nanjing Massacre.[36] The book contained newspaper articles Honda had published in the decade prior, which aroused some interest in Japan. His claim that the Chinese memories of the events were accurate and that the Japanese army was guilty of a major war crime did not meet acceptance, especially within the conservative field of Japanese

The Rape of Nanjing

professors. Some insisted that a count of 200,000 to 300,000 victims was too high, whereas others denied the crimes entirely. Suzuki Akira spoke of the Nanjing Massacre as being an illusion and tried to label Honda's book as fiction.[37] In 1984, Tanaka Masaaki, the former secretary of General Matsui Iwane of the Japanese army during the operations at Nanjing, claimed that the stories about the massacre were a fabrication to support anti-Japanese sentiments in the region.[38] The historical struggle has continued even until now, as different factions still argue about the truth of the events. The fact that the historical discussion about Nanjing never ceased caused other problems, chiefly that of presenting the historical events to a wider public.

Although there are museums in Japan that provide a critical presentation of past events related to the Second World War and Japanese war crimes, not all follow such a path.[39] To quote Roger B. Jeans, the Yasukuni Shrine Museum (Yūshūkan) "glorifies prewar and wartime State Shinto, the imperial cult, and wartime sacrifice in the name of the emperor" and does not provide "references to 'comfort women,' Asian and Western women dragooned by the Japanese military into serving as sex slaves for Japanese troops . . . massacres or other war crimes."[40] When I visited the museum in 2007 for the first time, I was shocked by the positivistic display of Japan's military history, but was not surprised that taking videos and photography were prohibited within the museum, where descriptions were not only historically inaccurate but actively misleading. Museums like the Yūshūkan "still prefer to emphasize Japanese suffering while ignoring the catastrophe their country inflicted on the Asia-Pacific area during the years between 1931 and 1945."[41] However, museums established by private initiatives since the 1990s counter this official Japanese stance; they provide exhibitions that critically highlight past Japanese crimes and actively engage in a more just and mutual discourse with victims and people from countries that suffered from Japanese rule during the war.

Another issue that regularly led to tension between Japan and China was the so-called textbook struggle.[42] This "ongoing textbook story also is not a simple one, but one of struggle between those who would confront Japan's past, painful as it might be, and those who, driven by irrational patriotism, practice willful amnesia."[43] This willful amnesia was continuously stimulated by arguments made in favor of the total denial of the events in 1937 and 1938, which was based on the assumption that it was mathematically inaccurate to assume that the Japanese army could have killed so many people in such a short time.[44] Instead of accepting the fact that Japanese soldiers had committed war crimes in Nanjing during December 1937 and February 1938, Japanese scholars continuously scrutinized the number of victims. When Chinese researchers claimed numbers between 100,000 and 350,000 were realistic, especially because the Nanjing War Crimes Tribunal had reported about 28 mass killings with 190,000 victims and more than 850 spontaneous or sporadic killings with a total amount of 150,000 victims, it could have been assumed that more than 300,000 Chinese men, women, and children had lost their lives.[45] Japanese conservative historians and deniers usually demand a number of fewer than 15,000 victims and consider that to be a "reasonable" death count of civilians in a war zone.[46] Historian David Askew also claims a low number—between 3,000 and 5,000 victims during the Nanjing Massacre—to be accurate, citing his estimations of the number of people officially living in Nanjing by the end of 1937.[47] I strongly disagree with his view because many more people might have been in the Chinese capital when the Japanese arrived, considering that those living between Shanghai and Nanjing had arrived in the city to escape the Japanese army. Masahiro Yamamoto's numbers range between 15,000 and 50,000 victims,[48] which also seems to be too low, but focusing on numbers takes attention away from the important fact that Japanese soldiers *committed* war crimes to begin with. It must be accepted that the exact victim count is not as important when one considers that every single life taken during the events was precious. Between 1946 and 1948, the International Military Tribunal for the Far East in Tokyo listed more than 200,000 Chinese massacred and approximately 20,000 rape victims during the six weeks after the city fell. Japan had seven decades to accept the guilt, but instead, historians and publicists chose to discuss numbers.[49]

The deniers regularly state that there is no Japanese documentary evidence for the events at Nanjing, claiming that the whole issue is a conspiracy based on foreign documents and forged eyewitness reports that were used during the postwar trials. The deniers' question is simple: Where are the sources?[50] However, numerous sources are available[51]—which are still being analyzed and need further work to complement our picture of Japanese war crimes—and despite some evidence being lost forever, photographs,[52] Chinese victim accounts of the events,[53] and reports from foreigners who were at Nanjing during the Rape[54] are valuable sources to analyze the atrocities more closely.

In contrast to these documents, official Japanese history related to the Rape of Nanjing barely mentions any hint of the atrocities committed by the army. Instead, they read like reports based on dates and troop advances.[55] Private documents by Japanese soldiers and officers also focus on victory, how it relates to military strategy, and the overall achievements of the Japanese Imperial Army. They do not mention anything about the violent eruptions within the Chinese city.[56] It is not surprising that the soldiers' ego documents (e.g., letters to their families) omit the realities of war and focus on glory and honor instead. The human community that shared the guilt was the previously described military machine that participated in the events, and family members were usually kept outside that inner circle of shared insight. The soldiers' relatives thus remained as common citizens who could continue their lives after the war ended, but their knowledge of the cruelty that happened at Nanjing was deeply buried in their conscience to keep their own personalities as ordinary as possible. Denying guilt would thus be common in a postwar society whose members were not interested in examining Japan's cruel past closely. A debate about Japanese war crimes in general and the Rape of Nanjing in particular led to reactions "ranging from pure denial to utter outrage,"[57] and those Japanese who raised the issue were considered traitors or worse. The Nanjing Massacre will remain a bone of contention within the international relations in East and Southeast Asia, but as Lu Yan correctly remarked, "although the question on the number massacred continues to be debated while the Japanese revisionists hold on to their denial of the massacre, it is beyond doubt that the event in Nanjing seventy years ago will remain in global awareness for the time being."[58] Although the awareness exists, not everybody is familiar with the historical facts related to the Rape of Nanjing, which is why I want to provide a short account of what happened before analyzing the specific forms of and reasons for the violence in this particular space-time continuum.

The Events at Nanjing

When the Japanese military prepared for war against China, they considered the war to be fast and victorious like their victory in the first Sino-Japanese War in 1894–1895 had been. They planned on hitting hard and conquering China in a *blitzkrieg* to spare Japan from sending large contingents of troops to the mainland—especially because the main enemy on the continent was supposed to be the Soviet Union—and a second faction within Japanese military circles, which was led by the navy, pushed for an expansion to Southeast Asia and Australia. However, the fight for Shanghai took the Japanese army longer than expected when Chinese forces bound Japan's troops to the city from mid-August to late November in 1937. Due to a high number of deaths and casualties, the soldiers of the Japanese Imperial Army were seriously shocked by the fierce Chinese resistance.[59] Nine thousand Japanese soldiers had died by November, and more than 30,000 were wounded. More disastrous was the fact that the so-called "Shanghai Incident" could not be ended with a true victory, as most of the Chinese troops withdrew from the city before being encircled by the enemy.[60] They fled, of course, for Nanjing.

Consequently, as Japanese historian Fujiwara Akira (1922–2003) put it, "glory-hungry, frontline units lusted to be first in the enemy capital and staged a mad day for it."[61] Violence already took place on the march toward Nanjing, and the *Japan Advertiser* reported about a special killing contest on December 7 and 14, 1937. Mukai Toshiaki and Noda Takeshi were described as having such a contest, and the two Japanese men would be the first to decapitate 100 Chinese on their way to Nanjing. Although Bob Tadashi Wakabayashi considers this contest to be fictional based on the newspaper's PR story, it is no proof that similar contests between Japanese soldiers did not exist, especially because such stories often possess a kernel of truth.[62] Leaving their victims behind them, the Japanese troops eventually reached Nanjing and began encircling the city that represented China's political center of power. The soldiers assumed that if Nanjing fell, the war would be over and they could return home as victorious heroes. Instead, they took the city on December 13, 1937, after it was bombed by Japanese air raids and destroyed by countless artillery shells. Once the capital was occupied, the soldiers, as the *Beijing Review* described it, "launched into a six-week campaign of destruction, pillage, rape and slaughter."[63]

The Japanese soldiers did not find the Chinese army they were pursuing since Shanghai, but they discovered uniforms that were left behind by enemy soldiers who tried to escape. Acting under the assumption that many Chinese troops had entered guerilla status, every noncombatant was perceived as a potential threat. The paranoid Japanese soldiers, confronted with their memories of Shanghai, took every Chinese person into custody and accused them of being Chinese guerilla soldiers. Civilians, however, were also attacked, even if there was no indication of them being involved in military acts against the Japanese Imperial Army.[64] Historian Yu Lan also emphasized the symbolic value of Nanjing as the Chinese capital as a reason for the Japanese soldiers' violence: "To demonstrate the conqueror's power, atrocious actions were used by the invading Japanese army with a calculated ruthlessness: the massacre of enormous number[s] of Chinese was accomplished through methodic killing that demonstrated efficiency."[65] The Japanese forced two extremely violent periods upon the Chinese civilians in the city, ranging from 1.) December 15 to 21, 1937, and 2.) from January 28 to February 3, 1938. They thereby "created a living hell for those who were trapped within"[66] the city. However, between these two organized forms of violence in which macro-violence was used to kill captured Chinese soldiers in mass killings, the period in between was full of micro-violence when groups of Japanese soldiers looted and wandered the city in search of victims for violent experimentation, torture, and rape. The poor women and girls who had not been able to escape the city eventually found themselves in a "historical situation in which, in fact, beauty was a curse rather than a blessing."[67] However, once the gang rapes by small groups of soldiers began, no girl or woman was secure anymore. Girls from the age of 10 to women aged 70 were gang raped multiple times before they were likely stabbed to death with the soldiers' bayonets. It is unimaginable what trauma such an experience might have had for the young girls and women who were victimized by these violent groups of young men during the Rape of Nanjing. Although many women suffered during the events, many were saved from a similar experience by the establishment of the Nanjing Safety Zone, where Europeans and Americans had forged an alliance to rescue and protect those who were in danger of sharing such a violent fate.

When the representatives of the Chinese municipal government of Nanjing fled the city, foreign residents from Britain, Denmark, Germany, and the

The Rape of Nanjing

United States formed a Safety Zone in the city where they would provide shelter for Nanjing's citizens and other refugees to protect them from the Japanese soldiers, who would supposedly raid the city after its fall. They eventually formed a Committee for the Nanjing Safety Zone and became acting authorities in an otherwise lawless environment.[68] Alongside the Western representatives of the Red Cross, the Red Swastika Society and some criminal organizations joined the committee and tried to secure supplies for those who could not have made it out of the city. A message was sent to the Japanese ambassador in Shanghai to inform the authorities about the creation of the Safety Zone, who was requested to accept it as a sphere within the city in which Japanese soldiers had no access. On December 8, the committee formally took over the city's government and also received money from the Chinese central government. Even before the city fell, its members tried to secure a truce with the Japanese military to avoid senseless casualties. Once the Japanese soldiers were in control of the city, however, the committee and its members did everything possible to save the civilians from rape or torture by wandering groups of soldiers.[69]

Over 50 foreigners who were involved in attempts to rescue Chinese civilians and hidden soldiers from Japanese violence were successful despite having risked their lives to keep Japanese soldiers out of the Safety Zone.[70] News about Nanjing was broadly circulated in English-language newspapers,[71] and official diplomatic reports described the situation well enough for others to understand what the Chinese had gone through. On January 7, 1938, a member of the U.S. embassy described the Japanese pillaging: "During the last week of December Japanese soldiers broke into both Embassy compounds frequently and in addition to taking the two motor cars previously reported took money and property, including jewelry and watches, belonging to members of the Chinese staff and servants totaling in value several hundred dollars Chinese currency."[72] A week later, on January 13, 1938, the U.S. Consul at Nanjing sent the following confidential message to the British Embassy at Shanghai:

> Very confidential.
> Situation here is far more difficult and abnormal than we had anticipated. Atrocities committed during first two weeks after occupation of city were of a nature and on a scale which are almost incredible. Condition as regards military nature and on a scale which are almost incredible. Condition as regards military unruliness are slowly improving but isolated cases of murder and other barbarities continue.[73]

Other reports proved that Japanese soldiers had entered the Safety Zone numerous times to find women and girls to rape.[74]

More and more people tried to enter the Safety Zone, as this seemed to be the only place where some security could be granted—save for the few times when Japanese soldiers snuck in to find victims for their cruel actions.[75] However, no life was safe from being taken at will outside the zone. Tao Baojin (1875–1948), who acted as president of the Nanjing Red Swastika Society, which supported the efforts of the Safety Zone Committee by setting up porridge kitchens at Mount Wutai Guangji Temple and Gulou University, described reality outside the zone:

> Since the Japanese army entered the city, they have slaughtered, burned, plundered, and raped without pausing for a day! The family members and refugees of the Nanjing City Red Swastika Society that live on my block number in the hundreds. Of the women old and young, every one has been raped. Many have committed suicide out of shame.[76]

The foreign missionaries, businessmen, physicians, and teachers did whatever they could to prevent a world of suffering from entering the Safety Zone, even if they bravely had to step between a Japanese bayonet and a civilian. Ying-Ying Chang, the late Iris Chang's mother, emphasized their roles when she mentioned "those brave Europeans and Americans who risked their own lives to protect thousands of Chinese refugees who were trying to escape the mass killings, rape, torture and systematic brutality of the massacre."[77]

One could not agree more, especially because these foreigners actively intervened on behalf of the Chinese people instead of being bystanders. Many of them would return from the war with scars that went beyond physical exhaustion, but rather irreparable trauma. Once the Japanese entered the city, people flocked to the Safety Zone "because the Japanese soldiers came to their homes to demand money and to rape."[78] Not all of them made it to the zone, as "quite a few people were bayoneted to death on the streets."[79] The American missionary Minnie Vautrin (1886–1941), who also served as president of Gingling College, a women's college in Nanjing, was one of the foreigners who stood up against Japanese demands. Ying-Ying Chang correctly remarked that "because of her admirable courage, humanity and tenacity, she saved thousands of Chinese women and children from rape and other crimes by Japanese soldiers in the Safety Zone."[80] However, she was also deeply hurt by the events and committed suicide after she returned to the United States in 1941. What she had experienced was obviously too cruel to live with for the rest of her life, being haunted by memories of women and girls beaten and raped by Japanese soldiers. On December 15, 1937, she wrote in her diary:

> From 8:30 this morning until 6 this evening, excepting for the noon meal, I have stood at the front gate while the refugees poured in. There is terror in the face of many women—last night was a terrible night in the city and many young women were taken from their homes by the Japanese soldiers. . . . The Japanese have looted widely yesterday and today, have destroyed schools, have killed citizens, and raped women. One thousand

disarmed Chinese soldiers, whom the International Committee hoped to save, were taken from them and by this time are probably shot or bayoneted.[81]

On the next day, she stated that "there probably is no crime that has not been committed in this city today."[82] Occasionally, shots could be heard at the Safety Zone, signaling the fates of those who had not made it before the Japanese found them. The stream of women who sought shelter from the Japanese soldiers did not stop. On December 17, Vautrin noted:

> A stream of weary wild-eyed women were coming in. Said their night had been one of horror; that again and again their homes had been visited by soldiers. (Twelve-year-old girls up to sixty-year-old women raped. Husbands forced to leave bedroom and pregnant wife at point of bayonet. If only the thoughtful people of Japan knew facts of these days of horror.) Wish some one were here who had time to write the sad story of each person—especially that of the younger girls who had blackened their faces and cut their hair.[83]

An increasing number of girls and women arrived, all begging Vautrin to be taken into the zone where they could find shelter and security.[84] What the American missionary experienced was far too cruel for the human mind to process: "Those of you who have lived in Nanking can never imagine how the streets look—the saddest sight I ever hope to see. Buses and cars upset in street, dead bodies here and there, with faces already black, discarded soldiers' clothing everywhere, every house and shop looted and smashed if not burned."[85]

However, Minnie Vautrin was not the only foreigner in Nanjing trying to protect the refugees from the danger posed by the Japanese. Reverend James McCallum was a missionary and physician who worked in one of the hospitals in the Safety Zone; he wrote a report on December 29, which he would later send home to his family, that explained "a foreigner must be on duty 24 hours here at the hospital to deal with the Japanese visitors."[86] Women and girls required constant protection from soldiers who would use any chance to get them out of the zone to rape them. What happened to the people of Nanjing was a nightmare:

> They have been in terror and no wonder. Many of them have nothing left now but a single garment around their shoulders. Helpless and unarmed, they have been at the mercy of the soldiers, who have been permitted to roam about at will wherever they pleased. There is no discipline whatever and many of them are drunk. By day they go into the buildings in our Safety Zone centers, looking for desirable women, then at night they return to get them.[87]

The women and girls seemed to have no chance to escape this fate, and as McCallum highlighted, "Resistance is fatal. A woman six months pregnant, who resisted, came to us with 16 knife wounds in her face and body, one piercing the abdomen."[88] The men's fates were not better, and they were treated in similarly cruel ways:

> Men who gave themselves up to the mercy of the Japanese when they were promised their lives would be spared—a very few of them returned to the Safety Zone in a sad way. One of them declared they were used for bayonet practice and his body certainly looked it. Another group was taken out near Ku-ling Sz; one who somehow returned, lived long enough to tell the fate of that group. He claimed they threw gasoline over their heads, and then set fire to them. This man bore no other wounds but was burned so terribly around the neck and head that one could scarcely believe he was a human being.[89]

Of course, not all Japanese were like that. McCallum reported that "[w]e have met some Japanese who have treated us with courtesy and respect. Others have threatened us, striking or slapping some. Although the Japanese Embassy staff has tried to help us out, they have been helpless. But soldiers with a conscience are few and far between."[90] Luck played a key role and was decisive for the survival of the people trapped in the zone surrounded by Japanese "sharks" who awaited the first signs of weakness.

To demonstrate that the available reports from Nanjing all describe a similar level of violence against civilians, I will provide some further descriptions. Dr. Robert O. Wilson (1904–1967), who received his medical degree from Harvard Medical School, worked at Drum Tower Hospital in Nanjing when the Japanese took over the city. In his letters to his family,[91] Wilson described the people's harsh living conditions, explaining that he had to deal with more than 10 severe surgeries per day to keep up with the steady stream of badly wounded people. He told his family that

> [t]he slaughter of civilians is appalling. I could go on for pages telling of cases of rape and brutality almost beyond belief. Two bayonetted cases are the only survivors of seven street cleaners who were sitting in their headquarters when Japanese soldiers came in without warning or reason and killed five of their number and wounded the two that found their way to the hospital. I wonder when it will stop and we will be able to catch up with ourselves again.[92]

He called the Rape of Nanking "the modern Dante's Inferno, written in huge letters with blood and rape," and directly or indirectly witnessed "murder by the wholesale and rape by the thousands of cases. There seems to be no stop to the ferocity, lust and atavism of the brutes."[93]

In a letter to his family on January 28, 1938, he described how the International Safety Zone Committee tried to bring a rape case to the attention of the Japanese authorities in which three Japanese gendarmes "took a woman to their headquarters and raped her three times before returning her."[94] The police investigated the case and took the woman into custody to question her:

> They brought her back to our house at about ten o'clock last night and listed five points of error in her story. These pertained to the color of the walls, the number of steps she went up, the position of the lamp in the room and the time of her abduction. As to the main points of the story there seemed to be no division of opinion. By bringing out these errors they saved their face, the woman was returned and I guess the incident is closed.[95]

The Japanese authorities had no interest in dealing with the cruel reality, and it is tragic that this attitude has not changed much since 1938. In contrast to such reports, the authorities had ordered Chinese citizens to go back to their homes until February 4. However, the danger for women and girls had not disappeared; Wilson stated that "a 53-year-old woman went back to her home and within an hour a soldier tried to rape her. She went on her knees and wept and wailed so that he contented himself with beating her up a little whereupon she immediately came back to the zone."[96] The Japanese soldiers also had their own sex slaves during this time, and Wilson reports a 22-year-old woman who had been "taken to some quarters in south city where she was raped about a dozen times daily for 38 days. By that time, she had developed bilateral purulent buboes, a vicious case of gonorrhea and a large raw ulcer of the vagina so that she was sent away as no more use."[97] The Japanese soldiers treated these women and girls like trash, and it is unbearable to imagine what their fates would have been without the Safety Zone.

Miner Searle Bates (1897–1978), who was a professor and vice president of the Nanjing University, also reported about the events and would later testify at the Tokyo Trials. He correctly argued that "at Nanking the Japanese Army has lost much of its reputation, and has thrown away a remarkable opportunity to gain the respect of the Chinese inhabitants and of foreign opinion."[98] Instead, the Japanese Imperial Army had created a living hell for those who could not escape the city fast enough (i.e., the weak and the poor):

> [I]n two days the whole outlook has been ruined by frequent murder, wholesale and semi-regular looting and uncontrolled disturbance of private homes including offenses against the security of women. Foreigners who have traveled over the city report many civilians' bodies lying in the streets. In the central portion of Nanking they were counted yesterday as about one to the city block. A considerable percentage of the dead civilians were the victims of shooting or bayoneting in the afternoon and evening of the 13th, which was the time of Japanese entry into the city. Any person who ran in

fear or excitement, and anyone who was caught in streets or alleys after dusk by roving patrols was likely to be killed on the spot. Most of this severity was beyond even theoretical excuse. It proceeded in the Safety Zones as well as elsewhere, and many cases are plainly witnessed by foreigners and by reputable Chinese. Some bayonet wounds were barbarously cruel.[99]

There was also a German witness to the events; he was the "Oskar Schindler of China,"[100] John Rabe (1882–1950), a member of the National Socialist Party and the director of the Siemens branch at Nanjing. Rabe had lived in Nanjing since 1911, and in 1931 he took over the Siemens factory before joining the Nazi Party in 1934. Following his later testimonies, he was no believer in Nazi ideology but joined the party to gain funding for some projects related to the factory.[101] As a German, he used his party relations to act as a representative of the German Reich, with which Japan was on good terms due to the Anti-Comintern Pact of 1936. The relations between Germany and Japan consequently "created a spatiotemporal niche that endowed the swastika with a positive function,"[102] and Rabe would use it as often as possible to save lives. He "often rushed to save women from being raped or properties from being ransacked by waving his swastika armband under the nose of Japanese soldiers."[103] Because not all Japanese soldiers were willing to respect such an intrusion without resistance, his own life was often at risk. In his diaries,[104] Rabe draws a similar picture of the Japanese soldiers as other Western observers did, which is why it must be accepted that even without sufficient Japanese ego-documents, the outrageous acts of violence and rape happened. There is no doubt about that.

However, as historian Takashi Yoshida correctly highlighted, "[T]he Nanjing Massacre has undergone continuous redefinition and reinterpretation in Japan, China, and the United States."[105] Nanjing nevertheless remains an "emblem of Japan's wartime aggression"[106] for both the victims and those who remember them. However, taking a closer look at the violence committed in the specific space-time continuum of Nanjing will help us better understand how and why it could become emblematic and what could be done to prevent similar violent eruptions in the future.

Violence and the Nanjing Massacre

As mentioned earlier, Japanese documents related to the Nanjing Massacre exist, but they do not often expose Japanese soldiers' violent actions.[107] The lack of command and active intervention on behalf of the leading officers (such as Iwane Matsui, who was later sentenced to death for his role during the events by the judges of the Tokyo Trials) is regularly cited as one of the reasons for the atrocities.[108] However, the events remain hard to understand, especially because "the tortures and atrocities of the Rape were so extreme they were unthinkable."[109] It took the Japanese army until the end of March 1938 to fully restore order, redefine the space-time continuum, and prevent the soldiers from committing further outrageous acts.[110]

Particularly disturbing for the reader are the reports that describe the behavior of the soldiers: "Some Japanese soldiers laughed and applauded at the sight of a still-living person who was burning to death after being shot and then doused with gasoline. Other Japanese soldiers beheaded refugees and put their heads on bayonets to parade through the streets."[111] Although the Japanese soldiers already began their killings on the way to Nanjing, it was there that the conflict fully erupted into a helix of death, causing increasing suffering. The troops hoped to encircle the enemy at the Chinese capital and force China's army to surrender to end the war quickly. Yet many soldiers in the Chinese army had escaped, and the Japanese were enraged by their missed opportunity to end the war. The massacre, in terms of the typology of violence as it was discussed in Chapter 1, can be separated into mass killings (10,000 to 50,000 victims) and sporadic killings (fewer than 10 victims). Whereas mass killings are usually orchestrated and require a larger group of soldiers, the second category entails spontaneous acts of violence committed by small groups or individuals. These "individual, sporadic acts of torture and killing included splitting, gutting, slicing, piercing alive, and dog biting."[112] If Chinese men were killed in "so-called mopping-up operations,"[113] they became victims because the Japanese believed they were soldiers who had thrown away their uniforms to become guerilla fighters. However, the Japanese soldiers needed another narrative to rape the women, many of whom were gang raped before being killed. In the first four weeks of the massacre, up to 20,000 women were raped, although the total number is usually estimated to have been 80,000.[114] Yet it was not just killing or raping that the Japanese soldiers indulged in; both organized and spontaneous looting also became quite popular. It is assumed that the Japanese looted more than 70 percent of the buildings in Nanjing between mid-December 1937 and late February 1938.[115]

We can identify several forms of physical violence against human beings and things—committed in ordered and nonordered ways, by individuals and groups alike. Therefore, micro- and macro-violence was possible, and very often sanctioned, in the space-time continuum of the Nanjing Massacre. Soldiers did not consider their violent acts illegal or outrageous, as though bayonet training with living subjects was obviously permissible. Scholars, victims, and activists have argued about the reasons for such inhumane acts, but claiming that the Japanese are evil is insufficient and biased, influenced by the belief that we are incapable of similar acts. I would like to discuss five reasons that might shed light on the "why" of the situation, although we can never fully understand the perpetrators' motives because we cannot examine their minds in the context of their space-time continuum.

The first reason for their excessive violence was revenge. The Japanese soldiers expected the war to be short, glorious, and honorable. Once they had fought in Shanghai, they knew that this was not the case. At that point, because the Chinese soldiers had abandoned their own capital, there was no chance for a decisive battle—like the Battle of Sedan—that could have ended the war against China.[116] The war had not been ended at Shanghai; therefore, "the predefined goal of the Japanese invaders was to use terrorist tactics to force China to submit."[117] Because the soldiers could not submit after the city fell into the hands of the Japanese, civilians automatically became the surrogates who suffered from the anger of Japan's soldiers, who punished those who could not escape them.

A second reason for the violence was the feeling of superiority in a racial and cultural sense. The "Japanese soldiers did not feel much sense of guilt," and "they even committed atrocities with a certain kind of pleasant sensation."[118] Japan had become a great power in the aftermath of the Russo-Japanese War in 1905, and it considered itself to be different (i.e. better than China). The Chinese civilians were regarded as subhuman and deserving of neither sympathy nor protection. The extreme forms of violence against the people at Nanjing are related to this sense of superiority, which, as a narrative, legitimized the outrageous acts. It did not matter for the Japanese if a living being was set ablaze or stabbed to death; because the victims did not share their Japanese group identity, their lives were less valuable to Japanese soldiers.

One reason that could explain the acceptance of sex-based discrimination and the raping of Chinese women might have been that in contemporary Japanese society, discrimination against women was not considered a severe offense. As Kasahara Tokushi remarked, "In this male-dominated society, the husband's sexual indulgence outside the home was socially recognized and the wife could not interfere."[119] Just as the men were punished for their cowardice with penetration from Japanese bayonets, women were punished for their very existence by being penetrated by Japanese penises. They were used as human supplies to serve the sexual desires of the Japanese soldiers before being dumped as human trash.

A fourth reason that is often cited to explain Japanese soldiers' violence is the "inhumane nature of the Japanese Army"[120] in which violence is delivered from top to bottom in the existing hierarchies. The "barbaric nature of Japanese militarism"[121] was based on punishment for every disobedience, existent or nonexistent. Although the soldiers were usually victims themselves, they took advantage of the chance to channel their violence and aggression toward others. On the field, they were in charge and could decide what was right or wrong—they were in positions of uncontested power, and they behaved using the same patterns of violence that indoctrinated them in the past. In their contemporary space-time continuum, they defined law and order for themselves, and rape and killing were essential parts of it that occurred daily.

A fifth reason might be the paranoia that some Japanese felt about being killed by Chinese guerilla fighters. Because many Chinese soldiers had fled and left their uniforms behind, the once-clear line between combatants and non-combatants became blurry. To secure themselves, Japanese soldiers acted violently against any potential threats. This paranoid fear stimulated unnecessary overkill reactions from the Japanese soldiers, thereby causing immeasurable suffering for the victims. Eventually, Japanese soldiers acted like "loosened barbarians" and "human beasts"[122] when they ripped apart every bit of civilized rule that a peaceful society might have been based on.

Although these reasons can help us better understand the eruption of violence at Nanjing, they will never be able to excuse the actions of the Japanese soldiers. Nanjing has consequently "haunted and influenced the conscience of the world"[123] and will remind us of the evils human beings are capable of. Kevin Ng also expressed the necessity of remembrance in the *Chinese American Forum*, where he stated that

> Japan's actions are a stain on humanity and a snag on human progress. The world's similar disregard and silence regarding Japan's actions and failure to take responsibility for its crimes signify a tacit approval and even encouragement. Sadly, it appears that the movement of time, coupled with the business and political imperatives of the contemporary world make it easy to ignore and forget the injustices suffered and the crimes committed against the older generation.[124]

It is our task to bring Nanjing back to the public eye and stimulate the conscience of those who could be involved in similar situations in the future. Only such people can prevent the previously mentioned reasons from reappearing in a space-time continuum in which violence is partially legalized. However, to fully understand the actions and reactions of the Japanese soldiers, we must continue analyzing what happened. Before taking a closer look at the sexual violence as it began in Nanjing and found its climax in the establishment of the comfort women system, it is essential to address some general considerations about rape as a special form of violence, particularly against women, in the next chapter.

CHAPTER THREE

Rape: A Theoretical Analysis

Rape is a by-product of war. Oftentimes, soldiers use sexual violence against women and girls who survive military conflicts. The reasons for this are diverse, but they always relate to the space-time continuum the soldiers are acting in. Many explanations focus on what American scholar Jonathan Gotschall called "a complex combination of causal factors" but do not include the sexuality or "the sexual impulses"[1] of the soldiers. Solely focusing on the individual perspectives of rapists and the victim of rape from a legal standpoint, Fiona E. Raitt and M. Suzanne Zeedyk argue that "it becomes sufficient to explain rape as an event between two isolated individuals and to ignore the societal context within which the rape, and a woman's (or man's) subsequent reactions to it, occurred."[2] Yet such a perspective does not provide much help in explaining why rape seems so common in war zones. Although rape is generally "a low-risk, high reward crime,"[3] it becomes an accepted practice for male soldiers for the sake of expressing male domination, military victory, and ultimate power.

Moreover, there are also credibility issues with victims and perpetrators alike, as society often considers rape to be "an accusation easily to be made and hard to be proved, and harder to be defended by the party accused."[4] Rape and its prosecution depends on victim statements; this is often criticized from a legal perspective because cases can be based on false confessions, which erodes the credibility of real victims. In addition, a Freudian interpretation accuses women as responsible for their own rapes. This interpretative analysis suggests that women consider rape to be an expression of their own masochistic and self-destructive desires and needs.[5] Such a perspective does not at all consider women as victims of a crime, and as Rochelle Semmel Albin correctly remarked, "The most striking legacy of the Freudian view of women as inherently masochistic is psychiatric theory that places blame for rape on victims, mothers, and wives of the sex offenders."[6] Very often, researchers overemphasize women's responsibility in rapes—if not the victims themselves, then the rapist's mothers, whose maternal shortcomings purportedly lead men to become rapists as a means to regain power over the feminine figures they have rejected since childhood.[7]

Older discussions of rape largely fail to accept raped women as victims. Instead, they see them as *agents provocateurs* who are partly responsible for their own rapes. This perception of rape in many societies makes it difficult for victims to confess what happened, as they tend to fear being perceived as responsible for their misery or even guilty of inviting the crime against them.[8] This might explain why it takes many victims a long time to share their experiences with the public, especially in the cases of former "comfort women."[9] Perceptions of rape are often biased and based on stereotypes related to male-female interrelations.[10] However, as Susan B. Bond and Donald L. Mosher emphasized, it is a "myth that women are secretly willing victims of rape, a myth generated by the false belief that rape is sexual in its essence, rather than violent in its motivation, execution, and consequences for the victim."[11] Rape is not often stimulated by sexual desire but rather by a wish for power and domination. Consequently, the erotic perception of rape as a fantasy must be replaced by the reality that it is a violent crime against women to establish domination and male-determined power dynamics.[12] Rape must therefore be defined as "a crime in which a sexually and violently callous man (or woman, F.J.), motivated by power, anger, or sadism selects a victim of opportunity, uses force, often excessive force, to overcome resistance and to degrade the victim."[13]

The consequent problem is one of perception and interpretation regarding the criminality of rape, and women as victims have been maligned, degraded, and ignored by mental health professionals in the past during rape discussions in their fields.[14] The legal system has also been criticized for considering rape in many cases a sexual crime instead of a violent one, blaming victims for having "invited" male abuse.[15] Instead of perpetrators being prosecuted, many rape survivors were victimized twofold by interrogative and accusatory prosecution styles that questioned their characters and motives instead of objectively examining their cases.[16] The Japanese police's aforementioned investigation in Nanjing is not different; instead of considering the traumatic consequences the rape might have had on the woman, investigators doubted victims when they could not remember details related to the incident. Juries and prosecutors alike omit such perspectives and assume that only women with dubious characters get raped.[17] Although our society argues that abusive behavior against women is learned through pornography—which, according to the feminist movement, is a foundation for the practice of rape[18]—such an explanation does not illuminate reasons for the abusive behavior of Japanese soldiers who committed rape in many parts of Asia during the war years between 1937 and 1945.

Rape is not only done on the basis of gender, but follows racist attitudes or narratives stemming from existing prejudices.[19] Rape also becomes more acceptable if preexisting hierarchies determine that rapists are superior to their victims, which means the act of rape expresses and confirms existing gender and race hierarchies. The Chinese and Korean rape victims in the comfort stations and in the occupied cities—such as Nanjing—were permissible to rape, and soldiers did not hesitate to claim their "prey" after their army's successful advance. Although identifying the causes of rape involves a deeper analysis of soldiers' educations, social preconditions, and behaviors within the war-related space-time continuum, it is important to emphasize that "sexual violence is defined to include any sexual activity, whether legally defined as 'rape' or not . . . committed by the use or threat of physical force,"[20] to quote legal scholar Frederick Schauer. Sexual violence therefore includes "rape, attempted rape, sexual acts that are not rape but involve actual or threatened physical coercion, attempted sexual acts involving actual or threatened physical coercion, and actual or attempted acts of nonsexual physical violence inspired by a search for sexual fulfillment."[21] However, there are legal issues when it comes to prosecuting sexual violence.

The sincerity of the prosecution, especially in the aftermath of the Second World War, was based on the question of who had been a victim of sexual violence and abuse. Whereas modern courts often distinguish between "the chaste and the unchaste,"[22] prosecutors in the postwar trials brought white victims of sexual violence to trial and Asian victims were mostly ignored. "Chaste" and "unchaste" women were thus racially determined. To quote David J. Giacopassi and Karen R. Wilkinson, "The rape of a chaste female brought the full force of the law; the rape of an unchaste woman not only went unpunished but often resulted in the trial being a public degradation ceremony of the 'nonvirtuous' female."[23] Next to the ostracizing of rape victims in Asian societies, this might have been one reason why the prosecution of wartime rapes and other sexual crimes against women were prevented.

By raping women, Japanese soldiers not only performed acts of sexual abuse that required punishment, but they physically expressed their perceived dominance over racially inferior victims who were allowed to be raped in the contemporary space-time continuum.[24] Although such circumstances legitimized abusive acts of sexual violence, the preconditions were established during times of peace, namely by gender roles and images of the female gender that were sanctioned by society. If women are not treated as members of society with legal and human rights, the preconditions for wartime rapes are sowed long before war itself. However, we should examine possible reasons for rape more intently before assessing consequences for victims and the specific interrelationships between war and rape.

Reasons

Psychological examinations of rapists in the 1950s showed that "sex offenders evidenced greater castration anxiety than other incarcerated criminals,"[25] which seems to emphasize the perpetrators' fears of losing power. A specific fixation on the penis was observed, and Oedipal feelings also played a role in the construction of female images.[26] The Japanese soldiers' practice of raping and killing victims by stabbing them with their bayonets underscores a specific obsession with the penis as an instrument of control and domination; they not only penetrate victims' vaginas with their penises, but also the female body as a whole with their bayonets.

Further studies with sex offenders, including tests like "the Rorschach, the Blacky Pictures Test, the House-Tree-Person Test, the Thematic Apperception Test-and paper-and-pencil tests, such as the Minnesota Multiphasic Personality Inventory and the Edwards' Personal Preference Scale," showed that "sex offenders were fearful, inadequate, sensitive, shy, impulsive, irresponsible, expected too much sex, lacked social skills, had a self-concept confused in psychosexual areas of identification, and were unable to evaluate the consequences of their own behavior."[27] In the Japanese soldiers' cases, their youth is one explanation for their sexual violence. Most of the soldiers were away from home for the first time and may not have had any sexual and/or social experiences with the other sex. Furthermore, their first sexual encounters with women might have been during gang rapes; due to this, their fears related to sexual power and performance were translated into violent behavior to impress other group members. Consequences were evaluated based on group norms, which, in the soldiers' specific space-time continuum, had already sanctioned violence against nonmembers of their group based on stereotypes and the supposed superiority of the Japanese over other Asians.

Although "male dominance, female precipitation, society, male sexuality, and male pathology"[28] are considered to be the main causes of rape, different explanations for the root causes of rape developed over time: "the feminist theory, the cultural pathology theory, the strategic rape theory, and the biosocial theory."[29] These theoretical approaches were used to explain the increase of rape during war without basing the explanation on human nature, as each theory emphasized different sociocultural factors as being the most predictive of sexual violence.[30] Regardless of these varying approaches, it must be highlighted that war itself is a precondition for the increase of rapes. Soldiers usually inflict sexual violence upon women who could not escape war and are considered the "prey" of the approaching soldiers, who, by having been victorious, not only claim occupied territory but also sexually dominate defeated female "enemies."[31]

Again, there is no national monopoly on war crimes, much like there is none on the use of rape in war by military or paramilitary forces. The list

Jonathan Gottschall provided in 2004 is very long: Afghanistan, Algeria, Argentina, Bangladesh, Belgium, Brazil, Burma, Bosnia, Cambodia, China, Congo, Croatia, Cyprus, East Timor, El Salvador, Germany, Guatemala, Haiti, India, Indonesia, Italy, Japan, Korea, Kosovo, Kuwait, Liberia, Mozambique, Nicaragua, Pakistan, Peru, the Philippines, Russia, Rwanda, Serbia, Sierra Leone, Somalia, Turkey, Uganda, Vietnam, Zaire, and Zimbabwe.[32] Rape exists in all parts of the world, which is why it cannot be considered a "Third World" problem but rather a by-product of warfare. War allows soldiers to interact with women who are not in-group members but become accessible once the soldiers have invaded their native territory. Furthermore, as Gottschall remarked, "[H]istorical and anthropological evidence suggests that rape in the context of war is an ancient human practice, and that this practice has stubbornly prevailed across a stunningly diverse concatenation of societies and historical epoch."[33]

The problem of mass rape following war is not new, but it was first and foremost feminist scholars and activists who raised their voices to address the issue. The "pressure cooker theory"[34] argues that rapists' acts follow biological instincts, that is, a biological imperative activated by war itself, because war affords men the opportunity to sexually abuse women whom they could not harm before. Another feminist interpretation was the idea that men's desires to oppress women were unleashed by war, and war caused women in out-groups to be the soldiers' enemies. This behavior is dependent on the social preconditioning of the soldiers, which means that only antifemale societies would yield such actions. However, such assumptions purport that only societies that do not accept gender equality deal with antifemale rape violence in war. This is untrue, because many soldiers who come from societies that officially accept gender equality still express antifemale sexual violence in war. Although it is true that society preconditions soldiers' values, social preconditioning is not the only deciding factor of the "rape potential" an individual soldier may possess. The simple idea rapists are created by chauvinist societies does not suffice in a critical analysis. All in all, "the feminist theory has poor theory-data fit. Not only does evidence indicate that peacetime rape (and its proscription) is a cultural universal, but it also shows that large-scale rape is a common outcome of conflicts among bands, tribes, chiefdoms, and state societies spread across continents and centuries."[35]

A second theoretical approach to explain wartime rape is the pathology theory. Such approaches, like in Iris Chang's book, tend to look back in time to find national preconditions that ultimately forced soldiers to commit acts of sexual violence against (foreign) women. Although Chang pointed to the samurai tradition and harsh military training as the preconditioning of the perpetrators who raped women during and after the Nanjing Massacre, similar explanatory models are used about national socialism and the war crimes of the Wehrmacht.[36] The weakness of the theory is its construction of inevitability, meaning it argues that social upbringing alone is responsible for

Rape: A Theoretical Analysis

violence. Such an argument, which is inherently based on national heritage, can then be easily abused to blame a nation's crimes on its historical past without accepting the possibility that violent acts are transnational and simply human. However, this would require the accuser to accept the universal existence of violent behavior and the personal capacity to commit violence.

A third theoretical approach to explain wartime rape is the strategic rape theory. This theory is based on the general idea that rape is just another form of weaponry within violent conflicts used to psychologically weaken the enemy by raping those the enemy soldiers are trying to protect. Rape is consequently used to achieve a strategic aim within conflicts. The soldiers use rape as a means of pressuring civilian noncombatants who live in the war zone and become victimized simply because they are strategic assets in the conflict.[37] Furthermore,

> [b]y raping women, soldiers split the familial atoms of which every society is composed. Raped women may become pregnant by the enemy, they may suffer grievous physical and psychological injuries, they may die, they may be abandoned or disavowed by shamed families and husbands, all of which degrade the ability of a culture to replenish itself through sexual reproduction.[38]

As victimology is usually defined by ethnic or religious factors—which means that women become rape victims due to their specific group identities—this form of mass rape in war is usually referred to as "genocidal rape" or "gendercide."[39]

Journalist Alexandra Stiglmayer accurately described the soldiers' perspectives in such a situation:

> A rape is an aggressive and humiliating act, as even a soldier knows, or at least suspects. He rapes because he wants to engage in violence. He rapes because he wants to demonstrate his power. He rapes because he is the victor. He rapes because the woman is the enemy's woman, and he wants to humiliate and annihilate the enemy. He rapes because the woman is herself the enemy whom he wishes to humiliate and annihilate. He rapes because he despises women. He rapes to prove his virility. He rapes because the acquisition of the female body means a piece of territory conquered. He rapes to take out on someone else the humiliation he has suffered in the war. He rapes to work off his fears. He rapes because it's really only some "fun" with the guys. He rapes because war, a man's business, has awakened his aggressiveness, and he directs it at those who play a subordinate role in the world of war.[40]

Very often—and as Benita Moolman has particularly shown in the case of South Africa—gang membership or other group identities can be based on or linked to "a violent, sexualised masculinity." Parameters like "domination, power, control, conquest, achievement and competition contribute to this masculinity,"[41] especially when they are expressed in a form of rape, an act that is often performed in groups. Such forms of sexual violence can also be instrumentalized as psychological warfare that is not only meant to hurt victims, but their in-groups as well. National superiority is thus expressed by raping a supposed racial and sexual inferior who becomes damaged by the act of foreign invasion (i.e., sexual penetration).[42]

The German sociologist Klaus Theweleit also tried to explain the rape of women with the sexualization of women in modern societies. He argued that soldiers were confronted with images of the female sex during times of peace, particularly in popular media like journals and film, that did not accurately depict reality. This is why men at war "would begin to take revenge for the false promises held out by women's bodies."[43] In public images of women, "it was in the breasts and vaginas of women sexualized in this manner that global seas began to flow for men of the era,"[44] eventually creating pressure for men that could only be answered by violently demanding the fulfilment of their fantasies in a space-time continuum that allowed them to dominate women as victims (i.e., in war).

The theories discussed thus far all agree that "rape in war is not incidental but functional."[45] Whereas Gottschall assumes that rape serves the collective goals of the soldiers first and foremost, I would argue it is hard to determine the difference, especially because the individual act often coincides with the collective's aims (as mentioned in Theweleit's discussion of a soldiers' collective). The fact that there are perverted sexual desires to torture female victims cannot fully be denied, but in most cases, other factors like power dynamics, hierarchies, euphoria resulting from violence, or strategic aims to diminish victims as representatives of enemy nations play a more important role.[46] Ruth Seifert emphasized this interrelationship even more clearly when she stated that rape "has nothing to do with sexuality but with the exertion of sexual violence directed against women."[47]

Another theoretical approach, the fourth and final one that will be discussed here, is the biosocial one. It is generally based on the assumption that "men possess instincts for sexual aggression that are restrained under normal conditions."[48] Following this theory, every man is a possible rapist and is only kept in check by the existing social and political norms that prevent him from raping a woman. Such a view, however, has been challenged by theories of evolutionary biology, which emphasize that all forms of behavior are related and influenced by environmental factors.[49] These arguments support the idea of a specific space-time continuum that might trigger specific forms of behavior, including a greater likelihood of using sexual violence by dominant men; namely, the soldiers who legally commit acts of violence and feel justified in raping women who are part of the enemy collective. Although Gottschall

Rape: A Theoretical Analysis

argued that there is a "biological determinism theory of wartime rape," its determining factors of wartime sexual violence are limited.[50]

We must acknowledge that every conflict has its own unique characteristics, but factors that stimulate rape in a war zone follow existing images of gender, racism, chauvinism, jingoism, sexual drive, individual sadistic tendencies, group dynamics, disorder, and simply the ability to get away with it. The fact that rape occurs in so many different conflicts is unrelated to economic, national, political, or social preconditions. Poor soldiers are not the only ones who rape, and neither are nonstate-related combatants (e.g., guerillas). Although the aforementioned theories help us formulate a general approach to explaining rape, they fail to provide a solid explanation for the specifics. This is why theoretical debates alone are insufficient and must be integrated into the context of actual events. Regardless of what is responsible for rape as a form of sexual violence in war, it is important to emphasize that such an experience has tremendous consequences for the victims once the space-time continuum reverts to peace; victims are physically and psychologically scarred in a society that might not feel sympathy for their experiences.

When we discuss wartime rape, we must consider the "sociocultural context in which women react to rape victimization,"[51] especially since Anne Wolbert Burgess and Lynda Lytle Holmstrom identified and defined the existence of rape trauma syndrome in 1974.[52] The trauma the victims endure is manifold; the experience of having been raped causes "emotional, cognitive, behavioral, and interpersonal trauma."[53] Women who have been raped also go through an array of emotions, for example, "shock, disbelief, anger, fear, and anxiety, while in the later aftermath, a woman's feelings might range from fear, humiliation, and embarrassment to anger, revenge, and self-blame."[54] Although the initial reaction to rape is an acute one and the intensity decreases with time, the trauma itself may not subside. Fear and anxiety become symptomatic of remembered events that usually never disappear.[55] It is particularly the loss of control and power—which are instrumental concepts in understanding rape as an act to redefine power hierarchies[56]—that helps clarify the long-term consequences for the victims. The absolute and enforced domination by a stranger may therefore be the most damaging result of the rape. However, the existence of such a situation is also made possible by war itself, which is why the relationship between war and rape requires further analysis.

Rape and War

As mentioned, young men act as a group in war—a military unit in a specific space-time continuum that legally permits them to be violent. Many young and sexually inexperienced soldiers seem to have no problems with the performance of sexual violence in a war zone; they rather consider their acts to be an expression of victory.[57] Legal scholar Catherine A. MacKinnon also emphasized that "[r]ape in war has so often been treated as extracurricular, as just something men do, as a product rather than a policy of war"[58] and thereby highlighted that our perception of rape in war is perceived and judged from our perspective within our space-time continuum. Although we like to see it as an extracurricular criminal act, we eventually have to accept that rape in war is rather the norm than the exception. In these circumstances, the normally individual act of rape becomes embedded in the group dynamics of the usually male perpetrators. This is why, as Larry May and Robert Strikwerda argued, the men involved in such acts share responsibility and why "rape should be seen as something that men, as a group, are collectively responsible for, in a way which parallels the collective responsibility of a society for crimes against humanity perpetrated by some members of their society."[59]

When soldiers as a collective participate in gang rapes, as Japanese soldiers did in China, the guilt might be shared and thus legitimized by the group. However, this also means that the whole group must be held responsible for the rape even if not all soldiers actively penetrated the victim. Larry May and Robert Strikwerda provided some explanatory models of how perpetrators, bystanders, and (postwar) societies as a whole tend to neglect collective guilt for such crimes:

> First, it is sometimes said that only the rapist is responsible since he alone intentionally committed the act of rape. Second, it is sometimes said that no one is responsible since rape is merely a biologically oriented response to stimuli that men have little or no control over. Third, it is sometimes said that everyone, women and men alike, contribute to the violent environment which produces rape so both women and men are equally responsible for rape, and hence it is a mistake to single men out. Fourth, it is sometimes said that it is "patriarchy," rather than individual men or men as a group, which is responsible for rape.[60]

Like the quoted authors, I disagree with such narratives. Of course, the guilt is shared by the group of soldiers who committed the rape, even if it is not perceived as such in their specific space-time continuum. The capacity for rape seems even higher in groups; group dynamics demand that men prove their masculinity, and the encouragement by fellow group members stimulates or even actively requests the act of rape. The social dimension of rape in war zones is therefore distinguished by soldiers as a group and not by individuals.[61]

Another reason for the violent male approach to sex during conflict might relate to the various sexualities of men and women alike. Whereas sex is rather easy for men and does not cause any direct consequences to their own bodies, women consider sex to be more cost intensive, especially because pregnancy is a natural possibility. These differing evaluations of sex might lend to male perpetrators' violent approaches to it "because women are more selective about mates and more interested in evaluating them and delaying copulation," and this is why "men, to get sexual access, must often break through feminine barriers of hesitation, equivocation, and resistance."[62] Gang rape can also be considered a latent punishment for limiting sex to the male group members of a peaceful society. Being in a different legal and normative context, perpetrators take revenge for their own sexual incapacities and limitations experienced during times of peace. In the figurative sense, they might also be taking revenge for their own suppression by women, like by their mothers or elder sisters, but that would require a psychological examination of the perpetrators and is therefore a mere speculation at this point. However, Sam Keen argued in favor of such an assumption when he stated that "men are violent because of the systematic violence done to their bodies and spirits. Being hurt they become hurters."[63] As outlined about the level of violence committed in war, the preconditions within perpetrators' societies are responsible for basic configurations that can stimulate a stronger eruption of violent behavior during war. The existence of these basic configurations also seems essential to the formation of dominant group dynamics; to quote May and Strikwerda again, "seeing men as collectively responsible may mean that men form a group in which there are so many features that the members share in common, such as attitudes or dispositions to engage in harm, that what holds true for one man also holds true for all other men."[64]

However, rape often becomes more than a spontaneous act of violence—it could become a threat to military success. In many such cases, those responsible for military planning realized the threat that rapist soldiers posed to victory and tried to control the sexual violence committed by their soldiers.[65] Although one concern was the spread of venereal disease (VD) among the soldiers, another was the antagonism of the civilian population in a region that should be controlled without much resistance from the locals. One solution was the attempt to regulate prostitution, because military leadership was well aware that they could not simply prohibit sex for the soldiers.[66] In the Japanese case, the comfort system is a well-documented case of prostitution in the military system meant to prevent Japan's Imperial troops from raping civilians on the mainland and in other parts of Southeast Asia.

The use of comfort stations all over the Japanese empire in Asia was, in fact, an attempt to answer mass rapes as they had occurred during the Rape of Nanjing, which is why the extension of the existing comfort system can only be fully understood when seen as a consequence of the events of 1937–1938 and as a reaction to the Japanese Imperial Army's actions in China. It was therefore not a rape strategy, but a strategy to prevent rape that further spread a system of sex slavery. This sex slavery entailed nothing but rape, except it was controlled and institutionalized. As such, rape was ultimately incorporated into the strategic considerations of Japan's military leadership.

The victims of this exploitative system of sex slaves even suffered greater trauma after having been raped by countless Japanese soldiers who visited comfort stations on a regular basis, because "traditional Chinese culture [. . .] morally mandated female virginity or chastity."[67] Girls and women who wanted to return to their own society after having been raped at Nanjing or who were comfort women were unable to do so; they were ostracized by society for having been victimized by the lust of the barbaric Japanese soldiers. Their trauma was consequently doubled. Historically speaking, the Chinese environment or the "Chineseness" of many victims was responsible for an even higher pressure on the victims. Luo remarked:

> In combination, fetish for female virginity or chastity with the institutional emphasis on the sexual component of rape contributes to a distinct cultural construction of rape in Chinese society. The cultural construction of rape in relation to female chastity has manifested itself in a socially sanctioned connection between rape and marriage in Chinese society. In ancient China, rape was often employed by men to acquire sexual access to desired women as a socially acceptable precedent to marriage.[68]

This obsession with virginity is so extreme that women in contemporary Taiwan can be forced to marry their rapists, as this provides them the only chance to supposedly preserve their chastity. Consequently, having been raped by a man—or in our specific case, by a group of Japanese soldiers—does not pose a problem in Chinese society in general because it is considered the female victim's personal issue. The raped women are therefore punished twice simply by being women: once for not being able to resist the rape, and another time by the carelessness of their own society that shows no sympathy for rape and sexual violence victims. What it actually means for young girls and women to be collectively drafted into a system of rape and abuse will be discussed further in the following chapter.

CHAPTER FOUR

The Comfort Women System

Using the term "comfort women" for the female "military sexual slaves"[1] of the Imperial Japanese Army during the Second World War is the first problem when discussing the sexual violence committed by Japanese soldiers in the wartime era. The Japanese government and other right-wing deniers usually refer to the victims of this system as prostitutes, arguing that they were volunteers who aided Japan's war effort by making their bodies "available" to the emperor's troops on the Asian mainland and in Southeast Asia.[2] The victims, who were often young and sexually inexperienced women and girls, were traumatized by being sex slaves. As Japanese historian Yuki Tanaka correctly remarks about the "comfort system," "sex becomes a source of brutality and oppression, instead of one of joy and life, when it is exploited in warfare."[3] He continues his evaluation by adding that "when out of control . . . sex becomes ugly and monstrously abusive."[4] Regardless of the fact that the "comfort women" were "an extreme case of this institutionalized sexual violence against women,"[5] their suffering and legacy received too little attention in the aftermath of the Second World War and remains a disputed issue between the Asian nation-states until today, especially because Japan's government is reluctant to accept guilt and take responsibility for its past wrongdoings.

Prostitution seems to be an endemic part of every war, but the Japanese government and military actively helped establish and run the "comfort women" system. They shipped thousands of women across Asia and created official policies that demanded an organized form of sexual abuse against "colonially exploited" young women and girls.[6] Japan consequently built what George Hicks calls a "brutal regime of enforced prostitution,"[7] and the Japanese term "ianfu" (military prostitute) is a euphemism to cover up the brutal realities of the young women and girls who were systematically raped by Japanese soldiers.[8] As Chunghee Sarah Soh remarks, the issue of "comfort women" came to symbolize Japanese war crimes in Asia, especially in Korea[9]

MANCHURIA

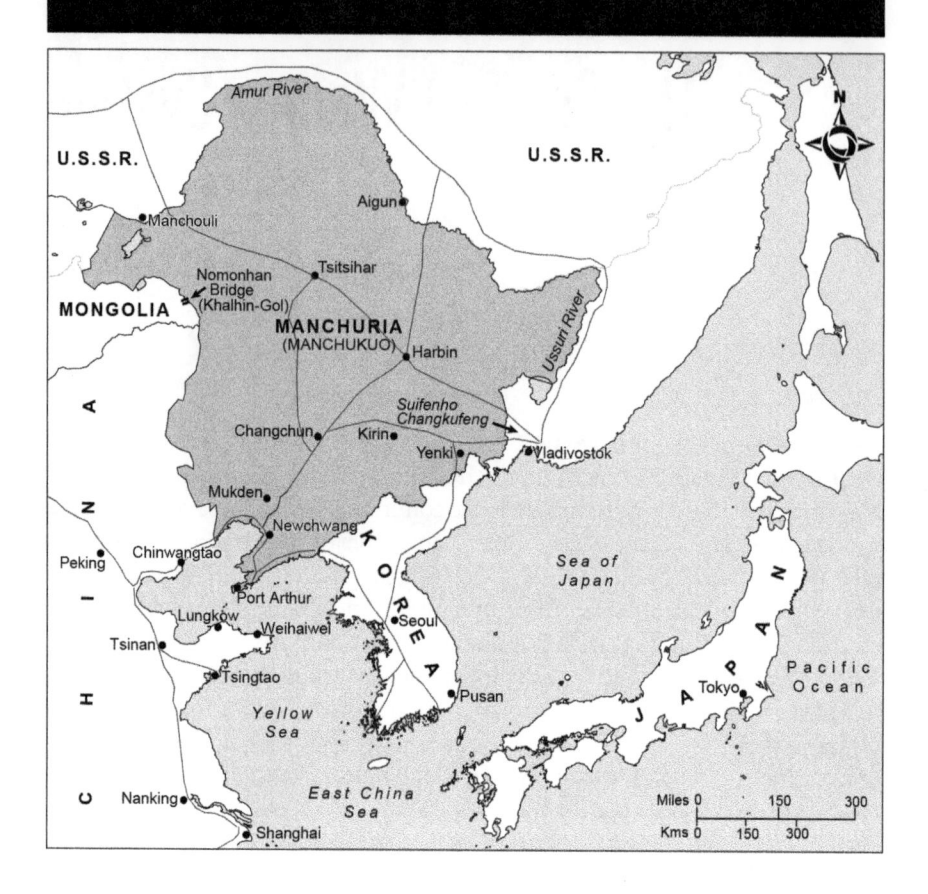

where most victims were forcefully "drafted" into their new lives as military sex slaves.

The women who suffered from sexual violence were victimized threefold:

1. they were violently forced to serve as sex slaves for the Japanese soldiers,
2. they suffered from mistreatment in the brothels, and
3. they were traumatized and often unable to return home after having lived through these experiences.[10]

Chunghee Sarah Soh highlights that such crimes are referred to as war crimes even though they can happen at any time, stating that "a war crime may take place during war, facilitated by the chaos and confusion of the time, but it is in fact a type of criminal act committed in everyday life under another

The Comfort Women System

name, such as murder, torture, rape, forced prostitution, or theft."[11] Although this basic observation might be accurate, I disagree with her because the specific space-time continuum of war enables the systematic rape of young women and girls, which would not be condoned in times of peace. The Second Sino-Japanese War and the Pacific War created spaces that offered Japanese soldiers the chance to "legally" commit sexual violence against female victims.

However, it is not only this fact that makes persecuting the perpetrators difficult, especially because Japan is officially uninterested in expressing guilt for these crimes. The "comfort system encompassed both commercial *and* criminal sex,"[12] so deniers usually fixate on the former to deny the existence of the latter. Yet the extension of the war over most parts of East and Southeast Asia led to the spread of the "comfort system," with brothels appearing all over the war zone. Of course, these crimes were made possible due to collaboration on the local level, where Chinese, Koreans, or Filipinos actively participated in the "recruitment" process of future "comfort women," which is why it is not possible to solely focus on Japanese perpetrators to understand the full picture of the sexual abuse and exploitation of so many young women and girls. This perception, to quote Chunghee Sarah Soh again, of the "story of comfort women as exclusively a Japanese war crimes issue has diverted attention from the sociocultural and historical roots of women's victimization in Korea, which Japan colonized from 1910 to 1945."[13] Deniers in Japan refer solely to the war time and use this chronological label as a way to disagree with the designation as criminal act, especially because rape seems to be something common in any war.[14]

Finally, the victims themselves and the women's movements in Asian countries, especially Korea, raised their voices to make the stories of past crimes heard again. The "comfort women" issue was then "highlighted . . . from a human rights viewpoint, eventually making it a diplomatic agenda for the countries involved."[15] However, the public doubted the women's late testimonies of their sexual exploitation, especially in Japan, where the evidence for these crimes had been destroyed in the last weeks before the Japanese surrendered. With almost no written sources to prove their claims, the government in Tokyo simply decided to ignore the stories about the systematic sexual abuse of so many Asian women in military brothels. The international community appeared uninterested in the suffering and trauma of Asian women, although the cases of Dutch victims in the Dutch East Indies garnered more attention.[16] The Japanese army closed brothels with Dutch women in Java in 1944 because the forceful recruitment of white women was considered legally dangerous. In comparison, forcing Asian women and girls into sex slavery was considered a bagatelle.[17]

Only in China were the Japanese war crimes related to the "comfort women" brought to trial after the end of the Second World War. Other Asian countries did not pay much attention to this matter until the early 1990s when a Korean redress movement requested an apology from Japan. It is estimated that anywhere between 20,000 and 400,000 women and girls were victimized by soldiers and by future generations that cared not for their fates. That said, the exact number of women and girls raped by Japanese soldiers is irrelevant; "from a moral standpoint, even the smallest number is huge,"[18] and the simple existence of an organized system of sex slavery run by Japan's military implies more guilt than a single individual could ever deal with. It is doubtless that the Japanese soldiers, military planners, government officials, and local collaborators who provided the "human supplies" for the appalling sexual exploitation of so many women and girls are guilty, and historians must instead focus on why this phenomenon occurred at all. As war crimes, the events related to the "comfort women" system must be explained in larger historical contexts; this includes not only the history of the Second World War in Asia but also the national history of perpetrators, victims, and bystanders alike.[19] It does not help to demonize the enemy—in this case, the Japanese—which Iris Chang did in her book; it is more helpful to understand under which circumstances such a system can be established to avoid similar developments in future wars. It is also important to explain the origins and reasons for this massive scale of sexual violence, which would better protect women and girls in future conflicts.

The Japanese army had multiple reasons for establishing the sex slave system all over Asia, but it was also a measure of colonial rule. As Kazuko Watanabe put it, "the Japanese army used other Asian women's bodies to protect Japanese women's chastity."[20] Young Japanese women and girls were not sexually exploited in military brothels, but colonized female bodies and minds were physically and psychologically harmed in these brothels through intense sexual abuse. Their stories were first made known to a wider public when Korean Professor Yun Jeong-Ok published some articles about "comfort women" in 1990. These publications also stimulated the formation of the first activist groups in South Korea, whose members demanded an official apology from Japan.[21] In the years that followed, many Korean scholars began to shed light on the dark past of Japanese sexual exploitation of Korean female bodies. In contrast to the idea that the Japanese did not care about this dark side of their own past, several historians in Japan began to research the "comfort women" issue and published numerous articles and books that critically dealt with their country's past evils.[22] However, these serious attempts at critical scholarship were overshadowed by Japan's general manner of confronting its past.

The textbook dispute in 1982 was responsible for an official policy to deny any Japanese war crimes in general, and the military brothel system in particular. The Ministry of Education ordered deletions of anything that might have referenced any Japanese criminal acts during the Second Sino-Japanese

The Comfort Women System

War or the Pacific War.[23] This could be done because "a vast number of relevant official records were destroyed immediately after Japan announced its surrender in August 1945,"[24] which made it hard for scholars to reconstruct the events. However, in 1992, Japanese historian Yoshimi Yoshiaki made public documents that proved the military's role in establishing the "comfort women" system.[25] In a later work, this important Japanese historian would also argue that Japan specifically chose Korean and Taiwanese sex slaves because their respective nations were part of the Japanese empire, and procuring women and girls from these territories would likely not cause legal issues with international laws such as the International Convention for the Suppression of the Traffic in Women and Children (1921).[26] The Japanese colonies of Korea and Taiwan were not included in this convention, which is why Japanese officials continued their inhumane recruitment of women and girls in these regions without fearing a clash with international law.

With documents now available and the first Korean eyewitness accounts gaining worldwide attention, the Japanese government can no longer deny the existence of the "comfort women" system. The nation offered an apology in 1993 but no financial reparations. The Asian Women's Fund was created to channel donations by Japanese civilians, which made it possible for the government in Tokyo to take on formal responsibility. Because "Korean women do not, however, want charity from Japan" but instead "a real apology with full acknowledgment of the transgressions and also monetary compensation,"[27] the establishment of the fund is considered another crime against the victims of Japan's military sex slavery system. Although Prime Minister Miyazawa Kiichi apologized for the sufferings of the "comfort women" for the first time, victims today still await an official state apology and official reparations. Regardless that it has been proven that the government, especially the Home and Foreign Ministries, the military, the navy, and other state-related officials—like the governors on the prefectural level and in the colonies, as well as police forces in Korea and Taiwan—the Japanese government has not confessed to anything or accepted guilt.[28]

To quote Japanese historian Hayashi Hirofumi, "the military comfort women system was clearly sexual slavery, organized and controlled by the military, and it constituted sexual, racial, ethnic, and economic discrimination and the violation of the rights of women."[29] This system not only violated international laws, especially in the case of the victimized girls, but it was also a war crime and a crime against humanity. Right-wing Japanese groups have rallied against this perception since the 1990s, denying research conducted on the topic and attacking any textbooks that dare discuss the issue.[30] The dispute was further internationalized in 2007 when the U.S. House of Representatives passed its resolution (H. Res. 121) that Japan was guilty of war crimes, urging the government in Tokyo to acknowledge the nation's guilt and formally apologize to the victims. However, Japan has yet to assume responsibility. In the following part, I would like to focus on the origins and structure of the "comfort women" system before discussing what caused the soldiers to sexually exploit young women and girls in the military brothels, as well as the lasting effects of this system.

The "Comfort Women" System

The establishment of "comfort stations," that is, brothels for the systematic sexual abuse of women and girls from China, Korea, Taiwan, and the Philippines, directly relates to the Rape of Nanjing, and the raping of these females by Japanese soldiers is among the cruelest of Japanese war crimes. The civil and military authorities in Japan knew the dangers of troops looting, marauding, and sexually abusing civilians in war zones, which is why leaders in Tokyo decided to provide countermeasures for such behavior and to avoid a second Rape of Nanjing.[31] Furthermore, the authorities wanted to prevent the spread of venereal disease (VD) among the soldiers, as this might have endangered the Japanese war effort.

Brothels that were privately run for the needs of the Japanese military go back to the Sino-Japanese War (1894–1895) when the first establishments opened in China to provide soldiers with sexual entertainment.[32] During the Russo-Japanese War (1904–1905), this practice of allowing brothels for military use in the war zone was continued. During the stationing of Japanese troops in Siberia in the aftermath of the Russian Revolution (1918–1925), military brothels were institutionalized when they were opened for each of the military barracks, and soldiers used them to fulfill their sexual desires.[33] However, in Siberia, prostitutes were brought from Japan and were often the children of poor families that sold them for this kind of "service." It can be assumed that this institutionalization of military prostitution was also done in part to prevent VD among troops.[34] The practice was continued in the 1930s, and as Yuki Tanaka correctly remarks, "it can be said that the establishment of military brothels in Shanghai in the 1930s, by both the Japanese Navy and Army, was a natural development from regulated prostitution in Siberia."[35] Although the brothels in Siberia were a by-product of Japan's intervention in the region, the establishments were also open for civilian use. However, once Japan's expansionist activities in China intensified after the Manchurian Incident in 1931, the brothel system was institutionalized and used exclusively by the military.[36]

During its aggressive expansionism in China, Japan used a "three sparkles policy" (*sankō sakusen*) that demanded soldiers kill, deprive, and burn everyone.[37] In Shanghai, the first real "comfort station" was established in early 1932. The idea can be traced back to Colonel Okamura Yasuji, who came up with a military brothel system after the Manchurian Incident.[38] He asked for Japanese prostitutes because Japanese soldiers had raped local women in the

Shanghai Incident. To prevent such events from being repeated and to protect the soldiers' health, the first military comfort stations were eventually established. With the geographical spread of Japan's war effort, similar establishments were erected in other parts of Asia.[39] In contrast to the former brothels in Siberia, the army stations were under strict regulation and control:

1. The brothels were solely to be used by soldiers or army-related personnel.
2. Condoms were to be used and soldiers had to pay an admission fee.
3. The time of use was limited to 30 minutes per soldier.[40]

Brothels became mobile and moved alongside the army. The Kantō Army Department, which was in charge of the military operations in Manchuria, also applied the first standards for the "comfort women" system. One woman or girl had to be available in the system for every 35 soldiers,[41] and more women were required to accommodate the increasing number of Japanese soldiers deployed in China. This stimulated the violent drafting of Korean women into the newly established system of military prostitution. After the Shanghai Incident, "comfort stations" were erected in northeast China and Manchuria.[42] Whereas private entrepreneurs had run brothels in Shanghai before the incident, the military later took control of the "buyable sex entertainment" its soldiers were permitted to access. The navy also established brothels to control the use and abuse of prostitutes by its personnel, and "these navy brothels seemed to be established primarily as a VD-prevention method, and operated under the close supervision of navy authorities as well as the Consulate-General's office (i.e. Japan's Ministry of Foreign Affairs)."[43] Yuki Tanaka discovered that the navy may have been the initial force behind the "comfort women" system and assumes that the army followed shortly afterward. Although the chronology is not reproducible, this does not matter much; both the army and the navy were responsible for sexually exploiting and abusing women and girls to prevent the spread of VD among their troops, as well as to provide them leisure and relaxation. This leisure and relaxation were paid for by the female victims, who were traumatized by the physical and psychological abuse stemming from being raped by 30 or more soldiers per day. Although prostitutes were initially supposed to be sent from Japan, particularly Nagasaki,[44] the growing demand necessitated a larger source of sex slaves—and Korea seemed perfect for this task.

Initially, the "army intended to use Japanese professional women, rather than Koreans," and "it is clear that the establishment of army comfort stations was initiated by top-ranking officers of the Japanese forces stationed in Shanghai,"[45] but once it was taken beyond the local level, the available prostitutes from Japan were not enough to meet demands. In April 1933, the first station in northeast China opened its gates. In addition to providing condoms to the soldiers, the "controlled intercourse" with 35 Korean and three Japanese women—the latter ones likely served the officers—was meant to prevent VD from spreading. The stations supposedly prevented soldiers from raping civilian Chinese women, and given what occurred in the Rape of Nanjing, more and more brothels were opened to contain the troops' sexual aggression.[46] Until 1937, the "Japanese forces adopted the military comfort women system as a general policy,"[47] and recruitment issues were also to be dealt with systematically. Although the events in Nanjing were a catalyst for the development of the "comfort women" system, the initial recruitment of Chinese "comfort women" caused trouble for the Japanese military in China. When the Chinese were violently recruited to serve in the military brothels, it created tension between the Japanese army and the local population. Korea was thus chosen as a new recruitment area to prevent local resistance in the future. Moreover, the Japanese military police (*Kenpeitai*) wanted to avoid using local women to minimize the danger of espionage by Chinese prostitutes who might have gathered information for the enemy.

Since March 1938, the number of Korean and Japanese women sent to China increased. In Japan, the Ministry of the Army had requested brothel owners to participate in the recruitment of Japanese women, who were to be sent to the war zone. Although some followed this request, like Kunii Shigeru, who left Japan with 53 prostitutes in January 1938, the number of professional prostitutes from Japan was far too low to match the demanded soldier-prostitute ratio.[48] Because the war in China was not set to end soon, the soldiers who stayed abroad would need constant access to brothels, whose numbers had to be increased to accommodate a longer war. Yuki Tanaka counts the existence of 4 stations in Hangzhou, 24 in Jiujiang, 6 in Wuhu, 20 in Wuhan, 11 in Nanchang, 8 in Zhenjiang, 1 in Yangzhou, and one 1 Danyang between 1938 and 1939.[49] The military brothels were not only established in the larger metropolitan areas of China, but also in mid-size and smaller cities. Although the military claimed that these "comfort stations" were effective in preventing large-scale mass rapes in China, they did not abolish sexual assault against civilians.

The existence and growth of the system also stimulated the future rapes of young women and girls who were not willingly drafted as prostitutes, in contrast to many of the Japanese women who worked under Japan's licensed prostitution system before being shipped to China by the military. However, in contrast to the argument of Japanese deniers, the women and girls from Korea were not voluntary participants in the military brothel system.[50] Chunghee Sarah Soh emphasizes that "in the conjuctural [sic] structure of imperial Japanese society the paternalistic state and its military leaders realized the comfort women system by instructing low-level local functionaries to enlist the help of profit-seeking entrepreneurs in Japan and colonial Korea who, in turn, unscrupulously recruited with false promises young women in search of wage-paying jobs."[51] To guarantee the success of this recruitment process, the transport of the women and girls, and the logistics of these operations, the Japanese Ministry of War had to be involved in the establishment of the "comfort women" system, especially because the ministry was most interested in its success.

Local police forces in Korea and Taiwan were also involved in recruitment. This was overseen by the Bureau of Police Affairs of the Government-General, which highlights how local administrations were also part of establishing the military sex slave system.[52] Furthermore, in January 1942, Tōgō Shigenori (1882–1950), Minister of Foreign Affairs, issued an official instruction for the ministry's staff that "comfort women" were to be provided with travel documents by the military.[53] As such, the military also controlled the bureaucratic measures involved in securing the human supply the system continuously needed. Until 1942, the system had grown tremendously, and the military had to oversee and organize recruitment for 100 "comfort stations" in north China, 140 in central China, 40 in south China, 100 in southeast China, 10 in the southwest Pacific, and 10 in southern Sakhalin.[54]

Chunghee Sarah Soh and Yuki Tanaka defined various categories for the existing types of "comfort stations,"[55] which can be combined to achieve a better typology for them (see Table 4.1).

Whereas Japanese prostitutes served in the first category (i.e., establishments in large cities) where "comfort stations" could be run by civilian guarantors, the other two categories mostly consisted of abused Korean and/or Chinese women and girls. Tanaka remarks that "it seems that the third category was often operated without obtaining permission of the central military authorities, as the troops were far away from headquarters,"[56] which also meant that these stations likely "recruited" victims in the hinterland of the front lines to rape them in these "wild" military brothels. The type of any given "comfort station" was largely determined by its geographical location and chronological context; space-time continua therefore play a key role in defining types of sexual violence, the environments in which it occurs, and against whom it occurs.

Table 4.1   Types of Military Brothels

Location	Status	Guarantor	Customers
Large cities (Shanghai, Nanjing, etc.)	permanent	military/civilian	military/civilian
Unit garrisons	semi-permanent	military/civilian	military
Immediate war zones, close to the front lines	temporary	military units	military

The motives for establishing a military brothel fall into various categories:

1. commercial profit for the entrepreneurs,
2. paternalistic accommodation by political and military leadership, and
3. criminal self-gratification for the soldiers.[57]

Prices for the "service" at a "comfort station" varied depending on who demanded it and by whom the "service" was to be performed. The Japanese empire's racism was also expressed in the sex slaves' prices. Whereas Japanese prostitutes were more expensive—two to three yen depending on the rank of the soldier/officer—Korean or Chinese women or girls were cheaper, with Koreans being 1 yen and 50 sen to 3 yen and Chinese being 1 yen to 2 yen and 50 sen.[58] Originally, the women and girls would receive half of the earnings, but the inexperienced sex slaves were often ripped off by their "managers," who claimed to be spending large sums on food, accommodations, and medical supplies. Although a ticket system was used to keep track of the females' "performance rates," the exploited women and girls could not ask for more income. The "managers" often profited from the "comfort women's" inexperience and lack of education. These women and girls were thus exploited both sexually and economically, and they were sexually abused daily not only by soldiers, but also by the guarantors of the "comfort stations" and even by the doctors who examined them for VD.

Chunghee Sarah Soh emphasizes that there are three periods in which the nature of the military brothels changed. Although the permanent establishments in the larger cities dominated between 1932 and 1937, the war in China between 1938 and 1941 caused the other two brothel types to come into existence. The Pacific War in the years that followed until 1945 spread the military brothel system all over Southeast Asia, stimulating a greater number of unofficial rape camps established by single units in war zones.[59] Soh argues that "the Japanese military comfort system must be characterized as fundamentally rooted in a masculinist ideology that privileged men's presumably uncontrollable 'biological need' for sex,"[60] but this alone does not sufficiently explain what actually led to the systematic sexual abuse of women and girls all over the Japanese empire. Therefore, the causes of its creation shall be analyzed in more detail.

As stated before, preventing VD from spreading among troops was one incentive for military authorities to create the military brothel system. Due to this practice, young women and girls were specifically "recruited" because unmarried and sexually inexperienced females had a lower risk of carrying diseases. It was thought that if they were infected, it would be easier to discover during routine medical examinations by military doctors, and the spread of VD could thus be prevented. However, the number of reported cases of VD increased from 11,983 in 1942 to 12,587 in 1944.[61] Because infected soldiers were demoted by two ranks as punishment for having "acquired" a disease, which usually occurred following intercourse with noncontrolled prostitutes or civilians, most of them would not report infections. Instead, most infected soldiers tried to acquire medicine from the black market and ask for unofficial treatment, often by prisoner-of-war (POW) physicians. Therefore, the strict rules meant to prevent VD led to further rapes, avoidance of the official brothel system, and looting to procure trading goods on the black market.

With their system, military leadership also intended to avoid mass rapes as they happened during and after the fall of Nanjing in late 1937 and early 1938. However, rape in the war zone was not fully discouraged, and the dispatch of more than 20 million condoms in 1942 was unsuccessful in preventing further cases of VD. The military brothel system did not discourage raping female civilians close to the war zone either, and the establishment of "wild" rape stations close to the front lines stimulated a growing number of cases in which local women and girls were violently drafted for sexual abuse by the Japanese army units.[62] Although the Japanese Imperial Army Criminal Law (Article 86, Clause 2) punished rape and looting alike with seven years to lifelong imprisonment, there were some problems with this punishment. First, rape was considered a secondary crime, only to be punished when it occurred alongside looting. However, as Yuki Tanaka remarks, it was "a general trend in the Japanese Imperial forces that looting and rape, especially during combat operations, were not only tolerated but even encouraged by many troop commanders as a means of arousing the fighting spirit in their men."[63] Consequently, few soldiers were punished for raping civilians—only 15 cases were filed in 1939. It took until 1942 for rape to be considered a primary crime once the written law changed, but the reasons for this change were not humanitarian. To quote Tanaka once more, the "rape of women in occupied territories was regarded as a crime under the revised Army Criminal Law mainly because it brought disgrace on the name of the Japanese Empire, not because rape itself constituted a serious crime against humanity."[64] All in all, civilian rapes did not disappear; the third type of "comfort stations," which were established close to the front lines, usually violently recruited local women and girls for rape. These women and girls, like those from Korea or abused in other parts of the Japanese empire, were treated as "military supplies,"[65] and a woman or a girl had to be present for every 35 or 40 soldiers. The number of "comfort women" during this period is estimated to be between 80,000 and 280,000.[66] The fate of these women and girls must be discussed in more detail to fully understand that they lived as sexual slaves, exploited by an imperialist army whose commanders believed it was permissible to sexually abuse women and girls to serve Japan's war effort.

Becoming and Being a "Comfort Woman"

Japanese deniers usually argue that the Japanese army and the government in Tokyo, whose ministries were involved in the recruitment processes, never forced nonprostitutes into the "comfort system" because all "comfort women" were supposed prostitutes who voluntarily participated in Japan's war effort. However, "a large number of women who were not prostitutes appear to have been forced to render sexual service to the Japanese troops."[67] It is crucial to closely examine the cases of the wartime women and girls who were stripped of their personhood and were solely considered "objects" for providing sexual pleasure.[68] Only some Japanese seem to doubt the justification of the sexual abuse of women and girls in the name of the war effort.[69] Most of the perpetrators and bystanders simply accepted the existence of this evil and cruel system of sex slavery within the Japanese Imperial Army.

Although women and girls were taken from all parts of the Japanese empire—Korea, China, Taiwan, Indonesia, Malaysia, and the Philippines—less than 30 percent of them survived the war. They were expendable "commodities," and once a soldier had damaged one, it had to be exchanged for a new one. Because nearly 80 percent of the women and girls were Korean, a closer look into their stories can show how the Japanese recruitment processes worked and why it was so successful.[70]

Korea seems to have been predestined for the "comfort system," and the trafficking of young women and girls was already widely practiced before the war and before Japan had military brothels. The economic changes after Japan's opening of Korea in 1876 led to the establishment of a financial upper class that dominated the poor, especially the peasant class whose members were impoverished by Korea's capitalist integration into the world trade system. Rice was predominantly sold and shipped to Japan; combined with bad harvests, this system increased the suffering of the local population, whose members often had to sell their daughters into prostitution to secure the family's survival.[71] Because the urban areas, which saw more people looking for work to make a living, could not provide sufficient stability for all, "many young Korean women turned to prostitution to provide the essential income for their poverty-stricken families to survive."[72] The families, who usually received an advance payment, sold their daughters to brothels, where they were to work for a number of years before being re-released into a chastity-obsessed society. These Korean girls' fates were thus determined once they entered prostitution, as nobody would marry them, considering their profession. Korea's impoverishment as a by-product of its economic transformation forced people to see prostitution as a last resort of survival, which primarily punished the daughters of poor peasant families.

An official and licensed system of prostitution was established in Korea in March 1916, which "created a tendency for the prostitution industry to be

The Comfort Women System

exploited by the Japanese administrators as a tool to foster Koreans who would collaborate with the Japanese."[73] Collaboration with the colonial rulers was therefore expressed through that system early on. In the 1920s, 5,000 to 6,000 "employment agents" worked for the Japanese to "fill the ranks" of the brothels in Korea. In these days, the so-called labor brokers would make the same false promises to young women and girls they would use in the future to draft them into the military sex slave system. The women and girls were usually bound to brothel owners by the payments their parents had received in advance, which also meant they could not escape prostitution without financially hurting their families. During the war, brothel owners left for war zones where they could make greater profits, especially because the license taxes for brothels in Korea had been raised. Regardless of the numerous pimps who decided to leave for the war zones with their entire businesses, the numbers were insufficient—so in 1938, the army decided to become more involved in the systematic recruitment of women and girls who would later be sexually abused in the military brothels. Consequently, local agents or "subcontractors" of the Japanese army would target "young daughters of poor peasant families, knowing that it was relatively easy to trick them."[74] The longer the war took, the more "comfort women" were needed, so the local police forces eventually also forced women and girls into sexual slavery. The future "comfort women" and their families were often left in the dark about the work the females were supposed to perform. The women and girls or their families were usually told they would become nurses, housemaids, or factory workers, leading them to think they had a real chance to escape poverty and improve the quality of life for themselves and their families.

However, it was not only poverty that motivated the young women and girls to leave their homes and trust the Japanese agents. As Chunghee Sarah Soh remarks, "Some women freely left home to escape domestic violence, grinding poverty, familial strife, or an arranged marriage; some of these self-motivated women who made life-changing decisions in search of better life chances, however, were deceptively recruited by Japanese and Korean traffickers for the military comfort facilities of imperial Japan."[75] Of course, the women and girls almost never volunteered, especially because most of them did not know what they would be drawn into. Many women and girls were promised factory work in Japan where they could be educated, but instead they were sent to military brothels in China or other parts of Asia where Japan's expansionist war had gained ground. The fact that so many young women and girls fell for the recruiters' spells had to do with their places in Korean society, where "industrialization and the modern capitalist economic system opened new doors for women into the public sphere," but the young females "found themselves subjected to domestic tyranny under battering fathers, bullying brothers, and/or unsympathetic mothers."[76] It is important to emphasize that "some [girls] chose to run away from home in order to escape domestic violence and maltreatment or the oppression of crushing poverty, fervently aspiring to become modern autonomous 'new women,'"[77] but it can hardly be believed that they chose sex slavery as an option for this escape. However, their vulnerability in such a situation was unscrupulously exploited by the Korean collaborators, who acquired money by selling them to the Japanese military brothels.

The lives of Korean women and girls were exploited in numerous ways. Having been victims of a patriarchal society that did not regard females as equals but rather as housemaids, those who wanted "a place of their own in the evolving public sphere of Korea's industrial revolution and colonial modernity"[78] did not achieve this through education or paid work; instead, they were exploited by Japan's colonial interests, as Japanese agents often violently drafted the young women and girls into a system of sexual abuse and violence. The licensed prostitution system, the spread of brothels in Korea during the Russo-Japanese War (in which Japanese soldiers in the Korean Peninsula demanded a growing number of prostitutes, with about 3,000 professional prostitutes arriving from Japan in 1908), and the establishment of formal pleasure quarters after Japan's annexation of Korea in 1910 also increased the number of Korean women and girls working as prostitutes. In 1916, the military then centralized the control of prostitution on the peninsula, because fear of VD already existed among military leaders. Once prostitutes could "perform" outside of the official pleasure quarters, "the business of prostitution could seep into society as part of everyday life."[79] That the "comfort system" was so easily established in the 1930s was thus owed to over five decades of Korean history that enabled such a system.

The minimum age for prostitutes was 17, although it was claimed that girls as young as 13 were the most popular among customers. Korean women and girls in the prewar prostitution system were also paid only a third of what Japanese professionals received. Christians began the first antiprostitution campaigns in 1924, demanding an end to the sexual exploitation of women. However, they could not stop the expansion of the contemporary system in which Korean women and girls were "exported" to Japan and Taiwan in the early 1930s, a few years before the military brothel system would increase its numbers extensively: "For young, uneducated women from impoverished families in colonial Korea, to be a victim of trafficking became 'an ordinary misfortune' in the 1930s."[80] The preconditions of the "comfort women" system were consequently in place, long before the war had begun. Sexual violence was nothing uncommon in Korea, as the licensed prostitution system had established the basic organizational structures for it to exist. The population's increasing poverty necessitated selling daughters to contractors, who would eventually trick young women and girls into joining army brothels characterized by sexual abuse and steady violence. Those who longed for

The Comfort Women System

emancipation and personal freedom in modern Korean society were thus led into the opposite reality, that is, physical and psychological torture based on their biological sex and age.

Pae Chok-kan (b. 1922) left her home to work in a cotton factory in 1938, yet ended up in a "comfort station" in China where she had to serve up to 30 men a day. The man who recruited her had promised her a bright future and even provided her with a Western dress, which made the girl feel good. These young women and girls' hopefulness made them easy prey for those looking to find victims for sexual exploitation. Since the 1920s, recruiters "often masqueraded as factory recruiters to pick up unsuspecting country girls at the labor exchange markets held at major provincial railway stations, whom they then sent to brothels."[81] No matter the arguments Japanese deniers use about voluntary recruitment, the acceptance of any contract was based on lies because "many young Korean women were mobilized under deceitful promises of well-paying factory jobs."[82] Korean collaborators were essential to the success of Japan's sex slavery system because they had to ensure that enough women and girls were led to the brothels. To deny that they were tricked into doing so is to deny common sense; not even the poverty and suppression of a patriarchal Korean society would have made the women and girls seeking personal freedom sign up for lives as sex slaves in a Japanese brothel.

The "comfort women" system was successfully based on the exploitation of several factors, including "gender, class, and labor in the colonial capitalist system" that caused the victimization of women and girls, "who, as aspiring youthful subjects, chose to boldly pursue financial independence and individual autonomy with [the] intention of crafting modern gendered selves."[83] When the Japanese military administration introduced a mobilization program for voluntary recruits to provide support for the empire's national defense, which provided volunteer work in Japan, it also provided an opportunity to recruit "comfort women" for the army and navy brothels. The program was further expanded in 1939, and between 1939 and 1942 almost 300,000 men were officially conscripted, whereas around 280,000 men voluntarily joined. Under the same program, women and young girls could have been drafted into the brothel system as well. The longer the war took, the more people were forcefully recruited to serve on behalf of the Japanese empire.

Chinese women and girls, in contrast to Korean ones, were usually kidnapped or abducted and directly forced into military brothels that were locally established by army units. They were mostly used during the war's initial stages before the authorities strongly opted for a change of policy after which more Korean women and girls were recruited to serve as sex slaves. This change of policy was supposed to

1. Avoid resentment from the local population, whose daughters' "recruitment" could have caused further trouble
2. Serve the Japanese's racist ideas, who believed Koreans to be racially closer to the Japanese soldiers than the inferior Chinese
3. Provide more security, as Chinese intelligence might have used the local women and girls to gather information from Japanese soldiers or officers.[84]

Despite these intents, many Chinese women and girls were still forcefully abducted to serve as sex slaves in rape camps within the war zone.[85] Li Xiumei was 15 when Japanese soldiers abducted her in 1942 and forced her to go through a living hell:

> One day, about five months after she had been abducted, she tried to refuse the commander who had been particularly wild in his treatment of the girls. He severely beat her with his waist belt. Her right eye was hit hard with the buckle, resulting in her losing the sight of that eye. When she continued to resist the officer, he clubbed her, knocking her to the ground. Later she was sent back home because her injuries made her physically unable to serve the Japanese men.[86]

Some battalions even took their sex slaves as hostages to demand money from parents in exchange for their daughters. Liu Mianhuan, who had been kidnapped for this purpose, was raped by the soldiers and the commander of the 14th Japanese Battalion in China for 40 days before her parents managed to gather the requested sum of money.[87] It is unimaginable what these young women and girls had to endure, and words can hardly describe the harsh realities of the Japanese rape camps in China and the Philippines, where a similar system existed.

There, army units would usually kidnap up to 10 young women or girls who then had to serve the sexual needs of the soldiers until the unit moved or exchanged the abused females for new ones. Of course, "none of the victims were ever paid and some were forced to cook and wash for the Japanese soldiers during the day and then provide sexual services at night."[88] Although the average age of the victims was 17.6 years, some of the girls were as young as 10 years. For the Japanese military, the advantage of using young girls was that they did not menstruate, so they could be raped at any time. In the Korean and Chinese cases, the memories of "Filipina comfort women" had been contained for a long time before the first victims reported about their experiences.[89]

It is now time to examine the testimonies of some of the "comfort women" or "comfort girls" and to describe the realities of their lives as the Japanese military's sex slaves. These reports may not even highlight the worst experiences, yet they are cruel enough to elicit tears of anger about the Japanese and

The Comfort Women System

tears of sympathy for the victims to the reader's eyes. The cruelties these young women and girls suffered cannot be forgotten, and their memory can be honored by simply not forgetting what was done to them. Mun P'il-gi,[90] a Korean "comfort girl," describes her recruitment process as follows:

> On an autumn day in 1943 a man in his fifties who lived in our village and worked as an agent for the Japanese approached me and told me that he could introduce me to a place where I could both earn money and study. His proposition was very attractive to me, an eighteen-year-old girl whose heart was filled with *han* [resentment and anger] over being denied an education. I decided to leave without telling my parents because I feared that my father would beat me if I told him about my plan.[91]

One Japanese policeman named Tanaka and the Korean agent eventually managed Mun's recruitment:

> The two men told me to get on the truck and took me to Pusan, where they took me to a beauty salon to have my long hair cut short despite my resistance. Afterwards, the man from my village left me with the policeman, telling me to be obedient to him since he would help me receive an education. The policeman brought a Western-style maroon dress for me to wear . . . I should change into clean and pretty clothes. The next day, after breakfast, I was put on a train together with four young women, in the compartment reserved for the military, and we were taken to Manchuria.[92]

Very often, it was the wish for freedom and education that made the girls leave home and go with the recruiters, as the report by Yi Sang-Ok (1922–2004) highlights[93]: "My family was well-off . . . Yet, when I started going to school at the age of nine, my older brother strenuously objected to it, saying it was useless to educate a girl."[94] The 15-year-old girl pursued the false promise of factory work in Japan but ended up in a brothel run by the Japanese military:

> I was fifteen, the youngest among the ten women when we left Seoul for Pusan, where we boarded a ship to go to Shimonoseki, Japan. There I was told to have my long hair bobbed so as to avoid being recognized as Korean. A week later, we boarded another shop that took us to Palau. The Japanese man who traveled with us delivered us to a Korean couple . . . known by the Japanese surname Hayashi: they were the owner of the brothel. They paid the Japanese man. The amount he paid for each girl determined the period of labor . . . Mine was one and a half years, but I never received any advance for that. Each of us was given a Japanese name, and mine was Nabuko.[95]

Many young Korean women and girls were the perfect victims, as society had prepared them to be. Kim Ok-Sil (b. 1926)[96] was another young girl who wanted freedom and a better life but ended up in the chains of Japanese sex slavery:

> I yearned to go to school and make friends, too. Later, I once again went to school secretly for a few days before my father learned about it. I half died from his assault. From then on, I hated seeing my father. I disliked being at home and wished to leave . . . After I had worked for nearly four years, my family started talking about marrying me off. I was sixteen, and I detested the idea of getting married to a man from another poverty-stricken family.[97]

The young girl had no qualms about being recruited for work in a Japanese textile factory, but instead of reaching such a factory, she was sold to a "comfort station" in Nanjing in 1942. The fear of being in an arranged marriage also drove Song Sin-Do (b. 1922)[98] to believe a female recruiter's story: "One day, a Korean woman in her early forties approached me . . . She urged me to go to the *senchi* ["battlefield" in Japanese] . . . She assured me that I could make a living there without getting married."[99] In Hankow she began to work as a "comfort girl" in 1938 and was only freed by the end of the war in 1945. In her seven years of "service," the 16-year-old girl became a 23-year-old woman who had been raped approximately 65,000 times.[100]

A similar experience marked the beginning of many Korean women and girls' adulthoods, as most of them were unmarried virgins at the time of their recruitment.[101] The majority of those abducted were between 11 and 20 years old; many units seem to have followed the slogan of "The younger, the better."[102] Hayashi Yōko is correct in her evaluation that "many of these girls were so young that they did not even know the meaning of sex."[103] Moreover, not only were the rapes of these young women and girls often their first sexual experiences, but they would face social ostracization if they were ever to escape. Chunghee Sarah Soh describes the crux of the issue clearly:

> In the traditional Korean patriarchy, the sexual culture condoned, if not encouraged sexual freedom for men (infidelity if married), while women's sexuality was rigidly controlled by standards of virginity/chastity. Unmarried women had to maintain their virginity until marriage and widows were expected to be chaste. Regardless of the individual circumstances, women who lost their chastity were considered sullied, made to feel ashamed, and likely to be ostracized even by their own families.[104]

The young women and girls became explicit targets due to their families' poverty, as the officials responsible for the recruitment system did not expect much resistance by the rest of Korean society.[105] The colonial government and the general public in Korea, as Pyong Gap Min correctly highlights, "emphasized the chastity of middle-/upper-middle-class women, but they believed lower-class women could be mobilized to public prostitution and at the same time protect the chastity of their daughters and wives."[106] Nobody seemed to care for the young women and girls who were treated as if they were "female ammunition," while their bodies were simply used as "public toilets" for the Japanese soldiers' sexual desires.[107] Moreover, they were victims of not only sexual violence and abuse but also of racist colonialism; Japanese women were reserved for the officers, whereas the "inferior" Korean and Chinese women and girls were allowed to be raped by everyone. This racism also fueled more violence, because the soldiers thought it was permissible to use force against the bodies of "colonial subjects."[108] The dichotomy of comfort and rape was the essence of the "comfort women" system. Whereas the soldiers enjoyed the "comfort" of having somebody to rape, the young women and girls were stripped of their humanity with each penetration.[109] The daily lives of these women and girls deserve more elaboration.

As stated earlier, each woman or girl had to serve approximately 30 soldiers per day. They had no privacy because soldiers would wait in line in front of their rooms, which were often only closed by curtains. When soldiers were unable to perform sexually, they often inflicted violence upon the female sex slaves. Consequently, the "comfort women" were "regularly subjected to torture, beating, sometimes stabbing."[110] Although some soldiers showed empathy for the victims, these rare displays of kindness disappeared in the helix of sex and violence like a tear would disappear in the ocean. Although the "comfort system" was meant to prevent the spread of VD, it could not be totally avoided, and numerous women died of infections, if they were not killed by enraged "customers" or had not committed suicide already. Japanese officers had perpetual access to the sex slaves, and there were even exclusive brothels in big cities for the higher military ranks. Soldiers could visit the local "comfort station" once a week. It has been reported in testimonies that only 10 soldiers might have shown up on slow days, but on other days—especially after battles—30 or even 40 men would wait in line to be sexually pleased.[111] One witness report of a "comfort woman" during the Battle for Okinawa provides insight into the routine of the female sex slaves: "Most soldiers finished within twenty or thirty seconds and came out one after another in an infatuated state which greatly contrasted their behavior while waiting. Some, however, took five minutes or more, although if they took too long a veteran soldier who acted as supervisor would grab the offending soldier by the scruff of the neck and drag him out of the room."[112] In these situations, the women and girls were not even allowed to clean themselves.

Yuki Tanaka evaluates that "there is no doubt that such extreme sexual abuse caused considerable physical pain and health problems [for] many of the comfort women."[113] However, what happened is a far worse manifestation of human cruelty than what he describes. For example, one testimony emphasizes that "there were some women whose vaginas were so swollen and were bleeding so profusely that there was no space for a needle to be inserted inside."[114] Usually, the women were supposed to have a break from their duties during their menstruation, but it can be assumed that such protocols were often violated. The soldiers had also been instructed to use condoms—ironically a brand that was called Assault No. 1—during intercourse, but many of them were unwilling to follow these orders and used violence against women and girls who insisted on it.[115] Therefore, many women and girls may have been infected with VD during their intercourse with such soldiers. Not only that, but they could also become pregnant. Abortion was ordered in such cases, and if it was too late, the children had to be born and given away. Another trauma was thereby caused for the "comfort women," who, after having been raped, were also forced to go through such cruel measures to keep them active. Another testimony highlights their experience of both actual and threatened violence:

> There were many times when I was almost killed. If I refused to do what one man asked, he would come back drunk and threaten me with his sword. Others simply arrived drunk, and had intercourse with their swords stuck in the tatami. This left the tatami scarred, but this sort of behavior was more a threat to make me accede to their desires and give them satisfaction.[116]

Such violent eruptions increased at the end of the war as the troops' morale declined with each defeat. Kim Hak-Sun (1924–1991), the famous Korean survivor who broke the victims' silence in the early 1990s, described the soldiers' behavior:

> They varied in the way they treated us: while one soldier was so rough as to drive me to utter despair, another would be quite gentle. There was one who ordered me to suck him off, while he held my head between his legs. There was another who insisted that I wash him after intercourse. I was often disgusted by their requests, but if I resisted they would beat me until I gave in.[117]

For many of the young women and girls, the only way to deal with this steady trauma was doing drugs—usually opium—or to commit suicide.[118] How else were they supposed to handle their treatment?

Another detailed report about the treatment of young girls in the brothels came from Maria Rosa Luna Henson (1927–1997), one of the Filipinas who had been raped by the Japanese army. With her testimony, which received

The Comfort Women System

media attention, she paved the way for hundreds of victims to talk about their experiences.[119] When she passed a Japanese army checkpoint, Henson reported that a "soldier raised his hands and signaled that [she] was the only one to come back."[120] The young Filipina was taken into custody and brought to a military brothel. There,

> The guard led me at gunpoint to the second floor of the building that used to be the town hospital. It had been turned into the Japanese headquarters and garrison. I saw six other women there. I was given a small room with a bamboo bed. The room had no door, only a curtain. Japanese soldiers kept watch in the hall outside. That night, nothing happened to me.[121]

However, Henson would not only be a hostage, but also serve the sexual needs of the unit that had taken her prisoner. On the next day,

> Without warning, a Japanese soldier entered my room and pointed his bayonet at my chest. I thought he was going to kill me, but he used his bayonet to slash my dress and tear it open. I was too frightened to scream. And then he raped me. When he was done, other soldiers came into my room, and they took turns raping me. Twelve raped me in quick succession, after which I was given half an hour to rest.[122]

Afterward, she was raped by another 12 soldiers in a gang rape before further soldiers waited outside to be "served." Henson was physically and psychologically overwhelmed by these assaults: "I bled so much and was in such pain, I could not even stand up . . . I felt much pain, and my vagina was swollen. I cried and cried, calling my mother. I could not resist the soldiers because they might kill me."[123] From 2 p.m. to 10 p.m. on the following days, she was forced to sexually please the Japanese soldiers. During these visits, Henson reported that she "did not even have time to wash after each assault. At the end of the day, [she] just closed [her] eyes and cried."[124] Her "torn dress would be brittle from the crust that had formed from the soldiers' dried semen."[125] It is miraculous that the young girl survived such treatment. Additionally, the Japanese soldiers who raped her were mostly young and sexually inexperienced, which worsened their anger and violence:

> Once there was a soldier who was in such a hurry to come that he ejaculated even before he had entered me. He was very angry, and he grabbed my hand and forced me to fondle his genitals. But it was no use, because he could not become erect again. Another soldier was waiting for his turn outside the room and started banging on the wall. The man had no choice but to leave, but before going out, he hit my breast and pulled my hair.[126]

No matter what the women and girls did, they were seen as responsible for the success or failure of their sexual assaults. Henson remembers another episode: "One soldier raped me, and when he was finished, ordered me to fondle his genitals. He wanted to rape me a second time, but could not get an erection. So he bumped my head and legs against the wall. It was so painful."[127] She "felt like a pig,"[128] especially when the soldiers tied up one of her legs with a belt to the wall and then raped her. Henson is one of many women who had to live through such treatment. Rape was everywhere, and even the doctor who tested her for VD raped her afterward. It is hard to imagine the pain Henson and others like her endured. Although it is difficult to remember these events and the emotions related to them, it should not be forgotten that women in the Philippines were also victims of Japanese war crimes, especially sexual violence.

Henson also describes the psychological impact of the continuous rapes and of the sexual assaults on her body: "By now I had served thousands of soldiers. Sometimes I looked at myself in the small mirror in my room and saw that [what] I had been through was not etched in my face. I looked young and pretty. God, I thought, how can I escape from this hell?"[129] Eventually, she was rescued from her misery, but it is a wonder that Henson survived her experiences—especially given that she had only one week of rest after suffering a miscarriage before being forced back to work. She had been a sex slave for nine months, a period in her life she can never forget and will likely never come to terms with. These victims have remained victims for their entire lives, and unfortunately nobody cared for them after 1945 when politics determined the importance, or lack thereof, of discussing "comfort women." Having analyzed the victims' perspectives in detail, it is now time to explore why the Japanese soldiers acted as they did.

Thanks to the important works of Japanese historians, it is clear that "the comfort women system was created and developed as a well-planned policy by a group of top Japanese military leaders."[130] These people decided to install a system of sexual exploitation and abuse that dehumanized countless women and girls from China, Korea, Taiwan, and the Philippines. Their decision to consciously organize systematic mass rapes is among the most horrible of war crimes. Although the Japanese soldiers claimed to be freeing Asia from white colonial powers like Britain, France, and the Netherlands, they demeaned and dehumanized their victims and caused psychological and physical damages that can hardly be described. What happened to the "comfort women" must be referred to as what it is: a crime against humanity. The system's organization was based on the Japanese military belief "that they were protecting the moral and physical character of their troops, and protecting Asian civilians."[131] In reality, they allowed Asian civilians to be systematically abused to protect troops from VD. As mentioned earlier, the number of civilian rapes in Japan's colonized regions did not decrease, especially because

The Comfort Women System

women and girls were violently drafted into the rape camps of the smaller military units.

For the common soldier, however, other factors were responsible for their cruel acts. As Yuki Tanaka emphasizes, the "ideology of masculinity is intrinsically interrelated with racism and nationalism,"[132] and the Japanese soldiers acted on their beliefs that colonial subjects, as well as women, were inferior; they considered it legitimate to abuse human beings who fell under these categories. Furthermore, the "sexual abuse of the bodies of women belonging to the conquered nation symbolized the dominance of the conquerors," and the penetration of the colonized female body mirrored the Japanese army's suppression of the colonial territories. One could argue that the soldiers' penetration of their victims was akin to the physical penetrations caused by bayonets and samurai swords on the battlefield or during the mass killings of civilians, for example, during the Rape of Nanjing—however, the women and girls were "killed" thousands of times over.

When we discuss the nature of the crimes committed by the common soldiers of the Japanese army, it is essential to emphasize that these crimes of sexual abuse were committed "by choice,"[133] especially because the men were neither ordered to use military brothels nor observed while using them. Every soldier decided to become an active participant in this systematic rape of Asian women and girls. In contrast to the punishment of POWs, which will be discussed in the following chapters, the soldiers had no direct orders to rape a woman and therefore feared no consequences for not participating in these acts. It is thus correct to assume, as Yuki Tanaka does, that the "personal responsibility in this situation is far more serious than in instances in which soldiers acted under orders to commit atrocities."[134] Nevertheless, many external factors pressured the soldiers to commit these cruel, violent, and sexually abusive acts.

First, masculinity had to be proved not only during battle, but also by sexual means in the "comfort stations." Most of the young Japanese soldiers were sexually inexperienced when they arrived on the battlefield, and they may have felt pressure to prove their abilities not only with rifles and bayonets, but also with their phalluses. Second, the group dynamics in the units could have led the young men to participate. In the case of the Japanese, strong group dynamics likely existed before the units were formed; as such, the soldiers could have been accustomed to following such strong group pressure, because it also existed during times of peace. Therefore, remaining behind when other group members visited brothels could have caused social ostracization, and many followed the group's actions to confirm membership. Considering the situation within the "comfort stations" where privacy rarely existed, the pressure to perform may have stimulated sexual abuse and other extreme forms of violence in the event that malperformance would be witnessed by other soldiers. It is hard to determine which psychological processes occurred in the soldiers' minds, especially because we have no detailed descriptions from the perpetrators' perspectives. Next to the individual responsibility of the soldiers, which should not be contested at all, there were external factors like group pressure and performance pressure that also played a role in their behavior. Moreover, in many cases, sexual assault and violence were legal in the existing space-time continuum; as such, soldiers unthinkingly accepted their roles in the military brothel system, which had been sanctioned by a higher authority. By the end of the war, soldiers would simply enter a new space-time continuum and continue their lives in a peaceful environment—and in a society that was uninterested in remembering the crimes of the past. The suffering of the victims therefore continued when they and their fates were largely forgotten.

The Aftermath of the "Comfort Women" System

A majority of the survivors of the "comfort women" system in South Korea "completely stayed out of the limelight," whereas some of them began to organize themselves in activist groups or other organizations like the Korean Association of Pacific War Victims and Bereaved Families.[135] The victims of sexual violence by the Japanese army had been suffering in multiple ways. First, they were victims of gender inequality at home, where a patriarchal system allowed their suppression. Second, many of the women and girls were poor and victims of capitalist-class exploitation within Korean society; many of the women and girls recruited for military brothels came "from poor families that belonged to the landless semitenant class in rural areas or to the jobless migrant groups in cities."[136] Third, because the women and girls were either recruited in occupied or annexed territory, they were victims of racial discrimination in the Japanese colonial system. Regardless of these three forms of victimization that related to the military brothel system, the surviving women and girls also suffered in a fourth way; they suffered when their perpetrators were not prosecuted in the aftermath of the war when Japan, like the United States, simply ignored the female victims of Japanese imperialism.[137]

Although politicians and military leaders of the postwar era were uninterested in making a case for the "comfort women," the victims themselves also had no interest in publicizing their lives as military sex slaves for the Japanese army. Those who did not immediately commit suicide "were resigned to keeping their deep *han* (resentment and anger) to themselves."[138] They had been victims of Japan's colonial rule[139] and became victims of the power game in East Asia during the Cold War in which Japan was needed as a U.S. ally. The women and girls who returned to South Korea after the war were very often "physically and mentally sick, most of them could not live normal marital lives," and "all victims suffered from a number of health problems and psychological traumas caused by their sexual slavery experiences . . . [suffering from] nightmares in which Japanese soldiers were chasing them."[140] The shame about their "loss of their virginity"[141] also forced them into lives of solitude and suffering, and it was this shame that kept many women silent about their pasts for so long, as survivor Lee Young-Ok told Pyong Gap Min in an interview:

> At that time, a woman's chastity was considered more important than her life. How could I tell people I was daily raped by many soldiers. It would have been a great humiliation to my parents. Many times I regretted I came back home alive. It would have been better for me to die there . . . Yet, looking back I am angry at the fact that because of traditional Korean customs I had to hide my past without myself doing anything wrong.[142]

The fact that only a few former "comfort women" married after the war highlights the level of continued suffering on the domestic level in South Korea's postwar society.[143] It took until the early 1990s when Kim Hak-Sun and others told the world about their pasts not only "in order to regain control over bodies," but also to recover their "past and their sense of themselves as victims."[144]

In the years since the first victims told their stories, it was what Alice Y. Chai called an "Asian-Pacific Feminist Coalition"[145] that helped spread the memory of the comfort women. As Margaret D. Stetz correctly remarks, "now the details of this systematic sexual abuse are being published everywhere, if not always in textbooks in Japan."[146] The Japanese government, on the other hand, initially denied any form of direct involvement in the "comfort women" system and claimed that only private recruiters or contractors had been responsible. It was only under the pressure of historians and the historical truth displayed in documents that forced the government in Tokyo to accept these facts. However, this did not change the Japanese wish to remain silent about the past, and similar trends can be observed in South Korea, where most citizens "generally accept the surviving comfort women as victims, [but] many people still believe it is a humiliation at the personal and national levels to discuss what happened to them in the hands of Japanese soldiers."[147]

During the war tribunals, the Allied powers failed to make a case for the sexually abused women and girls. If discussion of these women appeared in the powers' official documents, the women were usually dealt with as objects.[148] Although it was known to the Allies that the Japanese had systematically abused women and girls as sex slaves, only crimes against the European women in the Dutch East Indies were prosecuted.[149] Because licensed prostitution had been legal in Japan, some of the Allied investigators considered the "comfort women" system an extension of a genuine Japanese practice. Documents indicate that the Allied prosecutors were well aware of the existence of the military sex slave system but were not interested enough in this particular facet of Japanese war crimes.[150] Although "American interpreters did not regard it as a serious war crime against humanity,"[151] some of the U.S. military officials also played with the idea of establishing a similar military brothel system.[152] Yuki Tanaka refers to racism and chauvinism as the main reasons why the Allied powers were not interested in making a case against the mass rape of women and girls in Japanese military brothels, whereas the cases of European victims were prosecuted.[153] Silence was the consequence, and early publications about the fate of the Korean "comfort women" did not receive the appropriate attention for this crime against humanity.[154]

In Japan, there was no interest in dealing with the past after the war's end. Only when Korean survivors told their stories, which was organized by the Women's Voluntary Service Corps (WVSC), and demanded government action that the issue became more widely discussed in Japan and abroad. The WVSC demanded the Japanese government:

> (1) Admit to the historical fact that Japan forcibly drafted comfort women and took them to the battlefield, and apologize officially for the above facts. (2) Fully investigate the system under which comfort women stations were operated and publicize it. (3) Financially compensate the comfort women survivors and their bereaved families. (4) Continue talking about these facts, and do not repeat such atrocities in the future.[155]

The issue of comfort women received additional attention when the Vienna World Conference on Human Rights in 1993, the World Conference on Women in Beijing in 1995, and the UN General Assembly in New York in 2000 addressed it. It was the combination of feminist and democratic movements highlighting the victim's testimonies that established a strong redress movement that has since pressured the Japanese government to address the demands made by the WVSC.[156] The movement has become transnational in the last two decades and has put "comfort women" in the spotlight around the globe.[157] The apologies and compensation offered thus far do not indicate that Japan is willing to fully accept its historical past, and under the current government, a formal apology and reparations seem unlikely.

It was in 1995 when Kim Soo-Ja, another victim of the system, claimed that "it is more important to get a sincere apology than simply to get monetary reparations. I am not merchandise that can be traded for money. Even if they give me [money], they cannot compensate for my lifelong suffering."[158] Today, the "victims of Japanese wrongs often seem far from attaining reconciliation and closure,"[159] and in Japan, former soldiers "rationalized the atrocity as a natural part of warfare, and pointed out that everybody had suffered during the war."[160] This is a continuation of denial, and for the victims, this means a continuation of suffering and sorrow. Whereas conservatives and activists

The Comfort Women System

on the far right consider a discussion of the "comfort women" issue to be "a masochistic view of history,"[161] the common Japanese people "seem to have lost interest in Japan's war responsibilities."[162] Consequently, the few former "comfort women" who are still alive continue to suffer, and it is doubtful that they will ever gain an official acknowledgement of their cruel past by the Japanese government. It is thus even more important that historians around the globe address the issue and keep the memory of the system alive.

Women and children need special protection, particularly in war zones, where soldiers often use sexual violence to cause trauma—oftentimes, such trauma lasts longer than physical pain. Women and girls were not the only ones traumatized by Japanese war efforts, either. This will be demonstrated in the next chapters, which will focus on the treatment of POWs in the aftermath of the initial Allied defeats in Southeast Asia.

CHAPTER FIVE

The Bataan Death March

The Bataan Death March is considered one of the most severe Japanese war crimes; as Kevin Murphy correctly states, it "stands as one of the ultimate measures of Japanese wartime barbarity."[1] An army of 75,000 men—U.S. and Filipino forces alike—surrendered on the southern tip of the Bataan Peninsula in early April 1942 and were forced to march 65 miles from Mariveles in the South to Capas. There, they were loaded onto trains to be transported 30 miles farther north before being forced to march the last 5 miles to Camp O'Donnell, a prisoner-of-war (POW) camp. More than 10,000 of the 25,580 captured American POWs would die in captivity—a mortality rate of over 40 percent—and it is assumed that the first victims, which comprised about 650 U.S. soldiers, had already died during the Death March of Bataan.[2] Many veterans who were involved in the death march would later take up their pens to report the events, feeling the "need to have their suffering recognized and to define a place for themselves in the war's epic."[3] What all the reports show is a dichotomy between the barbaric Japanese soldiers and the sympathetic Filipinos, who would try to support the prisoners with food or water. The stories in these firsthand narratives constitute what Murphy called a "compelling reality": "Helpless Americans marched under the watchful eyes and cruel bayonets of the Japanese oppressor, and the Filipinos, in despair over the defeat of their defenders, wept in sympathy as they watched."[4]

Murphy is right to criticize this simplistic dichotomy, which does not accurately describe the "complex drama" of the Bataan Death March, "one that goes beyond the simplicity of 'oppressor—victim—sympathetic observer.'"[5] Some Filipinos tried to offer their American POW allies a chance to survive by providing them with food and water, but there were also those who pursued a business opportunity and "exploited Americans in their time of weakness and need."[6] The drama was "written by Americans" and "scripted from realities which included both wartime heroism but also a colonialism

BATTLES OF BATAAN AND CORREGIDOR

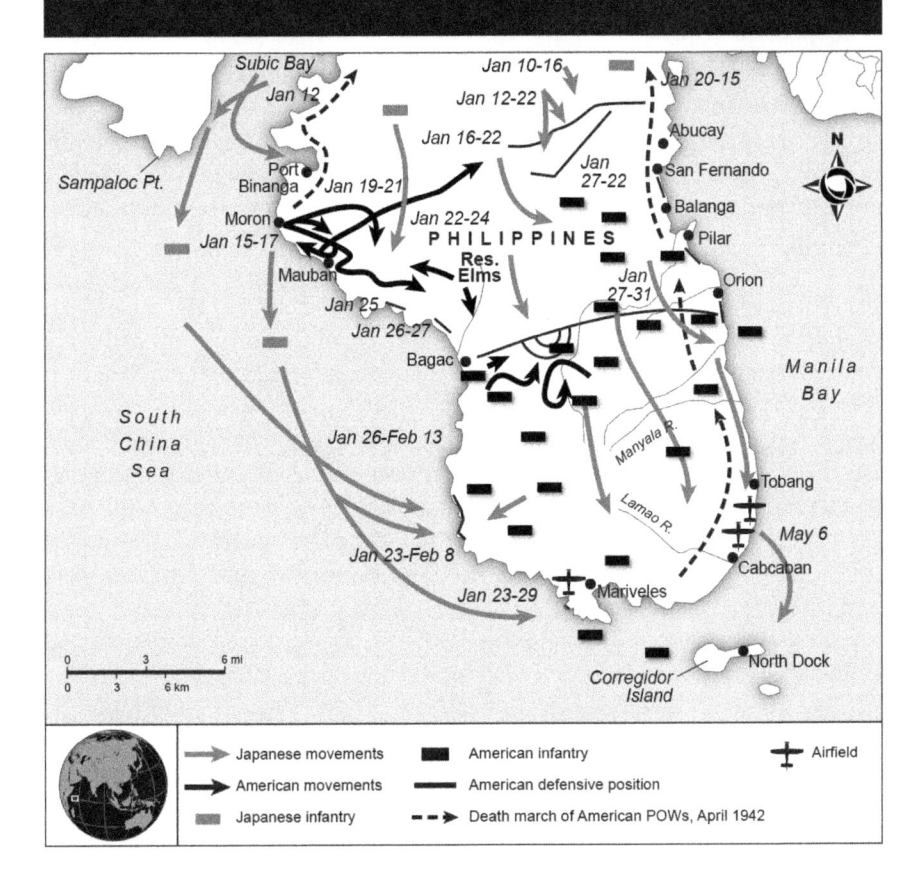

which was pleasing to American and Filipino elites."[7] However, due to the nature of selective memory, the memoirs also highlighted heroism while omitting unpleasant details about the American allies.

That said, all accounts related to the Bataan Death March have consistent descriptions of Japanese violence against the prisoners: "Numerous emasculations, disembowelings, decapitations, amputations, hundreds of bayonetings, shootings and just plain bludgeonings to death of defenseless, starved, and wounded soldiers were common on the march, in full view of their helpless comrades."[8] Enemy troops' reports about such violence were not rare,[9] but rather a common experience that all American POWs seem to have shared during their imprisonment in general, and the Bataan Death March in particular.[10] The Japanese soldiers are usually reported to have shown "unreasoning, unchristian brutality, deliberate cruelty and sadistic inclinations,"[11] and

Richard M. Gordon assures that "no survivor of Bataan will ever question the fact that the Japanese were to a man 'barbarians.'"[12] Other accounts even go a step further to explain that "the raw brutality exhibited by Japanese soldiers is incomprehensible and can only be explained by the existence of evil."[13]

Although there are some positive reports about Japanese soldiers and officers who tried to support the prisoners or the local Filipino population, such stories are uncommon.[14] Japanese soldiers rarely showed mercy, especially toward the latter group; they were more likely to massacre Filipino soldiers and officers than to help or support them.[15] Although the local population could expect violence upon them for helping American POWs, many U.S. narratives describe how the common people, regardless of the risks, tried to provide relief in the form of food or water. In the final stage of the march, the walk from Capas to Camp O'Donnell, containers of water were left along the route to ensure the POWs could drink something.[16] Those who were caught trying to help the Americans were punished for their kindness and "rewarded at the edge of a samurai sword or bayonet."[17] Some survivors of the Bataan Death March also reported how the Japanese soldiers treated the Filipino women and girls, who often became victims of sexual violence: "While the prisoners stood in line with Japanese rifles trained on them, a group of the guards seized some of the nearby Filipino women and dragged them into the brush . . . [the prisoners] heard the women scream and cry and [they] knew they were being raped and beaten."[18] The story of a young woman named Erlinda became particularly well known; she was "a village maiden of a remote barrio of Bataan, aged eighteen, a beautiful virgin. She was gang-raped by seven Japanese soldiers in a most bestial manner as she was washing clothes by the river. She was buried alive, naked, her head above the ground."[19]

The POWs' sympathy with the Filipino victims is evident, but it is also "clear that the ideal image of the sympathetic Filipino is incomplete and to some degree misleading,"[20] especially because many Filipinos tried to benefit from the suffering of the American POWs when they sold supplies to those starving in the camps.[21] However, the prisoners of the Japanese were thankful for any food, whether a mango or a few peanuts; despite paying for aliments, they were grateful and refrained from judging the Filipinos' business practices.[22]

Remembrances of the Second World War and of the Japanese occupation of the Philippines are tied to intense emotions that are often expressed during discussions of the war years.[23] Filipino collaboration with the Japanese military, the United States' failure to defend the Philippines against Japan's invasion, the fact that no reparations were made for the lost lives and material goods, and the increased focus on U.S. soldiers over their Filipino allies are all issues that can aggravate the Philippines' relations with Japan and the United States. As Ricardo T. José emphasizes, "[T]he government on the other hand has tended to belittle or even ignore the more sensitive issues, while selecting specific anniversaries for celebration,"[24] whereas the common population's discussions about the war usually revolve around "the Comfort Women, reparations from Japan, veterans' benefits from the United States, and the injustice Filipino veterans suffered under the Americans."[25] Veterans and their families usually meet at Mount Samat in Bataan to remember past events on April 9, commemorating the dead Filipinos who gave their lives to defend the peninsula and those who died during the Bataan Death March or in the POW camps.

Although the government of the Philippines often downplayed public controversies about the "comfort women" in past decades, it supported the annual Philippine-Japan Festival to establish good relations, which was supposedly more important than critically dealing with the past.[26] The Filipino victims of the Second World War were ignored for economic gain, which a good partnership with a major player in Southeast Asian trade could provide. In contrast to this political course of action, private associations began to seek "redress of grievances or justice."[27] Many women like Henson, whose cases were discussed in the previous chapter, were abducted and raped by the Japanese army in the Philippines. However, as the Korean women's stories were forgotten in the postwar order, so were those of the Filipino women who had been victimized by the Japanese soldiers. Since the 1990s, however, a redress movement also formed in the Philippines that demanded recognition, an apology, and reparations.

The Philippines offers an interesting example of official remembrance of the war and how this relates to nation building in Southeast Asia. The heroic cases of Filipino resistance against the Japanese oppressors was remembered, whereas any "sign of weakness" was avoided. However, for the victims of violence and destruction, the nation does not seem to have a place when only the strong are considered valuable.[28] April 9 is among the days in which the "strong public memory" of the war "is enshrined," and the national holiday is usually referred to as the "Day of Valour."[29] This is unsurprising considering that next to 9,921 Americans and 62,100 Filipinos endured the Bataan Death March, of whom 5,000 to 10,000 died after having defended the nation.[30] To this day, countless commemoration ceremonies are held throughout the Philippines, and "Filipino schoolchildren re-enact wartime suffering in plays and cultural presentations while adults and veterans walk the 104 kilometer Bataan Death March from Mariveles, Bataan, to San Fernando."[31] The cooperation between the Filipino elites and the Japanese occupational government is usually forgotten in the Philippines' narratives of national unity and suffering; moreover, former collaborators gained high-ranking governmental positions after the Philippines was "liberated" by the returning American forces under the command of the later Supreme Commander of the Allied Powers, General Douglas MacArthur (1880–1964), whose later Cold War–related decisions in Japan[32] would resemble his decisions in the Philippines after the Japanese occupiers were forced out again.[33] Regardless of the long-term implications of the Bataan Death March and its public remembrance, it is sensible to focus on the actual events that led to the death of so many POWs—Americans and Filipinos alike—on their way to reach the prison camps.

Defense, Fall, and Death March of Bataan

When the war in the Pacific began in 1941 following the Japanese attack on Pearl Harbor, U.S. forces stationed in the Philippines consisted of around 120,000 men, mostly Filipino recruits "who had never fired a weapon, and had barely any military training at all."[34] The American troops, besides the 31st Infantry Regiment, totaled 3,100 soldiers and were also recently drafted recruits with almost no training or equipment. Most of these recruits had been serving on the U.S. National Guard before, and they were hardly a match for the Japanese forces they were supposed to fight. The American forces' chief defense plan, which was last revised in April 1941, was based on holding Manila Bay and defending Bataan; these spots were considered the main priority.[35] However, as the war would prove, the "tragically inadequate supplies"[36] would make a prolonged defense of the Peninsula against the approaching Japanese forces almost impossible. Whereas the air force in the Philippines had received new planes—modern bombers and fighters—and was reorganized, most of the army remained underequipped and unfit for the coming weeks of the operation in 1942. This lack of preparation is surprising, especially considering what Benjamin Appel would ask in his 1957 novel about the events in the Philippines, specifically about Bataan: "Japanese armies and Japanese sea and air forces had invaded China and Indo-China. Who would be next?"[37]

Once the Japanese forces began their attack, there was little doubt about the Philippines' future. All the American forces could do was defend for as long as possible. It was Jonathan Mayhew Wainwright IV (1883–1953), "a genuine, old-fashioned, flag-waving, gun-toting American hero,"[38] who oversaw this task; while he organized the defense of the American positions, he had to face what Duane Schultz called "a hopeless situation." Wainwright understood that he was "fighting against impossible odds" but was also "considered expendable by his country."[39] Nevertheless, he slowed down the Japanese advance by five months despite lacking supplies and facing an increasingly diseased assembly of American troops. The defenders' memoirs paint a vivid picture of this situation, which was characterized by "starvation menus and ever-dwindling rations and . . . the mounting toll of disease from malaria and malnutrition."[40] The men's rations were cut in half in January 1942, and by the end of March everybody received less than a quarter of the usual rations for a serving soldier in the U.S. Army. By then, it was a

The Bataan Death March

matter of time until Bataan could no longer resist the Japanese attacks. Louis Morton described the situation in 1947:

> Malnutrition, malaria, and intestinal disease had lowered combat efficiency by more than 75 percent during the final weeks of the campaign. Men were getting 1,000 calories a day in March and the Luzon Force Surgeon estimated that they required at least 3,500 calories to fight effectively in the jungles of Bataan. The ration was deficient in vitamins A, B, and C, and beriberi was almost universal. Malaria accounted for a very large number of casualties. By April 1st the malarial rate had reached 1,000 cases daily, and there was little hope of securing additional supplies of quinine.[41]

The last two days of the defense were chaotic. The front lines destabilized, the army command was rarely informed about local developments, and orders went back and forth because they were either no longer timely or simply not executable.[42] Wainwright received pressure from Washington to resist for as long as possible—President Roosevelt and General MacArthur allowed no surrender—or to wage an attack against the Japanese if food supplies ran out, but the officers who remained in the Philippines knew better than that. Using starving and sick U.S. forces to attack the Japanese would lead to a "wholesale slaughter" and thereby had to be prevented. If the officers had known what would happen to their troops in the days, weeks, months, and even years after the surrender, they probably would have chosen differently.[43]

The only thing the Filipino and U.S. soldiers, not only those from Kentucky that James Russel Harris is referring to, could do was to continue "to fight—not with conventional weapons, but with courage, faith, and the bonds of community."[44] That seems to have been the only means of continuing the fight anyway, because fuel shortages limited the U.S. tank forces' mobility. Furthermore, the steady air raids by the Japanese caused a severe threat to the American and Filipino defenders, and "to avoid being spotted by planes, all light reflectors—windshields, headlights, and even belt buckles—were removed."[45] However, the outcome was obvious to everyone: the defenders would have no option but to surrender. Bataan surrendered on April 9, 1942—Corregidor was defended for an additional four months—and the soldiers had almost no choice but to become POWs of the Japanese Imperial Army.[46]

One account that vividly describes what happened in the aftermath is the so-called "Dyess Story,"[47] which "became the staple narrative of the Death March."[48] The eyewitness report by Lt. Col. William E. Dyess (1916–1943) was published in January 1944 and "burst upon a shocked nation." The story of the officer and his fellows about the "atrocities they had witnessed had been withheld for months by the government in the fear that its publication would result in death to thousands of American prisoners still in Japanese hands."[49]

Initially, the *Chicago Tribune* had secured its publication rights from the War Department, but it took more than four months for the story to become publicly known because they were barred from printing it. The story was extremely powerful and of broad interest because "here was a man who had lived behind the curtain of military secrecy the Japanese had drawn upon Bataan after the surrender and who could tell what actually had happened to the battered remnants of MacArthur's armies after the Stars and Stripes had been hauled down."[50] Furthermore, Dyess "was not reluctant to describe in full his personal experiences on the Death March and in the prison camps. This was because the sufferings he endured were typical of those visited upon thousands of other Americans."[51] The U.S. officer wanted the world to know of the daily war crimes in Japanese POW camps, which had happened before during the horrible Death March of Bataan. Dyess also clearly expressed the dimensions of the conflict's horrors: "If you triple my troubles and multiply the result by several thousand, you'll get a rough idea of what went on."[52]

It could be assumed based on little information that the soldiers, who had become prisoners of the Japanese Imperial Army, suffered from various difficulties throughout the march, including "dysentery, malaria, thirst, fatigue, heat exhaustion, and the cruelty of guards."[53] As prisoners of an army that considered surrender a dishonorable act, the U.S. soldiers could expect no kind treatment. In his introduction to the "Dyess Story," Charles Leavelle remarked that the book "stirred the nation more deeply probably than any event since Pearl Harbor, there can be little doubt."[54] The following description of the events related to the Bataan Death March will therefore follow Dyess' narrative to highlight some issues, which can also be found in other firsthand narratives about the march.

As previously mentioned, the soldiers who eventually surrendered at Bataan were used to low rations of food. Their diets mainly consisted of rice or thin salmon soup; their diets were sometimes enriched if somebody had been able to shoot a bird or a monkey, but their meals largely remained sparse.[55] Bataan's final surrender was unsurprising to the soldiers, and as Dyess remarked,

> There still was plenty of fight left in us. We were prisoners, but we didn't feel licked. I don't know what we would have felt could we have known that this was only the first of 361 days to be filled with murder and cruelty such as few American soldiers ever had endured. It was the start of the Death March from Bataan.[56]

The Japanese considered the soldiers who surrendered as less than human because they had not only lost the battle, but also accepted being POWs instead of committing suicide to escape the shame of being prisoners. This may partially explain the anger of the Japanese soldiers, who wasted no time in

The Bataan Death March

showing their disgust toward the American enemy. Dyess remembered the initial moments when the Japanese soldiers searched the prisoners for valuables, and when violence became a natural part of the POWs' lives:

> I noticed that the Japs, who up to now had treated us with an air of cool suspicion, were beginning to get rough. I saw men shoved, cuffed, and boxed. This angered and mystified us. It was uncalled for. We were not resisting. A few ranks away a Jap jumped up from a pack he had been inspecting. In his hand was a [supposedly Japanese] small shaving mirror. . . . The Jap stepped back, then lunged, driving his rifle butt into the American's face. . . . The Yank went down. The raging Jap stood over him, driving crushing blows to the face until the prisoner lay insensible.[57]

Yet this was not the only violent act Dyess witnessed that day, because another "Jap was smashing his fists into the face of another American soldiers who went to his knees and received a thudding kick in the groin."[58] These acts of violence were extreme, and the POWs did not understand why the Japanese beat somebody who already surrendered. Dyess, like many other prisoners, simply did not comprehend why they were treated with such brutality by an enemy so different from the one depicted in American propaganda since Pearl Harbor, and even before then:

> We were shocked. This treatment of war prisoners was beyond our understanding . . . an air force captain, was being searched by a three-star private. Standing by was a Jap commissioned officer, hand on sword hilt. These men were nothing like the toothy, bespectacled runts whose photographs are familiar to most newspaper readers. They were cruel of face, stalwart, and tall.[59]

They demonstrated their cruelty—like in the captain's case—whenever they felt that the Americans, who were searched for Japanese goods, could have harmed a Japanese soldier. The captain that Dyess refers to was punished when Japanese money was found among his possessions:

> The big Jap looked at the money. Without a word he grabbed the captain by the shoulder and shoved him down to his knees. He pulled the sword out of the scabbard and raised it high over his head, holding it with both hands. . . . Before we could grasp what was happening, . . . [the Japanese officer] had swung his sword. I remember how the sun flashed on it. There was a swish and a kind of chopping thud, like a cleaver going through beef.[60]

Without trial or legal defense, the Japanese killed the U.S. officer in cold blood: "The body fell forward. I have seen wounds, but never such a gush of blood as this. The heart continued to pump for a few seconds and at each beat there was another great spurt of blood."[61] For Dyess and his fellow POWs, the crime's legality was instantly clear: "This was the first murder. In the year to come there would be enough killing of American and Filipino soldier prisoners to rear a mountain of dead."[62]

Naturally, the prisoners hated the guards who regularly "beat and slugged prisoners" whenever they pleased, robbing them of their belongings such as "watches, fountain pens, money, and toilet articles."[63] Marching began once these tasks were done. There was no consideration for the well-being of the POWs, who were physically unprepared to travel the miles that lay ahead of them, and the Americans and Filipinos who had to march to Camp O'Donnell were not fed either. Requests for food, water, breaks, protection from the sun, or anything else were usually answered with violence, which is why

> it seemed worse than useless to ask the Japs for anything. An elderly American colonel did, however. He crossed the road and after pointing to the food and to the drooping prisoners, he went through the motions of eating. A squat Jap officer grinned at him and picked up a can of salmon. Then he smashed it against the colonel's head, opening the American's cheek from eye to jawbone. The officer staggered and turned back toward us, wiping the blood off.[64]

Even the last of those who believed in universal human values realized that the "Japs would respect neither age nor rank."[65] During the march, more and more corpses—mostly Filipino ones—appeared at the side of the road, but as Dyess noted, such "huddled and smashed figures beside the road eventually became commonplace to us."[66] The POWs also realized that complaining or disobeying Japanese orders could yield violence from the guards and their officers. However, marching for miles in the hot sun demanded its tribute, and water was one thing the soldiers needed more than anything else:

> The thirst of all had become almost unbearable, but remembering what had happened to the colonel earlier in the day we asked for nothing. A Jap officer walked along just after [a] thirsty soldier [who had left the lines] had been beaten. He appeared surprised that we wanted water. However, he permitted several Americans to collect canteens from their comrades and fill them at a stagnant carabao wallow which had been additionally befouled by seeping sea water. We held our noses to shut out the nauseating reek, but we drank all the water we could get.[67]

Every drop was valued at a fortune, because each one was a greater chance at life. Food was even rarer, and the Japanese came up with every possible

The Bataan Death March

excuse to avoid feeding the POWs—even the false claim to have found pistols in the possession of U.S. officer; however, even dirty water could make the difference between life and death.[68] The situation was so miserable that it even made no sense to assist those who were too weak to continue walking; not only were these people punished, but also those trying to help them. Once the march was in full procession, the violence against the marching POWs began: "It was not long until the advancing soldiers started beating us. Any Japanese who could reach an American hit him with a fist, elbow, or rifle butt. Their blows were strong; some broke jaws and bloodied noses. They were rewarded for these heartless acts with cheers of support from their comrades."[69] Gene Boyt, who also survived the Bataan Death March, described what happened to those who could no longer tolerate the hunger, the thirst, and the violence and had simply given up:

> I saw the first dead GI about an hour into the march. It was a horrible sight, indicating just how cruel our captors could be. The unfortunate American had been killed in the middle of the highway. What made the image so unnerving was the way the Japanese treated his body afterwards. It was lying prostrate, arms and legs outstretched like a gingerbread man's, and not more than an inch thick. Dozens of heavy trucks had crushed the corpse until it was flattened like a starched suit.[70]

Boyt began to fear a similar end for himself, leading him to stay under the Japanese guards' radar:

> I learned quickly to do as I was told, but it was not easy. Because of the language barrier, I could not understand anything the Japanese said. Kicks and punches often emphasized their incomprehensible commands. It was all very nerve-wracking. Half the time I was afraid to do anything, fearing [a] mistake would get me killed.[71]

According to Boyt's observations, the Japanese soldiers' violent behavior intensified the longer the march endured, and the number of beatings and the intensity of the violence increased.[72] Those who gave up walking were dead, and with a lack of food and water, a trace of dead bodies behind the marching party documented the death toll resulting from steady physical and mental torture, which, according to Boyt, destroyed the POWs' remaining dignity:

> [I]f a person needed to urinate or defecate while marching (and we all found ourselves in that circumstance at some point), he had to do it in his uniform as he walked. And there was no way to clean off afterward. That was

an awful experience, and it contributed dramatically to the spread of disease among the prisoners.[73]

However, the guards observing the marching party did not pay much attention to those who fell due to being unable to keep up with the march. The guards knew, as Dyess reported, that "skulking along, a hundred yards behind our contingent, came a 'clean-up squad' of murdering Jap buzzards."[74] Boyt had realized the increasing number of corpses on the morning of the second day of the march; some were killed immediately "and kicked into the borrow pits, along with the mud and feces,"[75] and he also witnessed what happened to one poor comrade who was simply unable to continue marching:

> When the man fell again, he effectively signed his death warrant. The others had no choice but to leave him behind. I, too, had to walk around him and keep going. As I looked back, a Japanese soldier appeared, Johnny-on-the-spot, to yell at him to get up. The condemned prisoner appeared desperate to live; he got to his hands and knees and attempted to crawl back into formation. The guard obviously relished torturing the doomed American, for he stabbed the man repeatedly in the buttocks with his bayonet. Moments later, when the prisoner lay flat on his back, I turned away. A horrific, high-pitched scream told me that the guard had impaled him, and he was dead.[76]

Regardless of such incidents, the soldiers mostly thought of only two things: food and water. The lack of water was particularly torturous to the soldiers, and the only water they were permitted to access was in wallows for the carabaos, where the animals usually gathered for a bath. Consequently, the water was "laden with animal waste [and] extremely filthy."[77] This did not matter at all to the dehydrated soldiers, some of which survived even this type of torture.

Boyt remarks that he "occasionally . . . met other kind guards who allowed prisoners to sit down when the column was stopped or to draw water from community wells in the various barrios" and that "these surprising acts of compassion spared American lives . . . [and] also kept me from viewing every guard as evil," but "most of the Japanese soldiers I encountered in the Pacific showed no mercy and treated the prisoners horribly."[78] Without the help of many Filipinos—who risked their lives by secretly providing something to eat or drink, even just a piece of sugar cane—more would have died. To the Americans, it was simple yet effective "water torture" for the Japanese to prevent the local population from helping soldiers by offering fresh water and disallowing POWs to access wells in the smaller villages.[79] POWs surviving the Bataan Death March depended on many factors: who their guards were, whether Filipinos helped them, and if they were physically and mentally strong

The Bataan Death March

enough to endure misery before giving up, thereby becoming victims of the death squads that followed the march and killed those too weak to continue. Some POWs simply lost their minds:

> In time, more of them became crazed for water and overcame their inhibition to drink from those polluted borrow pits. Most did not know it, but when they drank that untreated water they were committing suicide. Ingesting such slime was a sure way to contract dysentery, and like so many hazards on the Death March, dysentery was fatal.[80]

Other soldiers who went mad tried to retaliate against the Japanese, which was also fatal: "As the insane POW ran toward a Japanese sentry, the guards shot him. It was the only time during the march that I saw one of our boys killed with a bullet. At least he died instantly; I know I would rather have been shot than bayoneted."[81]

On April 12, 1942, the POWs and their guards reached Orani in the northeast of the peninsula. They had been marching for 21 hours on the third day of the Bataan Death March, starting at Cabcaben in the south. Dyess describes the arrival of the men, who looked more like ghosts than human beings:

> Near the center of the town the Japs ordered us off the road to a barbed wire compound a block away. It had been intended for five hundred men. Our party numbered more than six hundred. Already in it, however, were more than 1,500 Americans and Filipinos. The stench of the place reached us long before we entered it. Hundreds of the prisoners were suffering from dysentery. Human waste covered the ground. The shanty that had served as a latrine no longer was usable as such.[82]

The prisoners not only suffered from lack of hygiene; once the sun rose, the heat worsened, and the American and Filipino prisoners experienced delirium. Dyess outlines the symptoms of the deliria: "Their wild shouts and thrashings about dissipated their ebbing energy. They began lapsing into coma. For some it was the end. Starvation, exhaustion, and abuse had been too much for their weakened bodies. Brief coma was followed by merciful death."[83] In fact, death was salvation for many of the POWs, as many of the men had lost their faith in God and humanity alike. Those who grew delirious were ordered to be buried alive by their comrades, who had no other choice but to help dig graves for their friends and fellow soldiers.[84]

The prisoners received no food while they waited—most of them for death—but on one evening they accessed clean water for the first time in days, the night offering cool air to those who barely had space to sleep in the crowded camp. On the next day, however, the Americans and Filipinos "were desperate for something to eat ... The first day [they] felt empty, barren, vacant; the second day [they] had sharp pains in [the] esophagus; the third day [they were] obsessed with thoughts of food; the fourth day [they] felt nothing, a sure sign [they were] starting to starve."[85] Yet on the fourth day, the starving ended. All the men, Dyess included, looked forward to eating even the worst food:

> Out of one of the dirty buildings came kitchen corpsmen, dragging cans of sticky gray rice which they ladled out—one ladleful to each man. Those of us who had mess [kits] loaned the lids to men who had none. There were not enough kits and lids to go around, so some of the prisoners had to receive their dole in cupped hands. The portion given each man was equivalent to a saucer or small plate of rice. The food was unappetizing and was eaten in the worst possible surroundings, but it was eaten. Make no mistake about that. It was our first in many a day.[86]

It was only the second time in the 85 miles of the march that the prisoners received old rice. Meanwhile, the Filipinas and Filipinos who tried offering food to ease the pain of the POWs who looked like a "scarecrow procession"[87] were punished by the Japanese:

> The Jap guards went into a frenzy. They struck out right and left at the Good Samaritans, slugging, beating, and jabbing bayonets indiscriminately. Japs tried to stamp on all the food that hadn't been picked up. They turned their rage upon us. When the townsfolk saw their gifts were only adding to our misery they stopped throwing them.[88]

After these experiences, Dyess realized the "Japs were starving [them] deliberately."[89] On the morning of April 15, after the POWs had spent a night in San Fernando, they were neither fed nor granted access to water. Instead, the prisoners were brought to the train station and loaded 115 at a time into ramshackle boxcars, which were supposed to hold only 50 people. Because many of the POWs suffered from dysentery, the "atmosphere was foul,"[90] and the men could neither sit nor lie down, especially since the floor was covered in excrement. Eventually the train reached Capas, from where the survivors of the 30-mile train ride had "only" to walk the remaining 7 miles to reach Camp O'Donnell, "an even more deadly trial"[91] for the survivors of the Death March and a true hell for a prisoner of the Japanese empire.

Between the Loss of Humanity and Extreme Violence

Considering the experiences of the American and Filipino POWs after the fall of Bataan, one would understand anger or hatred against the Japanese. However, Boyt comes to a different conclusion:

The Bataan Death March

Bataan did not extinguish my faith in humanity. I still believe that most people, regardless of their race, are decent and desire peace. That is an idealistic goal, but we must strive for it anyway. A key to achieving global peace is to examine openly the barbaric deeds of the past, no matter how unpleasant, and vow not to repeat them.[92]

To fulfill the survivor's wish, it is important to discuss the reasons for the Japanese soldiers' extremely violent behavior. First, the surrender of Bataan established a new space-time continuum not only in which the Japanese were victorious, but in which new rules governing what was allowed or not had to be established, even from the POWs' perspectives.

Boyt also describes what happened within groups of prisoners:

In that unbearable climate, it was impossible to hold our forces together, and chaos ensued. The ruffians dominated for a while, but wiser heads ultimately prevailed, as new, more rational leaders emerged. Unfortunately, the transformation did not happen immediately, because our officers' corps had its share of bad apples. Prior to the war, some unqualified people were given positions of authority. . . . Some chastised subordinates needlessly just because they outranked them, and even instructed them to hand over any food and water they were hiding. Dealing with brutal Japanese guards was bad enough. Having to contend with unreasonable fellow prisoners made the Death March even worse.[93]

The Bataan Death March established a space-time continuum in which legal and ethical norms were reconfigured by the prisoners and guards alike. For the guards, this meant that they were able to use violence against human beings who were determined to be inferior, simply by the fact that they had lost the fight for the Philippines.

From the Japanese perspective, the American and Filipino soldiers who had surrendered at Bataan instead of dying an honorable death on the battlefield were no longer considered human. However, Japan's samurai culture, which is often referenced as one of the major reasons for the Japanese soldiers' violence during the war, is not the only reason for their brutal abuse of the POWs.

Like the Americans themselves, many Japanese were preconditioned by the propaganda that had shown the enemy as inferior beings undeserving of sympathy. Although some Japanese soldiers seem to have reacted kindlier than others, most of them considered it legitimate to use violence against POWs, and because Japanese soldiers thought themselves to be liberating Asia from Western imperialism, they naturally thought it was appropriate to punish the Americans.

The Imperial Japanese Army was unprepared for so many soldiers to surrender, and they were logistically unable to provide more food for them immediately. As such, the Japanese soldiers may have considered the prisoners a competing party for supplies, expressing their anger for this predicament through violence. This violence was also stimulated by the fierce resistance of the U.S. and Filipino troops who might have damaged the image of the Japanese army and its soldiers, who, like in Shanghai, had expected a swift victory over an inferior enemy.

As a group, the Japanese soldiers were also driven by specific group dynamics. Cheers for violence, steady surveillance of their conduct with the enemy, and exchanging stories about the enemy—to whom one might have lost friends or comrades—all played key roles in shaping the mind-sets of the Japanese soldiers. Some of them might even have accepted physical and mental torture as part of their own disciplinary treatment, because it was appropriate for the enemy.

Obedience was also a critical factor. The Japanese soldiers were ordered to guard the prisoners on their way to Camp O'Donnell, and they had a time schedule for this task. Knowing that any willing or unwilling disobedience of this schedule would lead to punishment, which was quite harsh in the Japanese army, the guards themselves punished anybody who did not follow orders quickly or accurately enough, who complained, or who could have otherwise endangered the success of the mission. Failure had to be prevented by all means, including violence.

It is therefore the specific space-time continuum that provided the Japanese soldiers with the reasons, the legal space, the possibility, and even the need to act violently against their prisoners. Again, if one does not focus solely on samurai culture or anti-Western and anti-American sentiments, the reasons for the soldiers' conduct were not determined by factors specific to the Japanese. The violence used during the Bataan Death March is a genuinely human form of violent behavior, and there is no guarantee that future wars will not see similar transgressions. For the Americans and Filipinos who survived the march, however, the real hell was yet to come: daily life in a Japanese prison camp, an existence that was also highly characterized by physical and psychological violence.

CHAPTER SIX

POWs of the Japanese

"Nobody knows what 'Auschwitz' is,
just as nobody knows what 'labour camp' is.
People vanish into both without a trace,
and that's the last that is heard of them."[1]

Yehiel De-Nur (1909–2001) was right in this evaluation about the lives and suffering of those who died during the Second World War in labor, concentration, or extermination camps under German or Japanese control. It is difficult to reconstruct the stories of those who perished in these camps, and many of them will never be told because only a minority of the victims survived. Although reports like the previously mentioned Dyess Story—which details the suffering of Allied POWs in Japanese camps—had been told, it took a while until they reached a broader public. On January 28, 1944, *The New York Times* published a story about the fall of Bataan and its aftermath based on the firsthand accounts of Commander Melvyn H. McCoy (U.S. Navy), Lieutenant Colonel S. M. Mellnik (U.S. Army Coast Artillery), and Captain William E. Dyess (Army Air Force), who had all "stunned their superiors with graphic descriptions of the savage treatment that the Japanese dealt out to helpless prisoners of war."[2] Yet these eyewitnesses were not allowed to report their stories immediately because President Roosevelt "feared that the disclosure of Japanese war crimes would provoke retaliation against American servicemen still in enemy hands"[3] and therefore demanded that the news be suppressed.

However, when the report was released in January 1944, *The New York Times* emphasized the enemy's barbaric nature: "The Japanese in war are not men we can understand. They are men of the old Stone Age, animals who sometimes stand erect."[4] The collected memories of the survivors of Japanese POW camps in Southeast Asia, especially the Philippines, represent what

Gregory J. Urwin called "a catalog of horrors so monstrous that it still has the power to elicit intense emotional reactions."[5] It has already been mentioned that the Japanese forces were simply unprepared for a large number of POWs; dealing with so many surrendering soldiers was uncommon for the Japanese army, but this cannot be the only reason why 10,650 out of 25,580 Americans in Japanese hands would not see the end of the war and instead die "slow, agonizing deaths from complications brought on by malnutrition, dehydration, disease, and physical abuse."[6] Most of those who survived the camps developed physical and/or psychological trauma, particularly because they lived under the steady fear of violent abuse or death: "At any time, the Japanese proved capable of executing prisoners on the slightest pretext."[7]

The discussion about POWs' mistreatment in Japanese hands remains controversial because deniers maintain that they never mistreated prisoners, claiming that those accusing Japan have based their accusations on massacres without witnesses.[8] Such views are strengthened by the fact that the "charges against the Japanese brought forward in the Tokyo War Crimes Trials were chilling,"[9] regardless of the fact that there were survivors whose appearances alone attested to their treatment, like some who had survived the building of the Burma-Siam Railway:

> That such skeletons could still retain a spark of life: staring eyes; beak-like noses; retracted lips; a green-grey skin; shoulder blades like knife-edges cutting through the skin; knee joints twice as thick as thighs; biceps thinner than wrists; and ribs almost devoid of covering. Yet, their ankles and stomachs were bloated horribly and these were the men not ill enough to go to the hospital.[10]

Although survivor testimonies are an important informational source, one must be careful when using them to avoid developing a one-sided perspective. As Van Waterford correctly remarks, many such accounts are "either biased by a speedy presentation or scattered by selective memory."[11] And yet a close reading of these sources will offer greater insight into the POWs' lives and suffering in the Japanese army's camps. It is important to include this perspective in the present analysis, as those who survived the Bataan Death March faced "an even more deadly trial"[12] in the months that followed. During this time, the POWs in the Philippines were initially transported to provisional camps before reaching the main ones, O'Donnell and Cabanatuan. The present chapter will not only discuss the American POWs' situation in the Philippines, but also compare them with the British's experiences related to the Burma-Siam Railway. The comparison will demonstrate which factors were critical in the POWs' survival; additionally, the forms of violence the Japanese soldiers used, as well as the possible factors responsible for this violence, shall be discussed. In other words, this chapter will add another specific

POWs of the Japanese

space-time continuum to the analysis of Japanese war crimes during World War II.

From Surrender to the Camps

John R. Bumgarner was a U.S. Army physician who was serving in Mariveles when the front began to collapse. More than 7,000 patients were assembled in the municipality's general hospital and awaited what would happen once the Japanese took them as prisoners of war. Once the enemy had taken over, soldiers visited the hospital as if it was a zoo:

> There were frequent visitations by Japanese officers, most of them carrying cameras. They seemed to enjoy promenading through the hospital, and at times they even paused in the middle of the hospital to rest. The Japanese enlisted men wandering through the hospital seemed to be more specifically interested in the watches, rings, and food. And as they made their way through the hospital, they collected every such item which anyone was foolish enough to expose.[13]

As Bumgarner put it, the Japanese soldiers did not consider the Americans worthy of humane treatment or respect: "The most obnoxious trait of our captors was their habit, whenever nature called, of squatting in their tracks and relieving themselves."[14] The hospital's cleanliness was of no concern, either—around 5,500 Filipino soldiers who would later join the Bataan Death March were forced out of the hospital immediately, and women in the hospital were treated worse:

> A few days before our surrender, a pregnant Filipino woman had wandered into our hospital obviously near term and in labor. She was delivered in the OR and put to bed in a small tent on one of the medical wards. She was so weak and sick after delivery that no one had the heart to send her away at the time of the surrender. The commanding officer of the hospital made every effort possible to keep her presence unknown to the Japanese, who wandered everywhere in the hospital, but the baby's cries brought her to the attention of the Japanese, who raped her repeatedly at gunpoint.[15]

Eventually, all remaining patients and physicians were forced to leave the hospital. Once on the march, they would witness the cruel realities their fellow Americans already had to endure. The road to the north was paved with corpses, some more obvious than others:

> From where we stood we could see what appeared to be a Filipino army uniform and a pair of shoes lying in the middle of the highway. As we darted

across the road we saw near the uniform a human head flattened across the road. Even in my haste I had to pause, if only momentarily. The face, a grinning, grotesque mask, was spread out to an absolute smoothness, having been run over repeatedly. In the few seconds we lingered in horror, it struck me that war dehumanized both victor and victim.[16]

On May 26, 1942, the party of American patients and physicians reached Bilibid Prison in Manila, where Filipino and U.S. POWs were imprisoned after the fall of Corregidor before being sent to Camp O'Donnell and Camp Cabanatuan.[17] To the imprisoned and those forced to march, it was clear that the Japanese sought to break the prisoners: "The idea seemed to be if they yelled, shouted, screamed, shoved, prodded, and hit, we would become totally intimidated." For men like Bumgarner, however, this was simply unnecessary: "I was already intimidated. I was also dirty, exhausted, and depressed."[18] Not only did some Japanese soldiers try to loot the POWs' belongings aggressively, but others reacted violently to any questions the POWs posed. They interpreted the questions as disobedience rather than products of language barriers, also failing to consider that exhaustion caused the POWs' delayed responses or lack thereof. It may be that some soldiers reacted violently because they feared the same violence from their superiors if they failed to carry out orders quickly enough. However, no matter the motive of the persistent violence, it was a severe problem for the POWs who were largely traumatized by their wartime experience.

The arrival at Bilibid did not comfort the POWs, as their diet continued to be "purely and simply, rice and more rice."[19] Yet the provisional camp was not the end of the prisoners' journey, who had survived the Bataan Death March like those before them, and those who spent time in Bilibid after the fall of Corregidor were transported to camps north of the Bataan Peninsula. Like other past prisoners, Bumgarner and his patients were also put on "small freight cars that seemed to be designed for horses and cattle," and the "Japanese crammed 90 into each car," leaving hardly any room for the POWs to stand. With six hours of transport in the heat of the Philippines—without any breaks and one provision of water—the trip itself yielded a high death toll.[20] Nevertheless, some of the soldiers considered death to be lucky, especially when they realized that the "Hell at O'Donnell"[21] awaited those who survived the trains.

The first impression of this prison camp was grisly: "Flies, maggots, and dead bodies were everywhere, and the odor was overpowering."[22] Gene Boyt was right when he claimed that the "Japanese had turned O'Donnell into the worst hellhole in the Philippines, with conditions even poorer than on the Death March."[23] The camp commander, Yoshio Tsuneyoshi, delivered a speech that explained the prisoners' state of affairs and expectations: "You are sworn enemies of Japan. Therefore, you will not be treated like

POWs of the Japanese

prisoners of honorable war."[24] He also emphasized his personal disgust toward the American surrender:

> None of you are honorable soldiers. You are all cowards who deserve to die. Instead, your lives have been spared by the benevolence of the Emperor! . . . You captives are our enemies and always will be. When given an order, you will comply with it immediately and without question. You will also salute all Japanese soldiers on sight. If you do not, you will be killed.[25]

The prisoners' regular treatment would serve as a daily reminder of the commander's words, who "treated [POWs] like archenemies and showed no compassion."[26] At Camp O'Donnell, the American POWs were forced to "live in filth," steadily surrounded by a "terrible odor of excrement"[27] because many of them suffered from dysentery. Another woe for the imprisoned Americans were lice, with which many got infected. Once a prisoner became too ill to kill the lice one by one, "lice overran their bodies," and it became easy to "identify the dying because they were completely covered with lice."[28]

To make sure that the prisoners would not attempt an escape from Camp O'Donnell, the Japanese authorities announced the so-called "Rule of Ten," which threatened to kill all members of a group of 10 men if one or more from that group escaped. However, because the prisoners were too unhealthy and hungry to attempt an escape, it did not seem necessary to enforce this rule. More importantly, the prisoners' survival was contingent on supplies, especially food and water, which were never sufficient in the first few months—which, again, points to the problems the Japanese authorities initially had in feeding so many prisoners. Their logistics were faulty and supplies were scarce, and the military staff's poor planning caused thousands of American deaths in Japanese camps. Whereas it was considered dishonorable for a Japanese soldier to surrender, the U.S. soldiers did so and remained alive. As such, these soldiers required supplies that were simply unavailable in the initial aftermath of the fall of the Philippines. For the POWs, this lack of planning and consideration meant a months-long struggle with death that many were unlikely to survive.

For Dyess and those who had survived the Bataan Death March, the situation was even worse. The survivors had made it, but they only received one mess kit full of rice for each man. After one week at O'Donnell, the death rate reached 20 men per day. The Filipino soldiers were treated worse, so their death rate reached 150 men per day. Another week passed, and the death rate climbed to 50 Americans and 350 Filipinos per day. Dyess was concerned from a pragmatic point of view: "The burial problem was serious."[29] New prisoners arrived every day, most of them starved and sick. In this condition, they were easy prey for numerous diseases like malaria, dysentery, and beriberi. Such illnesses were easily treatable, but without food and essential nutrients, most of the soldiers simply collapsed. Those with beriberi particularly suffered when their "feet, ankles, and legs were swollen almost double normal size" and their "faces were puffed up like balloons."[30] Within two months, more than 2,000 Americans had died in the camp, and the Japanese only promised to provide medicine for the sick. The only quinine that reached the camp and could be used against malaria among the patients was delivered by the Red Cross, and the only thing that could have helped against the spread of the diseases was food. However, food was as rare at Camp O'Donnell as any sign of humanity. Rice was provided three times a day, but rice alone did not suffice; meat was only provided twice within two months. The kitchens were also dirty, and flies and mosquitoes spread deadly germs throughout the facilities, which operated without being cleaned. That the prisoners had no water to spare for personal hygiene was the final blow. Dyess, who had spent 35 days at Camp O'Donnell before being able to take a bath in a gallon of stolen water, could never wash his clothes there.

For the POWs, however, hunger was probably the gravest problem. Some even suffered from food-related hallucinations: "Our talk and thoughts were almost continually of food; food we had enjoyed in the past, food we craved now, and food we intended to enjoy upon our release."[31] The fact that they were just given "enough" food to stay alive was considered torture from the Japanese, who "gave [them] just enough food to keep [them] in an agony of hunger at all times."[32] Nevertheless, the POWs did not give up. As John Henry Poncio and Marlin Young put it in their account, "As long as we were breathing, we had hope." In the meantime, there was nothing much more to do than obey the Japanese orders: "We got up on command, went to work on command, ate on command, and slept on command."[33] In the summer, the Japanese transferred the POWs from Camp O'Donnell to three camps: Cabanatuan 1, 2, and 3. Of the 50,000 American and Filipino prisoners, only 7,000 to 10,000 were held in the new camps. I do not want to stress the argument that the Japanese intentionally starved the American and Filipino POWs to kill them, but the military leaders responsible neither acted on behalf of the defeated enemy nor tried to treat them well or give them additional supplies. When logistics fail, it can be difficult to identify those responsible for problems caused by a lack of planning and foresight, but unpreparedness cannot excuse the loss of any life. Not all Japanese soldiers involved in the camp beat or physically abused the Americans, but the concurring reports show that violence was indeed part of the daily routine. The soldiers' motives to abuse others may have varied, including but not limited to, personal stress or abuse from higher authorities, anger, revenge, joy, or simply chance. However, without ego documents that reflect on the guards' actions, we can merely speculate. One thing for sure is that no higher military authorities prevented violence against the prisoners, probably because the POWs were never considered an honorable enemy.

POWs of the Japanese

Camp Cabanatuan was built to segregate the American POWs from the Filipinos. Transfers to the town, which was located 100 miles north of Manila, began in May 1942. The three camps had been erected within a 10-mile radius, and camps No. 2 and 3, which were 6 miles apart, were connected by a dirt road. Those like Burmgarner, who arrived from the field hospitals in Bataan after having spent some time in Bilibid, would usually end up in camp No. 3, whereas POWs from Camp O'Donnell were mostly gathered in camps No. 1 and 2. The men who surrendered in Corregidor after Bataan, who were already in Japanese hands, were also brought to No. 3. Eventually, No. 2 was used for naval personnel, whereas No. 3 was permanently closed in October 1942 with its prisoners moved to No. 1. In contrast to Camp O'Donnell, the prisoners at Cabanatuan were able to trade food "through the fence," which allowed them to improve their diets and obtain additional medicine so long as they had something to trade. Those who had nothing to trade faced serious problems, because "food was downright scarce"[34] at Cabanatuan as well.

When Bumgarner and the others arrived at camp No. 3, the sights before them seemed to promise nothing but death:

> Apparently the enclosure had been used before to hold prisoners. There were no latrines, and the ground was littered both with animal and human excrement. There was one single pit in the corner of the compound, which was full of maggots and liquid feces. We had just arrived inside the fence when the Japanese began wandering among us looking for loot, but most of our watches and rings were gone.[35]

Nevertheless, when Bumgarner saw the first survivors of the Bataan Death March, he could not help himself but believe that he and his group at least had a chance to survive in Cabanatuan:

> Seven hundred men, or shadows of men, walked into Cabanatuan from the railway station where they had arrived by train in cattle cars from Camp O'Donnell. These tired, sick, emaciated specters were lined up to be counted by the Japanese. Most of them were in shorts, many nude to their waists. They had pitifully few belongings, since they had long since been looted by the Japanese. Most of them, for unexplained reasons, were deeply tanned. Their ribs, which showed deeply sunken grooves between, were starkly outlined against their chest. Practically all subcutaneous fat was gone. Their legs and arms looked like pipestems.[36]

The Japanese soldiers "constantly patrolled the perimeter inside as well as outside the camp,"[37] but considering the prisoners' physical condition, none of them could fathom a realistic escape. The prisoners eventually divided the camp into three zones: one for prisoners, one for the Japanese, and one for those with no chance of survival, which was called the Zero War.

Because the Japanese had expected their captured enemies to "have their own rations," they "had far too little food to decently feed the prisoners."[38] The high number of atrocities in the camps during the remaining months of 1942 were a consequence of low rations and medical supplies, which eventually caused thousands of needless deaths. The diseases that plagued the POWs led to a particularly high number of deaths, especially because the prisoners "rarely dealt with a pure complex of any one disease; almost always it was a spectrum of various diseases."[39] The physicians could do nothing but try their best to ease the pain, knowing that they could hardly treat the illnesses successfully. One of them confessed that "[he] felt less like a doctor than a caretaker of the dying" and that the physicians' efforts "were a travesty."[40] Those who survived malaria or dysentery endured nutritional deficiencies; the diet provided by the Japanese would not change these issues, especially because "the diet of rice, soup flavored with a fish head or vegetable refuse, and occasional small portions of meat virtually invited beriberi, pellagra, scurvy, and other related maladies."[41]

The sick also affected other people's psychological states because they served as a vision of each prisoner's possible future. Bumgarner felt sympathy for the dysentery patients while fearing he would become one of them:

> The majority of those men had very frequent, very loose, watery stools, with no control. A good portion of them could not stand up, much less walk to a toilet 100 yards distant, so they soiled themselves repeatedly. A good percentage could stagger outside the building and make an attempt to reach the toilet, only to fail; consequently the ground was strewn with liquid feces covered with flies. However, the worst humiliation came to those who slept . . . below a patient with uncontrolled dysentery. The person in the lower bay could awake to find himself covered with liquid feces that had dripped down between the bamboo strips.[42]

In July 1942, half of the prisoners were infected with at least one disease, but the Japanese did not provide them with medicine. The only additional quinine the physicians could obtain had to be traded "through the fence."[43] In mid-June 1942, the death rate climbed to 30 POWs per day. The starved bodies could not resist the slightest infection, and the sick had no chance to survive and were usually brought to the Zero Ward. Four hundred to 450 men died of diphtheria, and their "deaths could be directly attributed to the wanton, deliberate neglect by the Japanese."[44] The Japanese remained adamant enemies in "a world where there was little to share than kindness,"[45] and the poor souls who were transferred to the Zero Ward reached "a place of zero medicine, near-zero supplies, and zero hope."[46] There,

POWs of the Japanese

the patients lay on the floor with only a blanket to cover them. There was one cold water tap at the front of the grisly ward, and during the day when the sun was shining and the weather was warm these men would be carried out, laid on the grass, and literally hosed down to remove the filth. They were without exception only ghosts of men.[47]

The only people who could offer at least spiritual support and relief were the chaplains, who were forbidden to perform Last Rites for the dying but tried to do them when the guards were not paying attention.

However, one day the Japanese intercepted a Greek Bible meant to be smuggled to Cabanatuan, and a chaplain was arrested. He would be severely punished for his disobedience:

> The chaplain was subjected to the most inhumane treatment in an effort to drag a confession out of him. He was placed in a 5 by 5 foot hot box with a half-crazed man who had been there for some time. . . . Day after day the chaplain remained in that place with the sun beating down on the metal roof. Their excrement lay around them. Their food, unfit for an animal, was limited.[48]

The chaplain, Preston Taylor, "spent many weeks in that hellhole"[49] before the other officers could intervene on his behalf. The prisoners believed that Taylor's survival was only possible through some miracle.

The Rule of Ten also existed in Camp Cabanatuan, and in August 1942, a man did escape. However,

> his nine mates were not killed. Instead he was caught and paraded on both sides of the camp. Led around like a dog with a Japanese soldier prodding him with a bayonet, he bore a large sign on his back proclaiming that he had been foolish enough to try to escape. The Japanese colonel lectured us all this while, maintaining that we were lucky to be Japanese prisoners of war, that no prisoners anywhere were getting the wonderful treatment we were enjoying.[50]

When three officers tried to escape, they were caught, bound, and presented at the camp's entrance, where passing Filipinos had to beat them. Rumors later had it that two of the officers were eventually decapitated, and the third one was killed with a bayonet. The prisoners had witnessed so much violent abuse from the Japanese during their camp life that these rumors needed no proof to be believed. In the eyes of the POWs, Japan's soldiers "were savage and totally unpredictable."[51]

Access to food determined life or death, and the occasional "muddy, fly-covered, freshly killed carabao" was simply not enough "to supply carabao stew for nearly 3,000 persons."[52] The available food could merely secure "a slow death of starvation,"[53] which a lack of medicine guaranteed. The 300,000 quinine tablets that arrived in July 1942 were only enough to treat 3,000 sick patients for 10 days. Afterward, the diseases reemerged. Lice and bedbugs added to the POWs' misery, as they kept the sick awake trying to seek solace from their "itchy, crawly annoyance."[54] The flies in the camp, which carried illnesses from toilets to the camp, guaranteed that the diseases never disappeared. When they severely affected the camps in the fall of 1942, the Americans had to bury 50 to 100 men per day. Many of them simply died of colds or from a small scratch that got infected.[55]

The diseases obviously bothered the prisoners, but what caused even more pain—psychological and physical—was their permanent lack of food. In the summer and fall of 1942, "food was so scarce, so poor, and so tasteless that some of the young and less experienced would resort to eating anything in order to quiet their hunger pangs."[56] Morale consequently decreased, and Second Lieutenant Charles W. Burris was shocked that his fellow POWs lost all signs of humanity: "That was one place where I learned that a human being is a marauder. I believe he would steal from his own mother if he was starving hard enough."[57] Because the rice was sometimes full of dirt and bugs, some prisoners turned to other food supplies, like John Henry Poncio and Marlin Young, who "also ate whistle weeds, which grew in the marshy places at the edge of camp, but I'll bet you couldn't find a vitamin or calorie in a ton of the stuff. We boiled it, added it to the rice—trying to spike up the meal—but our stomachs weren't fooled."[58] Another option was corn, but the Japanese guards were uncooperative when it was requested by the prisoners:

> The Japanese only grew corn for fodder, so we couldn't convince them of its goodness if harvested while still tender. By the time we got it, we could only make hominy, which we did by putting it in a barrel with wood ashes. The lye leached from the ashes dissolved the tough skin of the corn, making it edible. I never liked hominy, yet I loved fresh corn; everyone did. The vitamins and calories in it would have made a big difference in our conditions. It was another case of plain stupidity and unnecessary stubbornness on the part of the Japs.[59]

Nevertheless, the Japanese authorities allowed the prisoners to pursue their own farming project. Yet considering the number of sick POWs and the climate, working in the improvised fields caused more harm and yielded no extra food on the starving men's plates. The work was done "in the broiling sun during the dry season or in the pouring rain during monsoons, under backbreaking conditions and cruel, sadistic overseers" who forced the prisoners "to farm without shoes, tools, or protection from the elements." The tools were made "from scrap metal, wire, and bamboo," which made the farming more complicated and labor intensive, thereby increasing the death toll. It took little time until "everyone hated the whole idea of farming and would do almost anything to avoid the detail, especially when it became evident that the Japs were taking the lion's share of the crops."[60]

The POWs would usually try to escape their suffering in the camp by volunteering to work security details outside, but few were assigned to them. Most of the prisoners simply continued their daily routine of starving, dealing with lice, and getting abused by guards. Eventually, the men "began to look like animated skeletons with potbellies that hung over our shorts or G-strings"[61] and only humor could keep them alive. Laughing seemed to be the only way to avoid insanity, especially because death was everywhere. The men who died in the night were usually taken to the daily muster in the morning to be used as dummies to secure the dead men's rations. A dead comrade's last duty was simple: provide food for another day. For those who were still alive, this was no question of ethics—it was a matter of survival. Regardless of the lack of supplies, the Japanese kept the prisoners busy from dawn till dusk, and the only constant factors were work and sleep.

Their typical diets remained the same: "every day, every week, every month was rice mixed with a weed-like green called talinum."[62] Food therefore became "an ever-present topic,"[63] and dreams about new menus or future celebration dinners ultimately replaced sexual desire. Even a small amount of green tea purchased from a Filipino trader and secretly brought into the camp marked a highlight in the prisoners' lives and was celebrated as an invaluable event.[64] However, distrust and food rivalries were a natural consequence of the contemporary space-time continuum, which was marked by a lack of even the simplest food supply[65]:

> Who could be trusted? And not only about food, but about anything? That was becoming the question of all questions in the camps. As time went on, more and more the universe of trust, the moral community, came down to just the little subtribes, handfuls of men trying to stay human together in a world turning more and more inhuman.

The men simply wanted to survive and avoid the "triangle of death,"[66] which consisted of the morgue, the diphtheria ward, and the Zero Ward. Some went beyond the limits of immorality to achieve that goal. The Japanese therefore brought out the worst in the prisoners, because the human standards of American society did not apply in a Japanese prison camp.

For those who survived the camps in the Philippines, it was clear that "with few exceptions all those lives could have been saved by proper nutrition and proper medications."[67] In the eight months after the fall of Bataan, thousands of lives had ended due to insufficient food or medication. The end of the year, however, would improve the POWs' situation. In December they received money from the Japanese authorities—$20—to buy more food, which also improved the provisions of meat and vitamins in the future. Furthermore, on New Year's Eve, the prisoners received "ten-pound Red Cross food packages that contained very nourishing items such as cheese, corned beef, raisins, and chocolate."[68] In the months prior, 2,500 Americans had died in addition to the 1,500 who did not survive Camp O'Donnell. These deaths were a consequence of Japanese unpreparedness, and although the prisoners say that Japan's army with its "deliberate program of neglect and brutality [was] fully accountable,"[69] it is important to emphasize that the Japanese were unprepared for so many prisoners. This is by no means an excuse for their conduct, but it can explain the high death count in the camps in the Philippines.

Those who survived would eventually be transported to other locations, like Manchuria, where they continued to suffer, as the

> weather exerted a pressure as severe as the hard labor and beatings. Dead POWs were boxed up and placed in warehouses until spring, when the winter-frozen soil thawed enough for graves to be dug. . . . The eternal quest for food at Hoten proved as demanding as that for warmth. Dogs, cats, sparrows, and other small animals were added to the meager official diet.[70]

However, more prisoners were brought to the heartland of the empire: Japan itself. There, POWs would work in mines, factories, or shipyards while being officially imprisoned in one of over 100 camps throughout the country.[71] The POWs reached these prisons by sea, transported on so-called Hell Ships, in which they "were shipped the way animals were, in the hold, loaded along with all kinds of other freight: rice, coal, rubber, cinchona bark, cigarettes, steel tubing, gasoline, bombs."[72] During these journeys, the old ships were under "extreme overload" (chōmansai),[73] which decreased chances of escape if hit by an enemy submarine. The situation was unbearable, but as Gavan Daws described it, "[T]he Japanese said they did not overload POWs just for being POWs; they did it only because circumstances forced them to. But the POWs were foreign, they were white, they were prisoners of war, *disgraced individuals*, miserable objects." The prisoners were consequently "trapped in their own shit with the Japanese shitting down on them."[74] On the old and slow ships, the risk of dying on the way to Japan or Manchuria was almost as high as the risk of dying in the previous prison camps, and of the 50,000 men who had been transported, more than 10,000 never reached their destination.

The crowded ships added to the POWs' psychological stress, and the conditions caused more than simple anxiety:

> [The] ship was inhumanely crowded: a prisoner had to sit, legs extended, with the next prisoner's back almost touching his face. Darkness, crowding, and extreme heat caused some to go berserk. Fights broke out. A few

prisoners tried to climb ladders to the deck. Had others not restrained them, the guards would have had even more dead victims. Some prisoners, driven by thirst and madness, drank the blood of weaker comrades.... During air attacks the guards shut the cover of the hold, the only source of light and air. Added to the terror of explosions outside and darkness inside was uncertainty. If the ship was damaged or sinking, would the prisoners be freed, shot, or trapped? For thousands of unlucky prisoners on the tour ships sunk by bombs or torpedoes, the awful uncertainties became terrible realities.[75]

Those who survived the journey eventually reached the enemy's heartland. No possibility of escape existed there, and "[trying to escape] was meaningless because there was no way [they] could escape unless [they] had Asian features."[76] Rear Admiral Donald T. Giles shared his evaluation: "It would have been impossible for an occidental prisoner to escape into a society in which he would have stood out dramatically and in which he could not speak, read, or understand the language."[77]

The prisoners' hunger and humiliation did not end in Japan, where the guards continuously tried to break their spirits: "We were taken to work by a different route each day so more civilians could see us. They yelled and spit on us and threw things as we passed. Some who spoke English yelled at us that Japanese soldiers would never surrender."[78] Peter B. Marshall realized that the only chance of survival was staying under the Japanese radar, so he "decided to make [himself] as invisible as possible and never ask for anything from the Japanese such as food, clothing or cigarettes." He became a near-invisible prisoner, which the guards appreciated, but if something went wrong, they usually "took it out on some POW that looked familiar to them."[79] At Zentsuji Camp in Kagawa-ken, several prisoners had to share limited space—rooms designed for 8 people were usually filled with 14—and deal with a climate much colder than that in the Philippines. Moreover, what remained the same as the camps in Southeast Asia was the number of bedbugs and lice.[80]

The commander of the camp, Major General Mizuhara, gave a welcome note and made a few remarks to the prisoners: "As far as Japan is concerned, you must do away with the false superiority complex idea that you seem to have been entertaining towards the Asiatic peoples. You should obey me and other officers of the Japanese Army."[81] Obedience seemed to be the only thing the Japanese officers demanded, in addition to not wanting to lose face in front of their men and superiors. However, the guards in Japan were mostly reserve personnel, so prisoners were sometimes successful in stressing the Geneva Convention on behalf of their own situation. Nevertheless, the POWs "starved like the rest, and [they] were treated brutally from time to time."[82] For those imprisoned, like Giles, the physical abuse from the Japanese guards was the most unbearable part of life in Japan, especially because the starving was something the prisoners had already accepted as an elementary part of their lives. The violence and torture, however, could never be accepted as "normal":

> The Japanese must have worked hard thinking of ways to make us more miserable. They punished us for anything at all, without rhyme or reason. During our first week at Zentsuji they used one of our officers to demonstrate what we might expect as retribution for an infraction of regulations. They made him remove his shirt, tied his hands, and ordered him to kneel. Then a soldier beat him around the head with a bamboo pole and slapped his bare back with the bottom of a rubber-soled tabi until his back was raw and bleeding. As the first blows began to fall, several of the men surged forward in outrage. They were promptly restrained by soldiers and thrown into the brig to think about the error of their ways.[83]

It seems like these initial punishments by the Japanese guards served a Machiavellian plan to establish order by fear. Violence showed the prisoners the hierarchy between those who were permitted to use force and those who were ordered against it; as such, the guards may have felt obliged to be violent to underscore this particular dynamic in which an officer's punishment was an essential aspect of exhibiting dominance and power. Whether it was part of a diabolical construction of hierarchies or not, the Japanese used violence to control or react to disobedience from the American side, and any utterance from the prisoners could be interpreted as such. Giles consequently had "little doubt that the Japanese officers hated [their] feeling of superiority toward them," which is why emotions are another factor responsible for the guards' violent eruptions. In general, every conversation or meeting with the Japanese was "very delicate, because they did not like any display of superiority on our part," and the moment the Americans made a move to "register a complaint or to request something, the meeting frequently resulted in immediate punishment." As a senior officer in the POW camp, Giles had multiple contacts with his Japanese counterparts and "was frequently punished and was the target of many face slappings . . . [and] lost several teeth as a result of these slappings."[84]

For the prisoners, the climate was far more troublesome than the Japanese, whose violent behavior they had become accustomed to. Even if supplies should have been steadier in Japan, the prisoners still received no food on their first day at Zentsuji and froze in the Japanese winter.[85] Their diet hardly improved from what it was in the Philippines; "meat was never seen, nor was any form of seafood, except for the occasional fish head that found its way into the *benjo* soup."[86] As such, the prisoners' lifestyles in the Japanese camps were not too different from those in the Philippines: the poor weather, diseases, hunger, and violent Japanese guards were normal for the U.S. prisoners to deal with. However, even they could be considered lucky in comparison to most British POWs in the jungles of Burma and Thailand, who were forced to build a "railway of death."

The Burma-Siam Railway and the Murder of POWs

Although the American POWs in the Philippines suffered, the British POWs in Southeast Asia went through hell. They "were subjected to inhumane and brutal treatment"[87] that exploited them as a cheap and expandable workforce. Harold Atcherley (1918–2017) was a rifleman in the King's Royal Rifle Corps and later a divisional intelligence officer at the HQ of the 18th British Infantry Division. He arrived in Singapore two weeks before it surrendered to the Japanese and become one of the POWs who were brought to Burma and Thailand to build the Burma-Siam Railway, which is well known in the public eye from the film *The Bridge on the River Kwai* (1957). Atcherley's memoirs describe how he, like many other POWs, managed to survive a great deal of suffering—unfortunately, many other British POWs did not, which is why Atcherley could only preserve their stories.

Like in Bataan, the "Japanese were completely unprepared for so many prisoners—we should all have committed hara-kiri, according to them."[88] The Americans' British counterparts also suffered from low food rations, if any were provided at all. Nevertheless, the POWs of His Majesty's Army also felt the disgust that the Japanese soldiers felt for them:

> Our treatment soon became increasingly harsh under the influence of the Japanese military tradition of bushido. This held that any soldier allowing himself to be taken prisoner was guilty of dishonouring both his country and his family. There was only one way out for him and that was to commit suicide. This meant that the Japanese military regarded us as sub-human.[89]

Because the British who surrendered Singapore had failed to defend it, and failed again by becoming prisoners instead of committing suicide, the British soldiers were not considered honorable enemies, but rather dishonorable cowards who demanded to be fed by the victorious Japanese army. Consequently, many Japanese soldiers whose minds had been poisoned by anti-Western propaganda did not hold back their anger, using any excuse to physically express their hostility toward their foreign prisoners. Atcherley and his men were transferred to Thailand in early 1943 to work on the Burma-Siam-Railway.

Such a railroad connection "had been thought about as far back as the nineteenth century, but the country it would have to cross was fearsome," and the hours of labor required to build it would make it too expensive. However, "the Japanese in 1942 were doing their sums by the arithmetic of war. To turn the Burma campaign in their favor they had to have a railroad. . . . The military ordered it ready for use by the end of 1943."[90] The Japanese wanted to achieve something nearly impossible within only 18 months, and it was obvious that the construction "was going to be the worst work in the world, but the Japanese had scores of thousands of prisoners of war; they could work them like slaves, work every one of them to death, if that as what it took."[91] In the construction of 250 miles of tracks, 60,000 POWs—30,000 British, 18,000 Dutch or Indonesian, 13,000 Australian, and 650 American[92]— had to work to please the "Japanese pharaoh." The prisoners, who accounted for 45 percent of the POWs in Japanese camps, were supposed to build one of the most complex railroad tracks ever built by hand, and Colonel Nagatomo Yoshitada[93] had no doubt that the Japanese would "build the railroad . . . [even] if [they had] to build it over the white man's body."[94]

However, before working on the tracks, the POWs had to survive being transported to the work sites. Like the survivors of the Bataan Death March, the prisoners were transported by train:

> Twice a day, we were let out briefly to be given a small quantity of rice in onion water. There was no form of sanitation. Practically all of us were suffering from malaria, dysentery or both. The only way to relieve oneself was to hang precariously out of the wagon, the weaker ones being supported by others to prevent them falling out.[95]

Because not everyone could use this technique, the wagons were soon filled with excrement, and the diseases spread in the heat of the day as fast as possible. Those who survived the trains had to participate in a "200-mile march up to a camp just south of the Burma/Thailand border,"[96] and those who survived only did so to suffer even worse afterward. Yet during the march itself, scenes very similar to the Bataan Death March occurred and showed that the Japanese soldiers did not consider the POWs' lives valuable. Atcherley remembered that

> [e]very night of the march a number of prisoners became too weak to keep up. A few officers marched at the rear of the column to carry them on makeshift stretchers, but some had to be left behind because there was no one who had the strength to carry them. . . . [The] guards . . . insisted that we [keep] going by threatening us with their bayonets. Stragglers were set upon by marauding Thais and many were never heard of again.[97]

Of the 3,000 men in Atcherley's division, only 182 would survive the war. The others died in battle, on the trains, during the march, while building the railway, or in a hospital camp afterward. The duration of the building project was especially marked by extreme forms of violence; the Japanese soldiers beat the prisoners whenever they felt that an order had not been obeyed or if not

POWs of the Japanese

all tools that had been used during the day could be accounted for. Moreover, those who died in the daytime had to be returned to the camps so that the Japanese officers could account for all prisoners and ensure nobody had escaped.[98] They were obsessed with their prisoner tallies, and anything that might have threatened the accuracy of these end-of-day numbers was considered an obstacle to be violently removed.

It is remarkable that Atcherley developed no general hatred toward the Japanese and that he could distinguish between good and evil, even in an environment such as the deadly jungles of Burma and Thailand:

> I do not believe our treatment stemmed from any innate cruelty in the Japanese population as a whole. It was essentially due to brain-washing by the military commanders to ensure that the army fought with the extreme ruthlessness and brutality demanded. There were, of course, civilised Japanese who did whatever they could to help us. . . . I have learned that feelings of hatred among those who have to do the fighting are displayed far more by those who have never been directly involved, led by the media.[99]

These considerations are essential in understanding what happened during the construction period of the Burma-Siam-Railway. An objective discussion of the circumstances and the relevant factors of the perpetrators' violence is more important than a simple accusation, but the fact that the POWs' abuse during the railway's construction was legally a war crime needs no further discussion.

However, in August 1942, Atcherley and his men first arrived at a POW camp in Seralang. In the blocks that were supposed to hold 200 to 250 men, they "had up to 850 men, in not unduly unsanitary conditions." Two thousand prisoners had to live together in the Seralang labor camp, but when the men arrived, there "were no latrine arrangements whatsoever" and "the water had been turned off in all the blocks and [they] had only one water point per 800 men. No washing was allowed, and all drinking water had to be boiled. [They] only had enough fuel to last three or four days."[100] It was only a matter of time until most of the men were infected with a disease—before long, men were sick; recovering from a previous war wound; or suffering from beriberi, dengue fever, dysentery, or malaria. After three months, Atcherley was so accustomed to his camp and work routine that he felt his personal existence to be monotonous,[101] and he and his men began to doubt that there was any future at all:

> All we can see ahead of us is an endless procession of days, weeks and months stretching away into a hopeless future. It would be so much easier if we could be given a sentence of so many years. We could then settle down accordingly and watch the months bring us ever nearer freedom.[102]

Once the Red Cross food ran out, their diets were poor and consisted of a "particularly tasteless" breakfast based on "rice porridge, rice rissoles with perhaps a little fish flavouring and a handful of soya beans" and more rations of plain rice during the day.[103] Atcherley did not adjust to this diet and realized that he "miss[ed] bread more than anything else."[104]

Yet the routine of working and starving was regularly interrupted by violence. In December 1942, Atcherley noted an incident that seems beyond emblematic of the POWs' lives and of the violence guards used against them:

> More face slapping yesterday: three Nip privates . . . entered officers' messes and troops' living quarters and slapped faces for no apparent reasons. . . . Complaints were passed on . . . to the Nip officer. The latter received the complaints quite amicably and said there was too much face slapping, both in the POW camps and in the I[mperial] J[apanese] A[rmy] itself.[105]

This episode is important because it highlights the commonplace nature of violence in the Japanese army, and many guards seem to have merely reproduced the methods they themselves had been confronted with in the past. Questions or complaints were answered with slaps, disobedience demanded a slap, and not fulfilling a task fast enough earned a slap. However, in the camps and during the working details, the Japanese soldiers held the highest authority and used it to punish others instead of being the only ones getting hit by their own superiors.

Aside from these varying forms of violent abuse, the POWs suffered the most from nonexistent food supplies because eating could make the difference between life and death. On December 22, 1942, Atcherley and the men of the Seralang Camp received a fatal blow:

> Our meat ration, small as it was, has now been stopped altogether. Instead, we are supposed to receive a fish ration of 1oz per man, three times per week. I do not hold out much hope of ever seeing very much fish! First I have never known the I[mperial] J[apanese] A[rmy] to deliver such rations as often as they say they will, and second, a large percentage of the fish we do receive is so bad that it has to be thrown away the moment it arrives. We have now started drinking rice polishings in order to increase our intake of Vitamin B.[106]

Their diets remained poor for months, and the POWs' complaints were usually answered by the Japanese authorities by pointing out that Japan's soldiers were provided with the same rations. Atcherley did not doubt this argument but said that it "is possibly true of their basic ration, but in practice they [were] always able to add to it considerably."[107]

Starting in April 1943, Atcherley and his men were part of the F-Force, which was supposed to build the railway. After the train ride and the jungle march described earlier, they arrived at the labor force camp in the jungle. The prisoners barely had food and "just a small amount of bad rice and watery stew" was provided for them. The deaths began there—20 men or more died every day—and eventually, as Atcherley vividly remembered, "bodies piled up waiting to be put on the cremation fires. Not enough men to carry the bodies over from the camp, where they had been lying for over two days. How callous one became."[108] The lives of the prisoners were not taken into consideration. All that mattered was maintaining the timeline for the construction of the railway, which had to be finished on time. Any delay equaled disobedience. Furthermore, the situation in the hospitals eventually became disastrous.

Medicine was unavailable in sufficient quantity, and anesthesia usually consisted of the doctor "yelling louder than the patient."[109] However, the physicians such as those described by Gavan Daws dealt not only with incurable patients, but also Japanese guards:

> The same guards who would kick him in the crotch before breakfast wanted him to treat them. They came to him on the quiet, after dark, with VD. The Japanese Army did what most armies did to men with the pox or the clap—fined them and busted them. So the sorry guards would buy an ampoule of blackmarket Salvarsan and bring it to Doc to inject them. . . . Considering [that an ampule contained more Salvarsan than the soldier needed] . . . , would the guard mind if Doc used the leftover for his malarias, . . . for three of them? The moment Doc finished giving the shot, the guard grabbed the ampoule, threw it down, and stamped on it. . . . [Later on] Doc did not say a word, just stuck him, and fitnessed the rest of the ampoule for the three malarias.[110]

With time, the prisoners developed their own rankings for the deadliest diseases one could get in a camp: "Malaria kept knocking them (the POWs, F.J.) down; dysentery meant they had to keep trying to get up to run for the benjo; beriberi meant they were never going to make it. On top of all that, there was pellagra, dengue, fever, and scrub typhus. And then they ran into tropical ulcers."[111]

Besides being deathly sick, the POWs were still treated like slaves by the Japanese, and many were simply beaten to death when they could no longer work fast enough.[112] The POWs also renamed the sites along the track as remembrances of human suffering, such as Cholera Hill, Death Valley No. 1, and Shit Creek.[113] Only those who could work no more were sent to the hospitals, where "some were dead on arrival; others collapsed and died before they could get to the sick huts. The rest were walking skeletons, the whites of their eyes gray, pupils just a splotch in the middle, like broken eggs."[114] Among the Japanese along the railroad, 7 out of 100 died, whereas the death toll for POWs was much higher. The officers of Japan's army would claim that the Japanese "survived better because they were Japanese."[115] For their 12,000 soldiers—according to their narrative—only 6 medical officers, 20 noncommissioned officers (NCOs), and 20 orderlies were available, whereas 150 medical officers, 150 NCOs, and 700 privates took care of the 50,000 POWs. The Japanese considered themselves not guilty of any crime at all:

> Whatever happened on the railroad that might have been *wrong*, so these senior Japanese said, had nothing to do with them as officers. . . . It was a matter merely of individuals. Not all prisoners were good, so the senior officers said. They were even prepared to concede that not all individual Japanese were good.[116]

Following the Japanese narrative, everyone was personally responsible for his own life or death. At the same time, more than 10,000 POWs died during the railway project, but only two Japanese had been court-martialed for mistreating prisoners.[117] Consequently, from a Japanese perspective, "almost" nothing went wrong. In some instances, Japanese officers would later claim that Korean collaborators were responsible for the mistreatment because the diseases and the weather—especially the monsoons—were not controlled by the Japanese. As such, the "senior officers' arithmetic of life and death on the railroad"[118] was based on denial rather than reality.

Out of its initial strength of 1,602 men, F-Force lost 73 percent (1,175) of its men to diseases, starvation, and violent guards. Along the railroad, 6,318 British, 2,815 Australian, 2,490 Dutch, and 132 American POWs lost their lives.[119] Depending on their duties (i.e., cooks, truck drivers, physicians, etc.), some men had higher chances of surviving the jungle's hell, as did the officers of all nationalities. However, all of them had to go through what could only be described as a "hell on earth." When the rumor spread that the Japanese thought about building a canal in northern Malaya, the POWs were truly worried: "the Japanese pharaohs had just got through making them build the pyramids, and now they were ordering the Panama Canal dug."[120] However, in contrast to the violent realities along the railway and in the camps of the Burmese and Siamese jungles, it remained a rumor. Suffering violence was obviously a factor, next to starvation and disease, that all POWs of the Japanese Imperial Army shared. What is important about this specific factor is understanding why the soldiers and guards responsible for the POWs were so violent.

Japanese Violence

The prisoners usually "went on to suffer years of deprivation and brutality, most of them failing to survive."[121] Men over 40 hardly survived O'Donnell, but young men also died. Although "experience of life seemed to be important, too, and that was something that could only come with the years,"[122] luck seemed to be a decisive factor in survival. One could be lucky by not getting sick, lucky by acquiring more food, and lucky to avoid violent guards. Luck could, and would, make the difference between life and death. Furthermore, 90 percent of the prisoners were never inspected by the Red Cross,[123] and so even international help did not reach the POWs. Instead they lived and died on behalf of the Japanese, for whom "spirit was crucial."[124] Therefore, most of the POWs had been dead before they even began the death marches to the camps or to the railway, especially because "for a Japanese fighting man, death in victory was supposed to be glorious. In defeat—not that the word *defeat* was ever spoken—death rather than surrender was insisted upon. And to become a prisoner was unthinkable."[125] It was unacceptable that an honorable enemy would surrender and be fed by his antagonist. The POWs were consequently considered as good as dead (i.e., dishonored) from the moment they were taken prisoner by Japanese hands.

Before discussing the reasons for the Japanese soldiers' violent behavior, it must be underscored that not all Japanese were bad, but there was a grey area—much like the one Primo Levi identified about German destruction camps—which was discussed briefly in Chapter 1. On a Japanese prisoner transport, there may have been "a guard commander who saw it as his duty as a conscientious soldier to land his full tally of prisoners alive on Japanese soil. But for every one guard commander like that, there were any number just as happy to make up their final count from the dog tags of the dead."[126] Sometimes officers would intervene and prohibit violent acts against the POWs, and Japanese soldiers and civilians alike were more than able to show sympathy with their enemies.[127] Those who escaped the camps to deal with work details outside also experienced cases in which POWs were treated like human beings by the Japanese, but this was an anomaly. Naturally, the POWs often tried to take revenge on the Japanese guards. In one instance, the prisoners created placebos out of their APGs (all-purpose capsules) and sold them as anti-VD pills to their guards.[128] In most cases, however, the POWs were victims rather than the ones who caused suffering. Their treatment worsened, and the intensity of the violence against them seemingly increased the farther away their camp was from a center of power. The more peripheral the camp, the higher the chances of abuse, which is a trend in the post-WWII experiences of torture camps at the front lines of "old" and "new" wars alike. The soldiers, who had established their own space-time continuum under the control of the central authorities in Tokyo, determined what was allowed and what was not.[129]

The POWs perceived the members of the Kenpeitai (Military Police Corps) to be particularly violent. These men were regarded as "trained torturers"[130] who interrogated prisoners for valuable information:

> No POW ever had enough rice to eat, but the kenpeitai always had rice to spare for torture—they would force it down a prisoner's throat by the fistful, pour water into him by the gallon until he swelled up inside to bursting, then jump on his belly. POWs were forever short on cigarettes, but the kempeitai always had enough for burning ears and noses and eyes. And they had dynamos and batteries for electric shock, wired up with alligator clips for grabbing onto nipples and testicles.[131]

What made the use of violence for the Japanese soldiers easily acceptable was the racial propaganda that had been displayed to them in the years leading to the war, and even more so during the war years. The Americans were described as "epicurean wild beasts" and "Japanese soldiers looked upon the Americans as pleasure seeking, soft, and materialistic."[132] Van Waterford identified 10 factors responsible for the captor-captive relationships during the war years:

1. Economic strangulation of the Japanese by the West
2. Stereotypes and racism
3. Western colonialism
4. The Yamato belief
5. Bushido
6. Individualism of the Japanese within a group context
7. Dishonor of a captured Japanese soldier
8. Insularity of the Japanese soldier
9. Emotionality of the Japanese soldier
10. Tough military training[133]

The belief that the POWs were not "entitled to respect because they had lost their honor"[134] would have been stimulated by the first five factors, whereas the second five pertain to the Japanese soldiers as part of an army unit. This unit, as described by Theweleit and as discussed in the first chapter herein, acts as a part of a military machine whose components are expected to function according to pre-established norms in a given space-time continuum, especially in the case of the Japanese. Simply put, to a member of the Japanese army who can only feel disgust for a dishonored soldier of a foreign nation, violence need not be restricted due to sympathy or understanding. In other words, the Japanese soldier could not help but be violent, and "among the POWs the consensus of opinion seemed to be that the Japanese were brutal, rather than sadistic, and largely unaware of their own brutality, which found its target in an animal as readily as in a helpless POW."[135] It may be true that some "Japanese were arrogant in victory and obsessed with a desire to take revenge on individuals for the white race's galling pretensions to superiority over the colored,"[136] but most of the soldiers did not follow through with such abstract schemes. They simply considered it proper to treat the POWs as they did, as they were violently conditioned in their own army and expected to use violence against the inferior—against those no longer considered human. This effect was amplified within the groups in which Japanese soldiers functioned, which is why group dynamics should not be underestimated when discussing the level of violence used against the POWs. Ultimately, power and hierarchies played a key role in the Japanese soldiers' behavior, especially because these hierarchies could exist without the perpetrators suffering any consequences for enacting them. Within the contemporary space-time continuum, almost nobody would waste a tear for an American POW who was violently abused by a Japanese soldier. Conversely, groups of Japanese soldiers would rather applaud and cheer at the sight of their comrades behaving according to their pre-established violent norms.

In the end, many POWs died because the existence of different space-time continua was accepted by the Japanese authorities, who demanded no specific treatment or protection of the prisoners and instead allowed the local authorities to decide. Divided guilt usually has an amplifying effect on the level of a crime's violence, and something similar could be stated for the acts related to the POW camps. The Japanese soldiers' lack of sympathy is highly disturbing, but as explained before, many of them were exposed to propaganda that allowed no room for such feelings. The prisoners' punishments were simple: violence upon more violence. However, even they may not have been the most miserable victims of the Japanese empire—the final chapter will highlight the biological warfare program and experiments that the Japanese military and civilian physicians conducted to abuse human beings, POWs included.[137]

CHAPTER SEVEN

Unit 731

Unit 731, based on what Mark Felton called "the most infamous three-number identifier in history,"[1] is the last topic this book will cover. The code name covered the experiments of a branch of Japan's biological warfare program in Manchuria and is emblematic of the crimes against humanity the Second World War witnessed in both Europe and Asia. There is no doubt that Japanese scientists, who were given access to human test subjects by the military, conducted cruel experiments on Chinese, Koreans, and Russians, as well as British and American POWs.[2] What the unit's members did in Manchuria and other places in Southeast Asia, as Felton correctly remarked, "was nothing less than a horrific amalgam of sadism, murder and science gone very, very wrong."[3] One of the veterans working for Unit 731, Shinozuka Yoshio, remarked that the unit worked on multiple projects, with one deadlier than the rest: "There were a number of laboratories inside Unit 731 and each focused on producing a different kind of pathogenic germ. For example, the Ejima team was producing the dysentery bacillus, the Tabei team typhoid, the Setogawa team cholera, and so on."[4] In the meantime, scholars have shown that Unit 731 was not the only facility that worked on such projects, and other Japanese biological and chemical warfare units could be traced back to Beijing (Unit 1855), Nanjing (Unit 1644),[5] Canton (Unit 1688), and other cities[6] where scientists and military personnel worked on similar experiments as Unit 731's colleagues.

"In the name of science," as Mark Felton emphasized, many innocent men, women, and children lost their lives in the experiments of the Japanese biological warfare program, being abused as human guinea pigs in "every sort of medical experiment on live human beings; experiments that are normally proscribed by law, morality and political and public revulsion."[7] To this day, Japan's failure to officially accept responsibility for what happened in the Chinese and Southeast Asian facilities, acknowledge their denials in historical

Pacific Theater, 1941–1945

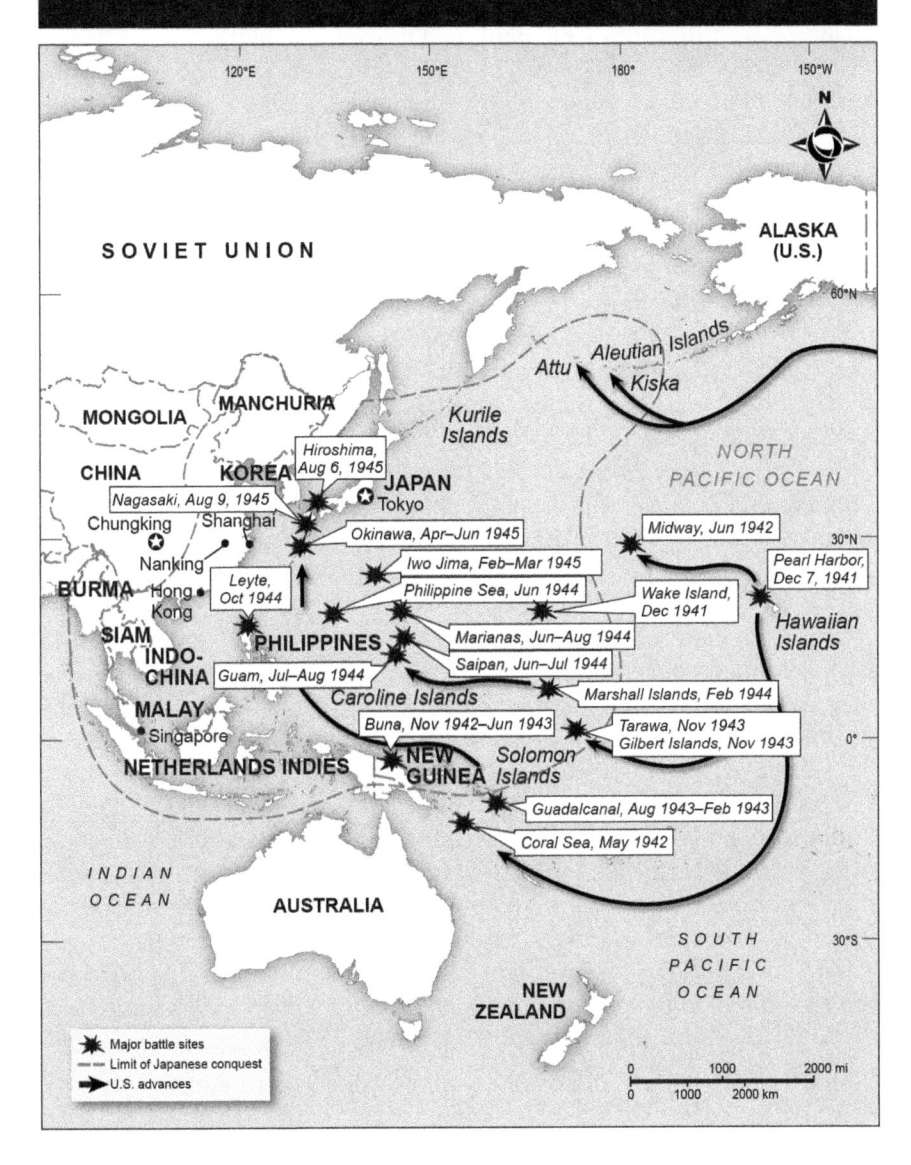

discourse, and apologize for its past evils continues to poison the nation's political relationships with its neighbors. Because "the Chinese government, for its own self-serving reasons, is determined that its people should never forget what happened,"[8] the topic will continue to elicit tension between the two countries.

The fact is that the possibility of their denial was generated by the postwar order in East Asia and the beginning of the Cold War in the aftermath of Japan's surrender. There was sufficient evidence of Japan's workings and experiments, even if they were only published in some camouflaged form during the war; a close reading of scientists' publications about Unit 731, or any other branch of Japan's biological warfare program, made it obvious what happened in the facilities and what kind of experiments took place there.[9] Even immediately after the war ended, evidence was presented that pointed to the crimes against humanity committed in the Japanese facilities. In December 1949, the government of the Soviet Union held a trial against 12 Japanese officers who had served in positions related to Japan's biological warfare program. In the trial's aftermath, documents related to the findings were published in several languages.[10] The publication even included copies of original Japanese documents related to the war crimes, but due to the Cold War, the publication's credibility—especially when the United States realized they needed Japan as a future Asian ally—was questioned.[11]

Furthermore, the American military was also interested in the results of the Japanese experiments because they could have been valuable in a conflict against the Soviet Union. Whereas China, whose government had tried "Kajiura Ginjirō, Commander of the 231st Regiment, 39th Division, . . . for using poisonous gas in combat,"[12] and the Soviet Union made no secret of Japan's criminal biological warfare program, the U.S. authorities in Japan suppressed related information during the War Crime Trials in Tokyo, especially because they feared being forced to share their knowledge about the results of Japan's wartime experiments. At the same time, the results of other trials "were publicly dismissed as false by the head of the Allied occupation forces in Japan, General Douglas MacArthur, and by the government of the United States."[13]

For the Japanese perpetrators, this was important because "data gained from human experimentation once again became ammunition: this time in the bargaining room, rather than on the battlefield. The Japanese hoped to use their knowledge as a tool for gaining freedom from prosecution as war criminals."[14] Although their crimes were often well known, they were not brought to trial to protect the experiment data for which the American leaders "wanted secrecy and exclusivity."[15] For that, the authorities risked granting high positions in postwar society to those who were nothing more than war criminals and had been responsible for the deaths of many innocent people. Daniel Barenblatt is correct when he states that Japan's "subsequent willful amnesia created a decades-long loss of vital history and led to needless suffering by the victims. This postwar complicity of the United States and its Western allies itself also constitutes a crime against humanity."[16] The wartime perpetrators simply continued with their lives in a new space-time continuum once the war ended; they were not burdened by their past sins and instead lived as ordinary men. Many of them held influential positions in Japanese pharmaceutical companies or major universities, while their crimes remained hidden to most of society. They were successful in transforming from murderers and ruthless villains into esteemed doctors and scientific researchers who worked solely for Japan's economic growth. Like Emperor Hirohito (1901–1989) himself, those "guilty of the most heinous acts of medical atrocity, filled top positions"[17] within Japan's society, protected by the silence about their previous sins.

Ishii Shirō (1892–1959),[18] the mastermind behind Japan's biological warfare program, was not prosecuted by the Supreme Commander of the Allied Powers (SCAP) in the Tokyo Trial, especially because he could provide experiment data that the American authorities were specifically interested in. Supposedly, it was Major General Charles A. Willoughby (1892–1972) and General Douglas MacArthur who ultimately decided to keep Ishii untouched.[19] It remains unknown what happened to the data and if it was transferred at all, even if some documents show that the United States obtained knowledge that was based on Japan's war crimes. Three of the documents—"The Report of A" (anthrax), "The Report of G" (glanders), and "The Report of Q" (bubonic plague)—were declassified in 1960 and became available through the Library of Congress,[20] where they can still be read and interpreted as proof that the United States received information from former Unit 731 members. Nevertheless, Japan's biological warfare program and its related documents received only minor attention until the 1980s. John W. Powell (1919–2008), an American journalist, was the first one to reconnect the documents and accused the U.S. government of having pardoned war criminals in exchange for information about their work.[21] The documents, housed at the National Archives and Records Administration (NARA) in the United States, were also translated by the Japanese historian Tsuneishi Keiichi, who thereby laid the groundwork for further studies in Japan.[22] Scholars and journalists, such as Kondo Shōji and Nishino Rumiko, traced the biological warfare program's activities, branches, and scientists to enable better access to documents related to the topic.[23] Between July 1993 and December 1994, an educational exhibit was shown throughout Japan that informed a wider audience of nonacademics in Japan about Unit 731's war crimes. Regardless of this attention and increasing academic discourse about Japan's criminal biological warfare program, further research is required to highlight the perpetrators' continued medical careers in Japan, as well as to evaluate the emperor's role during the establishment of the program and the military's role in providing human test subjects.

However, the Japanese government has proved unwilling to support these efforts. After a trial against the government that lasted from 1997 to 2002, Japanese courts denied the lawfulness of claims for compensation and for an official apology from the state and its representatives.[24] This denial has continued for more than seven decades; the existence of "the human experiments and large-scale biological warfare have been denied and marginalized," acts that by themselves "constitute[] a second crime against humanity and a crime against history itself."[25] The following pages will shed light on those involved in the biological warfare program and on the experiments that so many innocent people died from. It is essential to do this because history can never be totally forgotten, and as human beings, we will be judged by how we treated our past—which is why even the worst of humanity's sins must be remembered.

Ishii, the Mastermind of Biological Warfare

It is easy to morally judge Ishii in retrospect, who has been called "a brilliant but morally bankrupt scientist,"[26] a "rather eccentric young man" with a "reputation for brilliance and innovation,"[27] a "ladder-climber" who was a "pushy, inconsiderate, and selfish"[28] student, "free of every moral care," and a "flamboyantly corrupt man who considered himself a visionary."[29] At the considerably young age of 35, the man received a PhD in microbiology in 1927 from one of the leading institutions in Japan, Kyōto University. He was keen on his career and willing to go beyond the limits of contemporary medicine to rise in the ranks; as such, he was the ideal perpetrator in a space-time continuum that would provide him unlimited possibilities to obtain the results he wanted—and he soon found his field of interest. The Geneva Convention of 1925 had officially sealed the fate of biological warfare; it was condemned by the great powers, but Ishii took this development as an opportunity to do something else: "If the prospect of germ warfare created such dread, he reasoned, Japan must do everything in its power to *create* the most virulent germ weapons, as well as effective methods for destroying wartime enemies with lethal diseases."[30] With the help of influential friends, Ishii managed to change the course of Japan's research step by step. Although the "prevention of disease in the Japanese military was still an objective of the research," Ishii established a lobby for an offensive approach, and eventually "the center of gravity had shifted to development of bacteriological and chemical methods of warfare."[31] Ishii used the Geneva Convention as an argument for his own plans and often visited the "offices of Japan's top military officers, trying once more to persuade them that a program to conduct biological and germ warfare was the key to victory for Imperial Japan in any future wars."[32] He would usually argue that germs were so powerful that everybody feared using them, which is why biological warfare could become the Japanese empire's "secret weapon"[33] and allow Japan to fear nobody. Considering the world powers' neuroses about another world war in the late 1920s and early 1930s, such arguments found ears, especially in the aggressive circles of the Japanese military, where young officers were no longer willing to adhere to the military's official limitations.

Meanwhile, his "pleas to top commanders to create a germ warfare research division were consistent with his deep ambitions to move up in rank and further his own status in Japan's military and scientific strata."[34] He was willing to sacrifice whatever and whomever necessary to achieve his ambitious aims. The war prisoners he would sacrifice in Manchuria during his experiments were considered "subhuman and expendable," and his strong class consciousness must have "made it all the easier for him and the other Japanese perpetrators of lethal human experimentation to descend into a callous disregard for human life."[35] Early on, Ishii considered himself a genius and risked anything to show that to the world, but he was also "a mass of paradoxes: loud and rude, yet also a skilled social and career climber; an ardent nationalist and a devoted scientist, but a wild partygoer too."[36] That said, people often mentioned poor social skills when trying to describe Ishii and his interpersonal relationships. Ishii had invented a water filtration system that was supposed to prevent the spread of diseases during military campaigns, and he would usually demonstrate this filter's capacity by urinating into it and then drinking a glass of the filtered liquid afterward.[37] He therefore established his own "reputation as being the 'army's crazed surgeon.'"[38]

The older he got and the higher in rank he rose, the more entitlement Ishii felt. After his graduation, he joined military-run research projects and was even paid to do further research on biological warfare, including taking research trips abroad. When he returned to Japan in 1930, many military leaders were willing to listen to his promises that germ warfare could be used against the Soviet Union. The hawks among the new generation of officers gave Ishii greater attention, dreaming that his ideas could lead to Japanese world domination. War Minister Araki Sadao (1877–1966) and General Nagata Tetsuzan (1884–1935) were only two of such officers who backed Ishii and his demands.[39] Koizumi Chikahiko (1884–1945), the military physician and later Army Surgeon General of the Imperial Japanese Army (1934) and Minister of Health (1936), would also provide Ishii with important connections to higher military and governmental circles, funds, and other forms of support. At the age of 37, Ishii was promoted to the rank of major and appointed the chair of Tokyo Army Medical College's department of immunology, where he began his research for Japan's bacterial warfare program.[40] During his time at the Medical College, Ishii also received grants from the army to intensify his research, which brought Japan closer to creating biological weapons and secured him swift promotions through the ranks. Ishii can thus be considered a "willing executioner," a "murderous careerist" like Reinhard Heydrich (1904–1942).[41]

With the creation of Manchukuo, Ishii argued to have better chances of conducting assault research abroad while research for defensive measures against biological warfare could be continued in Japan. It was clear that Ishii wanted test subjects for his experiments on the Asian mainland, and the puppet state in northeastern China provided the testing grounds the Japanese researcher wanted. Once again, it was the specific space-time continuum that made men like Ishii possible; the experiments in Manchuria and other parts of the Japanese empire, as well as the military's willingness to accept them, only existed from the early 1930s until Japan's defeat in 1945.

When Ishii requested to have parts of his research facility transferred to Manchuria, he faced no obstacles. One could argue that the military planners were unaware of his ambitious experiments, but it is hard to believe that somebody as narcissistic as Ishii would not have pointed to the possibilities that such a transfer would ultimately lead to. It is also important to note that Japan's scientific world neither criticized the doctor nor his experiments once Ishii began publishing his research results, especially because anyone with medical knowledge must have been able to realize that the test subjects were not monkeys, but human beings.[42] The Kwangtung Army, known for its expansionist ambitions, also sponsored the biological warfare experiments in 1932. Ishii established his headquarters in Harbin, a cultural melting pot where 240,000 Chinese; 81,000 Russian; almost 5,000 Japanese; and smaller numbers of Manchurian, Mongolian, and even Jewish communities lived.[43] From Harbin, the program would soon spread all over Asia. Wherever Japanese occupational forces went, a branch of Ishii's program usually followed to collect further data for biological warfare through inhumane experiments.

The Experiments

Officially, Ishii and his men worked as an "Epidemic Prevention and Water Supply Unit of the Kwangtung Army," which was also referred to as the "Epidemic Prevention and Water Purification Corps." To mask the real experiments, all facilities were coordinated by the "Epidemic Prevention Research Laboratory" in Tokyo.[44] As soon as Japan's war effort spread over Asia—starting in 1937 for China and 1941 for Southeast Asia—facilities were established all over what would become the East Asian Co-Prosperity Sphere (e.g., Beijing, Changchun, Guangzhou, Xinjing, and Singapore).[45] Ishii himself worked in Beiyinhe and later Pingfang.[46] In 1941, the command of the Kwangtung Army gave the Pingfang facilities the code name Unit 731, a name that continues to represent the horrors of the Japanese army's biological warfare experiments.

Ishii was genuinely interested in four areas of experimentation: 1) cholera, 2) epidemic hemorrhagic fever (EHF), 3) plague, and 4) frostbite.[47] Although the latter seems surprising, it was quite natural if one considers that many military planners, especially in the army, envisioned war against the Soviet Union. Both military physicians and many of Ishii's former colleagues from the civilian sector arrived in Manchuria to participate in overseeing the experiments; the medical researchers were "attracted by the lure of expanding their research possibilities,"[48] even if "not all of them knew what they were getting into and were themselves used by Ishii and his henchmen." This especially applied to medical students who might have been "pressured by their professors to go work with Ishii's organization,"[49] but the men who participated in the experiments had a choice to be perpetrators and so their actions can only be considered voluntary. Although disobedience might have ended their research careers, one cannot claim that those involved could not make alternative choices.

The complex at Pingfang was gigantic—being six square kilometers, surrounded by electric fences, and equipped with armed guards, it took three years to build the facility. The Pingfang prison could hold 400 prisoners, who were used as a steady supply of test subjects to replace those who died unexpectedly or too quickly during the experiments. Those test subjects—men, women, and children—were simply referred to as *maruta* (logs of wood).[50] Bacteria were bred in special incubation ovens to be placed in special ceramic-walled bombs later, which would be used to spread artificial epidemics like the cholera epidemic in Yunnan Province in southwest China in May 1942. Not only were around 3,000 victims killed in the experiments at Pingfang, but several thousands, if not hundreds of thousands, of Chinese died because of biological warfare.[51]

Ishii had to work in an abandoned sake distillery in Harbin when he arrived, but the city venues made "secrecy and security difficult."[52] This is why the first facility was built at Beiyinhe in the hinterland of Harbin, where 300 male and female military and scientific personnel, among them 50 physicians, began their evil work. Chinese laborers were forced to build Ishii's dream, but those who constructed the medical facilities were shot once the work was finished. The Pingfang facility looked like a factory and even had a special laboratory that was used solely for experiments and research related to the anthrax bacterium. The main objective of the research in Pingfang was clear: "to have germ weapons employable in a wintry environment such as the Russian border, or for longer-term disease seeding of the Russian soil and animal life."[53]

Eventually, Ishii moved to Pingfang because the facility in Beiyinhe became too small for Ishii's needs; this emphasizes the extent of Ishii's experiments and his success in persuading his superiors of his work's merit. He was granted more space, more men, more equipment, and ultimately more money. At Pingfang, Ishii intensified his research on suitable biological weapons. To name just a few examples, cholera cultures were put in Chinese wells, infected food was left close to the roads to be picked up and eaten by civilians who would get infected with cholera, and bacteria bombs were dropped on Chinese territory to study the effects of deadly diseases on populated areas. Infected fleas were also bred and raised at Pingfang to infect the populations of entire villages and cities. Some authors estimate that more than 500,000 people died because of these experiments.[54]

Next to the medical experiments, as Daniel Barenblatt highlights, "many other medical experiments unrelated to germ warfare were conducted on the prisoners—studies involving human dehydration, starvation, frostbite, air pressure, animal-to-human blood transfusions, and a raft of other horrors that used human beings as lab rats."[55] The test subjects were very often provided by the Kenpeitai, whose members acted as Ishii's "human materials procurement arm"[56] and brought in Chinese, Russian, Mongolian, and Korean men, women, and children. Political prisoners and supposed guerilla fighters vanished forever to be brought to Pingfang, where, as Major Karasawa Tomio stated, "[plague] bacteria were ... isolated from the fleas and cultured in a ... laboratory and injected into the prisoners (three Chinese guerillas, F.J.). A cold and precise observation of the prisoners' physiological states were recorded by Ishii's team of doctors as the victims died in agony from the disease."[57] The life expectancy of a prisoner at Pingfang was seldom longer than 30 days, especially because copious amounts of blood were taken from them for research, which further weakened them and made them more vulnerable to the diseases they were already afflicted with. These experiments were cruel, especially considering one reason that Daniel Barenblatt was correct to highlight:

> Some experiments were simply based on scientific curiosity, as doctors had the opportunity to work on human subjects who were physically expendable; for example, one experiment involved seeing how deeply a person could be drained of his blood before he reached the point of death from low circulation or cellular deprivation.[58]

In the existing space-time continuum, such procedures would not raise moral concerns because they were thought to serve the greater good, especially from a Japanese perspective. Following Japan's racist views, the fact that the test subjects were Chinese made it easier to perceive them as expendable commodities rather than human beings.

Usually, when a "patient" had been infected with a disease, the researchers had to wait to experiment on them. A Pingfang veteran described the following procedure in some detail: "As soon as the symptoms were observed the prisoner was taken from his cell and into the dissecting room. He was stripped and placed on the table screaming, trying to fight back. He was strapped down, still screaming frightfully. One of the doctors stuffed a towel into his mouth, then with one quick slice of the scalpel he was opened up."[59]

Initially, the prisoners were kept in healthy, normal shape because they had to yield objective test results. Even so, the prisoners were stripped of their identities and became test subjects whose lives ended the moment they entered Pingfang. They were victims of a "scientific reductionism of his or her body,"[60] and like logs of wood, they were eventually burned. Nothing of their bodies would remain besides the data the Japanese had collected by performing crimes against humanity in the solitude of the Manchurian hinterland. The researchers acted like machines bound to an irreversible process who only cared about results. Consequently, there was "virtually no difference in the way a human subject was experimented on and the way a lab animal or plant would be treated, right down the vivisection and scooping out of organs for further weighing, probing, and examination of samples under the pathologist's microscope," and the "utter dehumanization of the victims and the dehumanizing effect on the perpetrators were official policy."[61]

The few witness reports by former perpetrators read like simple reports of a daily routine and rarely show emotional distress, let alone doubt. For instance, in 1997, the former technician Shinzuka Yoshio described one experiment as follows:

> This intelligent-looking man was systematically infected with plague germs. As the disease took its toll, his face and body became totally black. Still alive, he was brought on a stretcher by the special security forces to the autopsy room. Transferred to the autopsy table, the chief pathologist ordered us to wash his body.... The man's organs were methodically excised one by one and I did as I was ordered to. I put them in a culturing can we had already prepared.[62]

An anonymous veteran's statement also reveals that nobody in the facility truly cared for morals or ethics:

> At first we infected women with syphilis by injection. But this method did not produce real research results. Syphilis is normally transmitted through direct contact. Investigating the course of this disease can offer no useful results unless it is acquired this way. And so we followed a system of direct infection through sexual contact.[63]

Prisoners were thus forced to have sex with each other and thereby infected one other with syphilis.

When a specific experiment "accidentally" demanded more test subjects "or a particular body type, sex, or age was called for, the gendarmerie would, citing Unit 731 directives, snatch Manchurian citizens going about their daily business"[64] and send them to the hell of Pingfang. Sudden raids would occur on command to acquire more test subjects; nobody seemed to care that the lives and futures of human beings would be ended if it was to serve the perverted scientific interests of Ishii and his fellow researchers. The victims were simply numbers, and nobody cared for their personal stories because they became part of a data set. Their deaths were little more than a single count in the overall number of dead test subjects.

A witness in Beiyinhe observed what happened to the bodies' remains: "There was a big smokestack in the unit. On some days it poured smoke, sometimes there was none. It was far from our barracks. Once, we asked what was burning. The answer was 'prisoners.'"[65] Daniel Barenblatt made an analogy between Beiyinhe and the Holocaust, remarking that "each day the remaining flesh and bones of the eviscerated victims were turned to billowing chimney smoke and ash. Beiyinhe was an Auschwitz before there was Auschwitz."[66] Like Auschwitz, people knew about what happened behind the walls of Ishii's facilities long before the documents were reopened in the 1980s. Films of experiments were even shown in Tokyo, probably to members of the Imperial Family, but nobody intervened. It has also been argued that Emperor Hirohito could have been aware of the experiments, especially because he had a degree in biology and probably an interest in Ishii's studies. However, there is currently no evidence for this claim.[67]

The fact is that nobody stopped the experiments. With more and more support from the authorities—military and civilian alike—Ishii could expand his projects and experiments, branching out his biological warfare program to expand all over occupied Asia. Corporations like the Nihon Tokoshu Kōgyō in Tokyo also benefited from this trend, because Ishii had them build his new site. Ishii likely received substantial pushback for this deal, but it demonstrates the interrelationship between Japan's war and its private economy. This scenario may remind historians of IG Farben's role in building the KZ Auschwitz III Monowitz.[68]

At Pingfang, however, Ishii not only worked on his experiments, but produced around 20 million doses of vaccines per year. Although the inmates and *maruta* were "the fodder for the development,"[69] Japanese pharmaceutical companies sold these doses for widespread use, and it can be assumed that the civilian researchers who worked for Ishii financially gained from such deals.[70] In addition, the scientists could publish their research and boost their own careers, especially because results were easier to achieve at Pingfang than at any other research facility in Japan. The careerists thus had every reason to support Ishii's methods. However, the researchers who did not work in Pingfang and ignored the realities of the lab's publications are also guilty; the argument that they were unaware of the terrible things that happened in Pingfang cannot be accepted. To say the least, it is disturbing that "the Japanese plague makers were not solely military men; they were also many of the country's best and brightest doctors of the medical and biological research community who coldly violated every ethical precept of the healing profession."[71] They were not ordinary men, but intelligent men who became murderers. Most of them did this to stimulate their own careers, but all who participated did so in part because the existing space-time continuum neither judged nor prosecuted their actions.

Like many others, Ishii spent three months of the year in Japan offering his greatest up-to-date presentations, enjoying his fame as a star researcher in the academic world. For the rest of the year, he butchered innocent civilians to gain data for his future publications. It was clear what happened in Manchuria, especially because "Ishii's classroom lectures baldly revealed the unethical work being done in Manchuria, and potential recruits—medical students and microbiologists—were shown eight-millimeter films of biological warfare research processes."[72] For Ishii, however, these events were also ways to recruit new personnel; there was a steady rotation of physicians involved in the research at the Manchurian facilities.[73] Those who worked there, such as a hygiene specialist who was interviewed by Hal Gold, liked the work and the working environment there: "At the former unit we were always hit around by the senior soldiers, and it was rough. But at Unit 731, there was harmony. There were only medical officers and civilian doctors. There was no seniority among soldiers, no noncommissioned officers. The facilities and the food were good, and we didn't get hit."[74] Next to having the best possible laboratory equipment one could think of, Ishii's "lure of such unfettered, secret medical research proved to be quite strong for thousands of civilian scientists who traveled from Japan to Manchuria."[75] To quote Daniel Rosenblatt again, the reality in Pingfang can "perhaps best be described as a secret city devoted to human experimentation and the waging of biological warfare."[76] The facility itself, the laboratories, the libraries, the gardens, and even the ability to relax and have a family life in the area was attractive to many scientists at the time. Pingfang almost seems like "a resort spa enveloped in a biomedical death camp,"[77] a fact that makes its history even more disturbing and horrifying. Estimated numbers suggest that more than 20,000 civilians were employed in Ishii's system, so information about Unit 731 and its work must have spread—the explanation that nobody knew about it in postwar Japan is highly unlikely. However, most of the scientists who had left the former space-time continuum simply returned to their civilian lives in Japan as ordinary researchers. As Barenblatt correctly stated, they were "physicians, surgeons, nurses, biologists, microbiologists, chemists, veterinarians, entomologists, plant pathologists, and other scientists and technicians, all of them plunging the integrity and legacy of Japan's leading health institutions into a shameful darkness."[78]

The scientists' rationales may have differed case by case, but one factor seems to have been particularly strong: attaining research goals more quickly than under common experimental conditions. Pingfang provided an unethical and inhumane shortcut into the future of microbiology by using human test subjects instead of lab rats. Here, scientists could achieve and see results within their lifetimes, and the idea of being made immortal through memory legitimized many of the perpetrators' actions. Ishii, who promised everything a researcher of the time could dream of, lured honorable scientists into the rabbit hole of Unit 731. Once the guilt was shared, the scientists became part of a circle that would protect them after the war's end and obscure the horrible things that happened in Manchuria and other facilities in Southeast Asia.

Perpetrators like Yoshimura Hisato, who was responsible for the frostbite tests,[79] later defended himself against the accusation of being a war criminal, claiming that the experiments were executed for the greater good of Japan.

This is a natural defense mechanism for perpetrators who consider their acts necessary in fulfilling the common good.[80] Other perpetrators shared such ideas: "I killed people for the country—for the emperor. That was my belief then."[81] Another one made his feelings clear: "Personally, I feel no shame. I thought that I was really doing a good thing."[82] Yusasa Ken, a former field doctor, also expressed no inner turmoil about the past: "Sometimes I look at my hands and I remember what I have done with these hands. What's really scary is, I don't have any nightmares of what I've done."[83] A former professor at Osaka University, one of the country's leading research institutions, later confessed: "I believe that the Unit 731 research facilities were possibly the best in the world at the time." He added in an almost cynical way that "professional people, too, like to play."[84]

Eventually, the restless work of many researchers, journalists, and activists reminded people of what the Japanese had been so eager to forget, especially the politicians in Tokyo; these figures often preferred to ignore Unit 731 not only because of its shameful history during and after the war, but because former perpetrators simply continued their scientific careers untouched by the SCAP and unchallenged by the scientific community. Whereas the existence of Unit 731 shocked many Japanese who were unaware of what happened abroad, most of those in the scientific, pharmaceutical, and political circles of power were not shocked at all. Everyone involved relied on group dynamics to ease the shared guilt and knowledge of what happened, which most of the former members took with them to their graves. However, those who confessed decades later could not change history itself—they could only hope to change its remembrance.

Because there were no survivors from the experiments, it was difficult to force politicians to acknowledge the facts of the matter, and deniers would argue that there was no need for a trial without witnesses who could testify. Furthermore, the influential positions held by former perpetrators in Japan's postwar society laid a mystical dust of silence upon the topic for too long.[85] Regardless of these problems, it is essential to highlight these Japanese war crimes and the factors that made them possible, that is, the existence of a space-time continuum in which abusing others in horrible experiments was condoned by ordinary men and intelligent scientists who accepted making unethical scientific progress to further their careers. As is the case with the Japanese army's other war crimes during World War II, it will be the way the Japanese government and people treat their own past that decides how their actions and inactions are perceived by future generations.

Conclusion

Having discussed the Japanese Imperial Army's various war crimes—from the Rape of Nanjing and the establishment of the abusive "comfort women" system to the Bataan Death March, the violent psychological and physical abuse of American and British POWs and the horrible crimes of Unit 731 in which ordinary scientists killed innocents in the name of research and progress—my conclusive remarks will please neither deniers nor victims and their families. Instead, they will remind us all that anybody can become a perpetrator in the appropriate space-time continuum. Several factors were responsible for the Japanese soldiers' violence in different geographical and chronological contexts, which all have been comparatively elaborated and discussed in the present book. Were these factors specifically Japanese? No. Were they exclusively Japanese? No. Are they repeatable? Yes. Can we be perpetrators? Yes. Do we like this fact? No, of course not—but must we live with it? Yes, indeed.

All of us have the capacity to behave how the soldiers of the Japanese Imperial Army acted in their specific space-time continua. One's first instinct is to ask, "How?" It is possible because every human being possesses the capacity for violence; every human being, under the right circumstances and in a specific situation, is capable of murder. In the specific Japanese case, a conglomerate of factors that stimulated violence could be identified.

Anger

The Japanese soldiers were angry for many reasons: that the Chinese campaign did not entail a swift victory, that the Chinese soldiers in Nanjing had disappeared, that they could not sexually perform during their time with "comfort women," that so many American and British POWs had surrendered, that orders were not obeyed immediately, and so on. There were multiple situations in which anger stimulated violent reactions from Japanese soldiers, but that the anger led to immediate violence also related to the contemporary space-time continuum. The soldiers could use violent means to express their anger without fearing any repercussions for themselves, and the military leadership's lack of restrictions gave the soldiers' anger a vessel through which they could abuse human beings who were considered beneath the soldiers.

Power

Violence, in the Machiavellian sense, is always a tool to establish power hierarchies. Masculinity within the Japanese army was established through suffering, and the soldiers were confronted with violence—slapping was a particular problem in the Japanese army—during their conditioning period as soldiers. They were accustomed to power being expressed by force. With the creation of a new space-time continuum whose rules were determined by the fighting forces, new hierarchies were established on the battlefield, and so, too, were they established in POW camps and "comfort stations." Violence was considered a suitable means of doing that, and any form of willing or unwilling disobedience was punished without hesitation.

Joy

In every war-related space-time continuum, we can find those who simply enjoy violence and committing crimes for the sake of the joy they feel when they torture helpless human beings, like women, children, or defenseless prisoners. This would not apply to most of the perpetrators, but even a small number of such individuals can have a tremendous effect on the increase of violent behavior among soldiers, as specific group dynamics determine the way military units and their members act or react.

Group Dynamics

Group dynamics and group hierarchies are particularly strong in any military formation in general, but especially in the Japanese Imperial Army. As a whole, Japanese society is highly dependent on such group dynamics; as such, the social pressure to prove masculinity with violence and to demonstrate behavioral patterns that suit a turbulent space-time continuum increases the likelihood and level of violence. The stronger the group pressure, the more the unit might act on behalf of leading individuals. Moreover, potentially violent groups that reside farther from centers of political or military command have a greater chance of exhibiting extreme violence.

Preconditioning

Ideology also plays an important role here, and although samurai culture can be determined as exclusively Japanese, the chauvinist ideas the soldiers grew up with were not exclusive to Japan. As such, the Japanese Imperial Army held no monopoly on conducting sexual violence in a war zone, and the same could be said about the racism that stimulated violence against Chinese, Korean, or Filipino soldiers and citizens alike. Therefore, regarding the ideological preconditioning of the soldiers, some, but not all, factors that determined the violent behavior of the Japanese soldiers was rooted in specifically Japanese issues—strict hierarchies and obedience in the military and society per se; abusive behavior toward women, who were considered inferior; etc. What many of the perpetrators believed, however, was that they were acting on behalf of something bigger and more important than themselves.

Belief in a Greater Cause

The almost religious belief in the greater cause, that is, the sake of the Japanese empire, the Japanese emperor, the Imperial Family, and the *kokutai* (usually translated as national essence, national body, or national community), led to the soldiers' acceptance of violence. Their actions in the war-related space-time continuum were legitimized by the belief that cruelty was a necessary evil to achieve a greater good.

What, then, can be said about the war crimes discussed in the present book? They are all war crimes, no matter what deniers or politicians in Japan say. The soldiers may have considered their acts as legitimate as per their contemporary space-time continuum, but according to any ethical or moral standards, their abuse of various victim groups constitute nothing but war crimes. Therefore, only one question remains: What needs to be done?

Hannah Arendt knew the answer long ago: "Pardon between humans can only mean: The abdication to take revenge, to be silent, and to pass by, which is to say: the fundamental parting."[1] Conciliation demands equality, but mere forgiveness would only create inequality among those who require conciliation to overcome the past.[2] Conciliation also demands acceptance of the past by victims and perpetrators alike. In accepting the past, both sides agree on and accept what happened, and this agreement must be established between the victims of the Japanese war crimes and Japan's government. Only if this acceptance is established can conciliation be achieved on equal terms. Arendt emphasized that injustice becomes guilt when the acting party is unwilling to correct what happened, and the harmed party continues to face inequality.[3] It is therefore impossible to reach conciliation if victims and perpetrators favor accusation and denial over acceptance and correction.

The Japanese government must accept that the Japanese army committed war crimes between 1931 and 1945. The politicians in Tokyo cannot undo the past, but they can act based on their acceptance of the past and try to correct the wrongdoings of their predecessors by seeking a path to conciliation. Once this has been done, it might be easier for the few remaining victims and their families to accept an honest apology and truly begin to heal. Only alongside one another can the present generations undertake the historical task of remembrance and acceptance, and if they succeed in this regard, they make up for past wrongdoings.

We must all remain mindful of our human nature, which affords us the chance to reach conciliation, but can also cause us to act violently in the future. Where there is war, there is violence. To restrain this violence within a war-related yet legal context is a task that military planners, politicians, and soldiers alike must work on. Limiting the variables that cause violence and steadily controlling the space-time continua of war can help decrease war crimes. However, that they will fully disappear is a hope that stems from the same human nature that causes us to be violent in the first place.

Notes

Introduction

1. Iris Chang, *The Rape of Nanking: The Forgotten Holocaust of World War II* (New York: Basic Books, 2011 [1997]).

2. Kevin Ng, "The Great Denial: How Japan's Policies Regarding Its Actions during WWII Are Denying Both Its Own People and the World of Moral Betterment, Social Progress and Political Integration," *Chinese American Forum* 23, 3 (2008), 33.

3. Gayle K. Sato, "Witnessing Atrocity through Auto-bio-graphy: Wing Tek Lum's The Nanjing Massacre: Poems," *Inter-Asia Cultural Studies* 13, 2 (2012), 212.

4. Comparisons with the Holocaust are usually used for two purposes: either 1) to increase the importance of the event that is being compared to the systematic destruction of the European Jews or 2) to diminish the importance of the Holocaust. Regarding the singularity of the Holocaust, German scholars waged the "Historikerstreit" (historians' quarrel) in 1986–1987. For a documentation of this quarrel, see Ernst Reinhard Piper, ed. *"Historikerstreit": Die Dokumentation der Kontroverse um die Einzigartigkeit der nationalsozialistischen Judenvernichtung* (Munich/Zurich: Piper Verlag, 1987). Recently, the argument for the comparability seemed to re-emerge when Jörg Baberowski, professor of Eastern European history at the Humboldt University in Berlin, claimed that Ernst Nolte (1923–2016), whose statements had partially initiated the "Historikerstreit," was "historically correct." See Dirk Kurbjuweit, "Der Wandelt der Vergangenheit," *Der Spiegel* 7 (2014). Accessed September 25, 2017. http://www.spiegel.de/spiegel/print/d-124956878.html. Students protested against the right-wing extremist content of some of Baberowski's publications and talks in 2017 (especially with regard to some of his statements about the so-called refugee crisis) and were being taken to court for their acts by the Humboldt professor, who lost in the second instance and can now legally be considered a right-wing extremist. Meanwhile, other historians expressed their opinions in favor of or against Baberowski's position in the debate. Götz Aly, "Beistand für Professor Baberowski," *Stuttgarter Zeitung*, June 19, 2017. Accessed September 25, 2017. http://www.stuttgarter-zeitung.de

/inhalt.kolumne-von-goetz-aly-beistand-fuer-professor-baberowski.c58443d8-02da-44a3-8c87-2e5e496bc472.html; Wolfgang Benz, "Streit um Thesen zur Migration: Professoraler Populismus," *Der Tagesspiegel*, June 21, 2017. Accessed September 25, 2017. http://www.tagesspiegel.de/wissen/streit-um-thesen-zur-migration-professoraler-populismus/19957412.html.

5. Sato, "Witnessing Atrocity," 212.

6. Bob Tadashi Wakabayashi, "The Nanking 100-Man Killing Contest Debate, 1971–1975," in *The Nanking Atrocity, 1937–38: Complicating the Picture*, ed. Bob Tadashi Wakabayashi (New York: Berghahn Books, 2008), 145. For a more detailed and nuanced discussion of the reasons leading to the violent eruption of Japanese soldiers at Nanjing, see Frank Jacob, "Banzai! And the Others Die—Collective Violence in the Rape of Nanking," in *Global Lynching and Collective Violence*, Vol. 1: *Asia, Africa, and the Middle East*, ed. Michael J. Pfeifer (Urbana: University of Illinois Press, 2017), 78–102.

7. Edward Drea, "Introduction," in *Researching Japanese War Crimes Records: Introductory Essays*, ed. Edward Drea et al. (Washington, D.C.: National Archives and Records Administration for the Nazi War Crimes and Japanese Imperial Government Records Interagency Working Group, 2006), 4–5.

8. Chang, *Rape of Nanking*, 5.

9. Jacob, "Banzai," 80.

10. Jürgen Habermas, *Eine Art Schadensabwicklung* (Frankfurt: Suhrkamp, 1987), 163, cited in Paul Betts and Christian Wiese, "Introduction," in *Years of Persecution, Years of Extermination: Saul Friedländer and the Future of Holocaust Studies*, ed. Christian Wiese and Paul Betts (London/New York: Continuum, 2010), 8.

11. Saul Friedländer, *The Years of Extermination: Nazi Germany and the Jews, 1939–1945* (London: Harper Collins, 2007), xv.

12. A recent study that takes on this endeavor for Malaya and Singapore is Takuma Melber, *Zwischen Kollaboration und Widerstand: Die japanische Besatzung in Malaya und Singapur (1942–1945)* (Frankfurt am Main: Campus, 2017).

13. Bob Tadashi Wakabayashi, "The Messiness of Historical Reality," in *The Nanking Atrocity, 1937–38. Complicating the Picture*, ed. Bob Tadashi Wakabayashi (New York: Berghahn Books, 2008), 3.

14. Ibid., 8–11.

15. To name a few of these denials from the past few years: Nakagaki Hideo, "Nankin jiken no shinsô (The Truth about the Nanking Incident)," *Defense* 31, 1 (2012), 232–257; "Nankin jiken kôkoku kyohi ha Chûnichi shinbun no jisatsu da (The Veto Against Announcing the Nanking Incident Is the Suicide of the Chûnichi Newspaper," *Monthly Will* 91 (2012), 104–112; "'Nankin Jiken' no kyokô ha kantan ni setsumei dekiru (One Can Easily Explain the Fiction of the 'Nanking Incident')," *Monthly Will* 89 (2012), 76–81; "'Nankin Jiken' shôko shashin ha subete decchiage (The Photographic Proof of the 'Nanking Incident' Is Definitely Fiction)," *Monthly Will* 89 (2012), 82–89; Watanabe Hisashi, "Nankin jiken no gyakusha wo saikô suru (Revaluating the Slaughterers of the Nanking Incident)," *Chôkiren: Sensô no shinjitsu wo kataritsugu* 16 (2012), 85–103.

16. To name just a few among many: Honda Katsuichi, *Sensō o okosareru gawa no ronri* (Tōkyō: Gendai Shiryō Sentā Shuppankai, 1972) and Yoshimi Yoshiaki and Hayashi Hirofumi, *Kyōdō kenkyū Nihongun ianfu* (Tōkyō: Ōtsuki Shoten, 1995). For a broader discussion of the historiography of the Nanjing Massacre, see Joshua A. Fogel, *The Nanjing Massacre in History and Historiography* (Berkeley: University of California Press, 2000).

17. Masahiro Yamamoto, *Nanking: Anatomy of an Atrocity* (Westport, CT: Praeger, 2000). For a survey of the global perception of the Rape of Nanjing, see Takashi Yoshida, *The Making of the Rape of Nanking* (New York: Oxford University Press, 2006).

18. To name just one example, Enhan Li, *Ribenjun zhanzheng baoxing zhi yanju* (Taipei: Taiwan shangwu chubanshe, 1994) provides an early study for Taiwan.

19. For a detailed discussion, see Bob Tadashi Wakabayashi, "The Nanjing Massacre: Now You See It . . . ," *Monumenta Nipponica* 56, 4 (2001), 521–544; Daqing Yang, "Convergence or Divergence? Recent Historical Writings on the Rape of Nanjing," *American Historical Review* 104, 3 (1999), 842–865.

20. Daqing Yang, "Documentary Evidence and the Studies of Japanese War Crimes: An Interim Assessment," in *Researching Japanese War Crimes Records: Introductory Essays*, ed. Edward Drea et al. (Washington, D.C.: National Archives and Records Administration for the Nazi War Crimes and Japanese Imperial Government Records Interagency Working Group, 2006), 22.

21. Drea, "Introduction," 3–6.

22. On MacArthur's policy in Japan, see Frank Jacob, "MacArthur's Legacy: Japan and the Early Years of the Cold War," in *Peripheries of the Cold War*, ed. Frank Jacob (Würzburg: Königshausen & Neumann, 2015), 207–227.

23. Drea, "Introduction," 3.

24. For a comparison of dealing with guilt and memory between Germany and Japan, see Ian Buruma, *The Wages of Guilt: Memories of War in Germany and Japan*, new edition (New York: New York Review Books, 2015); Christoph Cornelißen, Lutz Klinkhammer, and Wolfgang Schwentker, eds., *Erinnerungskulturen: Deutschland, Italien und Japan seit 1945* (Frankfurt am Main: Fischer, 2003).

25. Maria Gabriela Romeu, "The Japanese History Textbook Controversy amid Post-War Sino-Japanese Relations" (MA thesis, Florida International University, Miami, FL, 2013). Accessed September 25, 2017. http://digitalcommons.fiu.edu/cgi/viewcontent.cgi?article=1952&context=etd.

26. Akiko Takenaka, *Yasukuni Shrine: History, Memory, and Japan's Unending Postwar*, reprint edition (New York: Columbia University Press, 2017) provides an excellent introduction to and discussion of the issues related to Yasukuni Shrine.

27. Yang, "Documentary Evidence," 22.

28. Drea, "Introduction," 6–7.

29. Ibid., 10; Yang, "Documentary Evidence," 23.

30. Greg Bradsher, "The Exploitation of Captured and Seized Japanese Records Relating to War Crimes, 1942–1945," in *Researching Japanese War Crimes Records: Introductory Essays*, ed. Edward Drea et al. (Washington, D.C.: National

Archives and Records Administration for the Nazi War Crimes and Japanese Imperial Government Records Interagency Working Group, 2006), 151.

31. Tanaka Hiromi, *Bei gikai toshokan shozo senryō sesshu kyū rikukaigun shiryō sōmokuroku* (Tokyo: Tōyō shorin, 1995), x.

32. Chūgoku kikansha rengokai, *Sankō* (Tokyo: Kōbunsha, 1957).

33. Shi Young, Margaret Stetz, and Bonnie Oh, eds., *Legacies of the Comfort Women of World War II* (Armonk, NY: M. E. Sharpe, 2001).

34. Tanaka Akira and Matsumura Takao, eds., *731 Butai sakusei shiryō* (Tokyo: Fuji Shobō, 1991).

35. Yang, "Documentary Evidence," 29.

36. Jose Ma. Bonifacio Escoda y Minguez, *Warsaw of Asia: The Rape of Manila* (Quezon City, The Philippines: Giraffe Books, 2000). Also see Richard Connaughon, John Pimlott, and Duncan Anderson, *Battle for Manila* (Novato, CA: Presidio Press, 1995).

37. Yang, "Documentary Evidence," 31.

38. For a survey on the events and battles leading to the fall of the Philippines, see Donald J. Young, *The Fall of the Philippines: The Desperate Struggle against the Japanese Invasion, 1941–1942* (Jefferson, NC: McFarland, 2015).

39. For the Burma-Thailand Railway, see Gavan McCormack and Hank Nelson, eds., *The Burma-Thailand Railway: Memory and History* (St. Leonards, Australia: Allen & Unwin, 1993).

40. On this issue, see Linda Goetz Holmes, *Unjust Enrichment: How Japan's Companies Built Postwar Fortunes Using American POWs* (Mechanicsburg, PA: Stackpole Books, 2001).

41. On this change of the Japanese attitude toward POWs, see Ikuhiko Hata, "From Consideration to Contempt: The Changing Nature of Japanese Military and Popular Perceptions of Prisoners of War through the Ages," in *Prisoners of War and Their Captors in World War II*, ed. Bob Moore and Kent Fedorowich (Washington, D.C.: Berg, 1996), 253–276.

42. Yang, "Documentary Evidence," 33.

43. An extensive collection of materials related to forced Chinese labor in wartime Japan is provided in Tanaka Hiroshi, *Chūgokujin kyōsei renkō shiryō*, 5 vols. (Tokyo: Gendai shobō, 1995).

44. There are also documents in American archives that offer new perspectives on Japanese war crimes. See Robert Hanyok, "Wartime COMINT Records in the National Archives about Japanese War Crimes in the Asia and Pacific Theaters, 1978–1997," in *Researching Japanese War Crimes Records: Introductory Essays*, ed. Edward Drea et al. (Washington, D.C.: National Archives and Records Administration for the Nazi War Crimes and Japanese Imperial Government Records Interagency Working Group, 2006), 120.

45. Ustinia Dolgopol, "Women's Voices, Women's Pain," *Human Rights Quarterly* 17, 1 (1995), 127.

46. Mina Chang, "The Politics of an Apology: Japan and Resolving the 'Comfort Women' Issue," *Harvard International Review* 31, 3 (2009), 34.

47. Ibid.

48. Kali Erstein, Cheryl Lindsey Seelhoff, Angie Manzano, and Karla Mantilla, "JAPAN: Comfort Women Demand Justice," *Off Our Backs* 36, 4 (2006), 3.

49. Ibid.

50. Ibid.

51. Hirofumi Hayashi, "Disputes in Japan over the Japanese Military 'Comfort Women' System and Its Perception in History," *The Annals of the American Academy of Political and Social Science* 617 (2008): *The Politics of History in Comparative Perspective*, 123.

52. Ibid., 124.

53. Katō Norihiro, "Haisengoron," *Gunzō*, January 1995.

54. Bessho Yoshimi, "The Logic of Apologizing for War Crimes 'as a Japanese,'" *Review of Japanese Culture and Society* 11/12 (1999–2000): *Violence in the Modern World*, 33–34.

55. Ibid., 37.

56. Adalbert Rückerl, "Einleitung," in *NS-Prozesse: Nach 25 Jahren Strafverfolgung, Möglichkeiten—Grenzen—Ergebnisse*, ed. Adalbert Rückerl (Karlsruhe, Germany: Verlag C. F. Müller, 1971), 9.

57. Ibid., 11.

58. Adalbert Rückerl, "NS-Prozesse: Warum erst heute?—Warum noch heute?—Wie lange noch?," in *NS-Prozesse: Nach 25 Jahren Strafverfolgung, Möglichkeiten—Grenzen—Ergebnisse*, ed. Adalbert Rückerl (Karlsruhe, Germany: Verlag C. F. Müller, 1971), 17.

59. Ibid., 26–27.

60. Benjamin Wittes and Gabriella Blum, *The Future of Violence* (New York: Basic Books, 2015), 5–8.

61. Steven Pinker, *Gewalt: Eine neue Geschichte der Menschheit* (Frankfurt am Main: Fischer, 2011), 19.

62. Ibid., 90.

63. Michael Geyer, "Eine Kriegsgeschichte, die vom Tod spricht," in *Physische Gewalt: Studien zur Geschichte der Neuzeit*, ed. Thomas Lindenberger and Alf Lüdtke (Frankfurt am Main: Suhrkamp, 1995), 136.

64. Georg Klute, "Kleinkrieg und Raum," in *Begegnungen und Auseinandersetzungen: Festschrift für Trutz von Trotha*, ed. Katharina Inhetveen and Georg Klute Rüdiger (Cologne, Germany: Koppe Verlag, 2009), 86.

65. Bärbel Clauss, Katja Koblitz, and Detlef Richter, eds., *Kriegsansichten—Friedensansichten. Vom Umgang mit Konflikten in Theorie und Realität* (Münster, Germany: LIT Verlag, 1993), 12.

66. Klaus Schlichte, "Krieg und bewaffneter Konflikt als sozialer Raum," in *Kriege als (Über)Lebenswelten. Schattenglobalisierung, Kriegsökonomien und Inseln der Zivilität*, ed. Sabine Kurtenbach and Peter Lock (Bonn, Germany: J. H. Dietz Verlag, 2004), 186.

67. Trutz von Trotha, "On Cruelty: Conceptual Considerations and the Summary of an Interdisciplinary Debate," in *On Cruelty, Sur la cruauté, Über Grausamkeit*, ed. Jakob Rösel and Trutz von Trotha (Cologne, Germany: Rüdiger Köppe Verlag, 2011), 4–5.

68. Thomas Klatetzki, "Cruel Identities," in *On Cruelty, Sur la cruauté, Über Grausamkeit*, ed. Jakob Rösel and Trutz von Trotha (Cologne, Germany: Rüdiger Köppe Verlag, 2011), 196.

69. Anne-Sophie Friedel, "Editorial," *Aus Politik und Zeitgeschichte* 67, 4 (2017): *Gewalt*, 3.

70. Ibid.

71. Alan Kramer, "Mass Killing and Genocide from 1914 to 1945: Attempting a Comparative Analysis," in *Years of Persecution, Years of Extermination: Saul Friedländer and the Future of Holocaust Studies*, ed. Christian Wiese and Paul Betts (London/New York: Continuum, 2010), 213.

72. John W. Dower, *War without Mercy: Race and Power in the Pacific War*, seventh edition (New York: Pantheon Books, 1993), xi, 3.

73. Ibid., 4.

74. Kramer, "Mass Killing," 213.

75. Ibid., 228.

76. For several examples of that impression related to different cases and forms of genocide, see Hannah Arendt, *Eichmann in Jerusalem: A Report on the Banality of Evil* (New York: Penguin, 1978); Christopher R. Browning, *Ordinary Men: Reserve Police Battalion 101 and the Final Solution in Poland*, new edition (New York: Harper Perennial, 2017); Alexander L. Hinton, *Man or Monster? The Trial of a Khmer Rouge Torturer* (Durham, NC: Duke University Press, 2016).

77. Lawrence Langer, "Redefining Heroic Behavior: The Impromptu Self and the Holocaust Experience," in *The Holocaust: Origins, Implementation, Aftermath*, ed. Omer Bartov (London/New York: Routledge, 2000), 235.

78. Ibid.

79. Heda Kovály and Erazim V Kohák, *The Victors and the Vanquished* (New York: Horizon Press, 1973), 1.

80. Langer, "Redefining Heroic Behavior," 242.

81. Primo Levi, *The Drowned and the Saved* (New York: Vintage International, 1988), 157–158.

82. Betts and Wiese, "Introduction," 1.

83. Ibid., 2.

84. Primo Levi, "Grey Zone," in *The Holocaust: Origins, Implementation, Aftermath*, ed. Omer Bartov (London/New York: Routledge, 2000), 253.

85. Ibid., 259.

86. Ibid., 264.

87. Ibid., 265.

88. Ibid., 267.

89. Dan Bar-On, *Legacy of Silence: Encounters with Children of the Third Reich* (Cambridge, MA: Harvard University Press, 1989), 2.

90. Ibid., 4.

91. Samson Munn, "Post-Genocide and Related Dialogue: What Dan Bar-On Began," in *Nationalsozialistische Täterschaften: Nachwirkungen in Gesellschaft und Familie* (Reihe Neuengammer Kolloquien 6), ed. Oliver von Wrochem (Berlin: Metropol, 2016), 262; Ding Ying, "History in Japanese Eyes," *Beijing Review* May 28, 2009, 18.

92. Folke Schimanski, "Zum Fortdauern nationalsozialistischer Ideologie in der Familie: Die Folgen von Täterschaft in der zweiten Generation," in *Nationalsozialistische Täterschaften: Nachwirkungen in Gesellschaft und Familie* (Reihe Neuengammer Kolloquien 6), ed. Oliver von Wrochem (Berlin: Metropol, 2016), 381; Oliver von Wrochem, "Einleitung," in *Nationalsozialistische Täterschaften: Nachwirkungen in Gesellschaft und Familie* (Reihe Neuengammer Kolloquien 6), ed. Oliver von Wrochem (Berlin: Metropol, 2016), 11.

93. Astrid Messerschmidt, "Selbstbilder zwischen Unschuld und Verantwortung: Beziehungen zu Täterschaft in Bildungskontexten," in *Nationalsozialistische Täterschaften: Nachwirkungen in Gesellschaft und Familie* (Reihe Neuengammer Kolloquien 6), ed. Oliver von Wrochem (Berlin: Metropol, 2016), 118–119.

94. John Keegan, *Die Kultur des Krieges* (Berlin: Rowohlt Verlag, 1995), 30.

95. Hannah Arendt, *Über das Böse: Eine Vorlesung zu Fragen der Ethik*, fourth edition (Munich: Piper, 2010 [2007]), 79.

96. Ibid., 86.

97. Ibid., 95, 101.

98. Ibid., 121.

Chapter One

1. Hannah Arendt, *Macht und Gewalt*, 20th edition (Munich: Piper, 2011 [1970]), 63.

2. Cited in Robin R. Vallacher and Christopher Brooks, "Adaption and Coherence: Evolutionary and Dynamical Perspectives on Human Violence," in *The Evolution of Violence*, ed. Todd K. Shackelford and Ranald D. Hansen (New York: Springer, 2014), 188.

3. Ibid., 190.

4. Hannah Arendt, *On Violence* (New York: Houghton Mifflin Harcourt Publishing, 1970), xx.

5. Arendt, *Macht und Gewalt*, 15.

6. Ibid., 22 and 45.

7. Karl Heinz Metz, *Geschichte der Gewalt: Krieg—Revolution—Terror* (Darmstadt, Germany: Wissenschaftliche Buchgesellschaft, 2010), 7.

8. Arendt, *Macht und Gewalt*, 52.

9. Ibid., 53.

10. Michaela Christ, "Gewaltforschung: Ein Überblick," *Aus Politik und Zeitgeschichte* 67, 4 (2017): *Gewalt*, 10.

11. Zygmunt Bauman, "Alte und neue Gewalt," *Journal für Konflikt- und Gewaltforschung* 2 (2000), 28–42.

12. Christ, "Gewaltforschung," 11.

13. Ibid.

14. Wolfgang Knöbl, "Gewalt erklären?" *Aus Politik und Zeitgeschichte* 67, 4 (2017): *Gewalt*, 8.

15. Christ, "Gewaltforschung," 9.

16. Knöbl, "Gewalt erklären?" 4.

17. Ibid.
18. Ibid., 5–6.
19. For a more detailed discussion of this issue, see Jack Katz, "Criminal's Passions and the Progressive's Dilemma," in *America at Century's End*, ed. Alan Wolfe (Berkeley/Los Angeles/Oxford: University of California Press, 1991), 396–417.
20. Knöbl, "Gewalt erklären?" 6.
21. Ibid.
22. Jack Katz, "From How to Why. On Luminous Description and Causal Inference in Ethnography (Part 1)," *Ethnography* 4 (2001), 445, cited in ibid.
23. Thomas Lindenberger and Alf Lüdtke, "Einleitung: Physische Gewalt—eine Kontinuität der Moderne," in *Physische Gewalt: Studien zur Geschichte der Neuzeit*, ed. Thomas Lindenberger and Alf Lüdtke (Frankfurt am Main: Suhrkamp, 1995), 15–17.
24. Daniel Hohrath and Daniel Neitzel, "Entfesselter Kampf oder gezähmte Kriegführung? Gedanken zur regelwidrigen Gewalt im Krieg," in *Kriegsgreuel. Die Entgrenzung der Gewalt in kriegerischen Konflikten vom Mittelalter bis ins 20. Jahrhundert*, ed. Daniel Hohrath and Daniel Neitzel (Paderborn, Germany: Ferdinand Schöningh, 2008), 9.
25. Susanne Kussß, *Deutsches Militär auf kolonialen Kriegsschauplätzen. Eskalation von Gewalt zu Beginn des 20. Jahrhunderts* (Berlin: Ch. Links Verlag, 2010), 12.
26. Ibid., 14–15.
27. Ibid., 16.
28. Ibid., 16–18.
29. Ibid., 32–34.
30. Ibid., 46–48
31. Hohrath and Daniel Neitzel, "Entfesselter Kampf," 10–15.
32. Udo Fink, "Der Krieg und seine Regeln," in *Kriegsgreuel. Die Entgrenzung der Gewalt in kriegerischen Konflikten vom Mittelalter bis ins 20. Jahrhundert*, ed. Daniel Hohrath and Daniel Neitzel (Paderborn, Germany: Ferdinand Schöningh, 2008), 40.
33. Seyom Brown, *The Causes and Prevention of War*, second edition (New York: St. Martin's Press, 1994), 14–16.
34. Ibid., 61–62; Volker Sellin, *Gewalt und Legitimität: Die europäische Monarchie im Zeitalter der Revolution* (Munich: Oldenbourg Verlag, 2011), 15.
35. James J. Sheehan, *Kontinent der Gewalt: Europas langer Weg zum Frieden* (Munich: C. H. Beck, 2008), 17.
36. Knöbl, "Gewalt erklären?" 7.
37. Ibid. For a more detailed discussion of violent spaces (*Gewalträume*), see Jörg Baberowski and Gabriele Metzler, eds., *Gewalträume: Soziale Ordnungen im Ausnahmezustand* (Frankfurt am Main: Campus, 2012); Timothy Snyder, *Bloodlands: Europa zwischen Hitler und Stalin* (Munich: C. H. Beck, 2011).
38. Knöbl, "Gewalt erklären?" 8.
39. Johan Galtung, "Gewalt, Frieden und Friedensforschung," in *Kritische Friedensforschung*, ed. Dieter Senghaas (Frankfurt am Main: Surhkamp, 1971), 55–104. For a critical evaluation of Galtung's ideas, see Michael Rieckenberg, "Auf

dem Holzweg? Über Johan Galtungs Begriff der 'strukturellen Gewalt,'" *Zeithistorische Forschungen/Studies in Contemporary History* 5 (2008), 172–177.

40. French sociologist Pierre Bourdieu (1930–2002) considered a form of "symbolic violence" to be an essential part of all social interactions, especially to establish a form of rule. Stephan Moebius and Angelika Wetterer, "Symbolische Gewalt," in *Österreichische Zeitschrift für Soziologie* 4 (2011), 1–10.

41. Teresa Koloma Beck, "(Staats-)Gewalt und moderne Gesellschaft: Der Mythos vom Verschwinden der Gewalt," *Aus Politik und Zeitgeschichte* 67, 4 (2017): Gewalt, 16.

42. Ibid., 17.

43. Ibid.

44. Ibid., 19.

45. Ibid., 21.

46. Trutz von Trotha, "Zur Soziologie der Gewalt," in *Soziologie der Gewalt, Kölner Zeitschrift für Soziologie und Sozialpsychologie*, Sonderheft 37 (1997), ed. Trutz von Trotha (Opladen, Germany: Westdeutscher Verlag, 1997), 10.

47. Ibid., 14.

48. Ibid., 19.

49. Ibid., 20.

50. Ibid., 25.

51. Ibid., 26–31.

52. Birgitta Nedelmann, "Gewaltsoziologie am Scheideweg: Die Auseinandersetzung in der gegenwärtigen und Wege der künftigen Gewaltforschung," in *Soziologie der Gewalt, Kölner Zeitschrift für Soziologie und Sozialpsychologie*, Sonderheft 37 (1997), ed. Trutz von Trotha (Opladen, Germany: Westdeutscher Verlag, 1997), 72–83.

53. Trotha, "On Cruelty," 5.

54. Ibid., 11.

55. Trutz von Trotha, "Dispositionen der Grausamkeit: Über die anthropologischen Grundlagen grausamen Handelns," in *On Cruelty, Sur la cruauté, Über Grausamkeit*, ed. Jakob Rösel and Trutz von Trotha (Cologne, Germany: Rüdiger Köppe Verlag, 2011), 126.

56. Ibid., 135–136.

57. Jürg Helbing, "The Tactical Use of Cruelty in Tribal Warfare," in *On Cruely, Sur la cruauté, Über Grausamkeit*, ed. Jakob Rösel and Trutz von Trotha (Cologne, Germany: Rüdiger Köppe Verlag, 2011), 150.

58. Norbert S. J. Brieskorn, "Grausamkeit—Gewalt—Macht," in *Globalisierung der Gewalt. Weltweite Solidarität angesichts neuer Fronten globaler (Un-)Sicherheit*, ed. Matthias Kiefer and Johannes Müller (Stuttgart: Verlag W. Kohlhammer, 2005), 73.

59. On this interrelationship, see Matthias Häussler, "Grausamkeit und Kolonialismus. Zur Dynamik von Grausamkeit," in *On Cruelty, Sur la cruauté, Über Grausamkeit*, ed. Jakob Rösel and Trutz von Trotha (Cologne, Germany: Rüdiger Köppe Verlag, 2011), 511–537.

60. Brieskorn, "Grausamkeit—Gewalt—Macht," 80.

61. Heimo Hofmeister, *Der Wille zum Krieg oder die Ohnmacht der Politik: Ein philosophisch-politischer Traktat* (Göttingen, Germany: Vandenhoeck & Ruprecht, 2001), 26–29.

62. David M. Buss and Joshua D. Duntley, "Intimate Partner Violence in Evolutionary Perspective," in *The Evolution of Violence*, ed. Todd K. Shackelford and Ranald D. Hansen (New York: Springer, 2014), 2.

63. Lawrence H. Keeley, "War Before Civilization—15 Years On," in *The Evolution of Violence*, ed. Todd K. Shackelford and Ranald D. Hansen (New York: Springer, 2014), 24.

64. Steven A. LeBlanc, "Warfare in Human Nature," in *The Evolution of Violence*, ed. Todd K. Shackelford and Ranald D. Hansen (New York: Springer, 2014), 87.

65. Ibid., 91.

66. Carlos David Navarrete and Melissa M. McDonald, "Sexual Selection and the Psychology of Intergroup Conflict," in *The Evolution of Violence*, ed. Todd K. Shackelford and Ranald D. Hansen (New York: Springer, 2014), 99.

67. Jost Dülffer, *Im Zeichen der Gewalt: Frieden und Krieg im 19. und 20. Jahrhundert* (Cologne/Weimar/Vienna: Böhlau Verlag, 2003), 2.

68. Klute, "Kleinkrieg und Raum," 296; Manfred Prisching, "Einleitung," in *Krieg, Konflikt, Kommunikation: Der Traum von einer friedlichen Welt*, ed. Gerold Mikula and Manfred Prisching (Vienna: Passagen Verlag, 1991), 13.

69. Amélie Mummendey, "Macht—Konflikt—Gewalt: Eine sozialpsychologische Betrachtung von Individuen und Gruppen," in *Krieg, Konflikt, Kommunikation: Der Traum von einer friedlichen Welt*, ed. Gerold Mikula and Manfred Prisching (Vienna: Passagen Verlag, 1991), 33; Prisching, "Einleitung," 14.

70. Peter Imbusch, *Moderne und Gewalt: Zivilisationstheoretische Perspektiven auf das 20. Jahrhundert* (Wiesbaden, Germany: VS Verlag für Sozialwissenschaften, 2005), 31–35.

71. Wolfgang Sofsky, "Gewaltzeit," in *Soziologie der Gewalt, Kölner Zeitschrift für Soziologie und Sozialpsychologie*, Sonderheft 37 (1997), ed. Trutz von Trotha (Opladen: Westdeutscher Verlag, 1997), 104.

72. Frank Bajohr, "Neuere Täterforschung," in *Nationalsozialistische Täterschaften: Nachwirkungen in Gesellschaft und Familie* (Reihe Neuengammer Kolloquien 6), ed. Oliver von Wrochem (Berlin: Metropol, 2016), 19. The two opposing positions of the controversy can be found in Christopher R. Browning, *Ordinary Men: Reserve Police Battalion 101 and the Final Solution in Poland*, new edition (New York: Harper Perennial, 2017) and Daniel J. Goldhagen, *Hitler's Willing Executioners: Ordinary Germans and the Holocaust* (New York: Vintage Books, 1997). On the controversy, see John C. G. Röhl, "Ordinary Germans as Hitler's Willing Executioners? The Goldhagen Controversy," in *Historical Controversies and Historians*, ed. William Lamont (London: Routledge, 1998), 15–22.

73. Bajohr, "Neuere Täterforschung," 20–21. Studies for Germany have shown that this narrative is not correct. For one important study about this topic, see Peter Longerich, *"Davon haben wir nichts gewusst!" Die Deutschen und die Judenverfolgung 1933–1945* (Munich: Pantheon, 2007).

74. Thomas Kühne, "Dämonisierung, Viktimisierung, Diversifizierung: Bilder von nationalsozialistischen Gewalttätern in Gesellschaft und Forschung seit 1945," in *Nationalsozialistische Täterschaften: Nachwirkungen in Gesellschaft und Familie* (Reihe Neuengammer Kolloquien 6), ed. Oliver von Wrochem (Berlin: Metropol, 2016), 33–34.

75. Ibid., 34.

76. On the Frankfurt Auschwitz Trials see Raphael Gross and Werner Renz, eds., *Der Frankfurter Auschwitz Prozess (1963–1965): Kommentierte Quellenedition*, 2 Vols. (Frankfurt am Main/New York: Campus, 2013).

77. Kühne, "Dämonisierung, Viktimisierung, Diversifizierung," 36.

78. Ibid., 37.

79. Ibid., 38–42. On the latter narrative, see (among others) Michael Wildt, *Generation des Unbedingten: Das Führungskorps des Reichssicherheitshauptamtes* (Hamburg, Germany: Hamburger Edition, 2003). For one example detailing the competition for the best possible form of destruction among perpetrators, see, as one example among many: Frank Jacob, 2013. "A Crossroad on the Way to Destruction: The Impossibility of the Madagascar Plan and the Destruction of the European Jews." Accessed October 10, 2017. http://www.academia.edu/7438779/A_Crossroad_on_the_Way_to_Destruction_The_Impossibility_of_the_Madagascar_Plan_and_the_Destruction_of_the_European_Jews.

80. Kühne, "Dämonisierung, Viktimisierung, Diversifizierung," 47.

81. Bajohr, "Neuere Täterforschung," 24.

82. See, as one example: Lord [Edward Frederick Langley] Russell of Liverpool, *The Knights of Bushido: A History of Japanese War Crimes during World War II* (Barnsley, UK: Frontline Books, 2013 [1958]).

83. Bajohr, "Neuere Täterforschung," 26.

84. Ibid., 27.

85. Arendt, *Macht und Gewalt*, 53 and Bajohr, "Neuere Täterforschung," 28.

86. Christian Gerlach, *Extremely Violent Societies: Mass Violence in the Twentieth-Century World* (Cambridge, UK: Cambridge University Press, 2010), 1–2.

87. Mummendey, "Macht—Konflikt—Gewalt," 37, 42.

88. Kühne, "Dämonisierung, Viktimisierung, Diversifizierung," 50–51.

89. On the trial, see Hannah Arendt, *Eichmann in Jerusalem: A Report on the Banality of Evil* (New York: Penguin 1997 [1963]); Christiane Grosse, *Der Eichmann-Prozess zwischen Recht und Politik* (Frankfurt am Main: Peter Lang 1995); Deborah E. Lipstadt, *The Eichmann Trial* (New York: Schocken, 2011).

90. Gerhard Paul, "'Dämonen'—'Schriebtischtäter'—'Pfadfinder': Die Wandlungen des Bildes von NS-Tätern in Gesellschaft und Wissenschaft am Beispiel von Eichmann und Höß," in *Nationalsozialistische Täterschaften: Nachwirkungen in Gesellschaft und Familie* (Reihe Neuengammer Kolloquien 6), ed. Oliver von Wrochem (Berlin: Metropol, 2016), 61.

91. Ibid., 60–61. See also Haim Gouri, *Facing the Glass Booth: The Jerusalem Trial of Adolf Eichmann* (Detroit: Wayne State University Press, 2004); Daniel H. Magilow and Lisa Silverman, *Holocaust Representations in History: An Introduction* (London: Bloomsbury, 2015), 63–72.

92. Elissa Mailänder, "Unsere Mütter, unsere Großmütter: Erforschung und Repräsentation weiblicher NS-Täterschaft in Wissenschaft und Gesellschaft," in *Nationalsozialistische Täterschaften: Nachwirkungen in Gesellschaft und Familie* (Reihe Neuengammer Kolloquien 6), ed. Oliver von Wrochem (Berlin: Metropol, 2016), 103.

93. Jan Philipp Reemtsma, "Grußwort: Zur Eröffnung der Ausstellung über Fritz Bauer," *Einsicht* 12 (2014), 58.

94. Sebastian Winter, "Lieber 'Kriegskind' als 'Täterkind'? Sozialpsychologische Überlegungen zur affektiven Funktion erinnerungskultureller Generationenkonstruktionen," in *Nationalsozialistische Täterschaften: Nachwirkungen in Gesellschaft und Familie* (Reihe Neuengammer Kolloquien 6), ed. Oliver von Wrochem (Berlin: Metropol, 2016), 104.

95. For Germany, see as a short introduction Alyn Bessmann and Jeanette Touissant, "Weibliche und männliche Täterschaft im Familiengedächtnis: Überlegungen zu Geschlecht als Kategorie der Auseinandersetzung mit NS-Verbrechen," in *Nationalsozialistische Täterschaften: Nachwirkungen in Gesellschaft und Familie* (Reihe Neuengammer Kolloquien 6), ed. Oliver von Wrochem (Berlin: Metropol, 2016), 232–236. For Japan, a more detailed discussion of female collaborators, especially with regard to the comfort women system, will follow later.

96. Harald Welzer, *Täter: Wie aus ganz normalen Menschen Massenmörder werden*, fifth edition (Frankfurt am Main: Fischer, 2011), 9.

97. Ibid., 37.

98. Ibid., 67.

99. Ibid., 113 and 147.

100. Ibid., 160.

101. For a general survey of the development of the Japanese army after the First World War, see Satoshi Hattori, "Dai-ichi-ji Sekaitaisen to Nihon rikugun no kindaika: Sono seika to genkai," *The Journal of International Security* 36, 3 (2008), 25–50.

102. Klaus Theweleit, *Male Fantasies*, Vol. 2: *Male Bodies: Psychoanalyzing the White Terror* (Minneapolis: University of Minnesota Press, 1989), 143–144. I follow Theweleit's study, regardless of the fact that his assumptions are related to Prussian and Germany military training, especially because they can easily be applied to the Japanese case as well. Donald G. Dutton argues that "[d]esensitization was part of the Japanese military training" as well. Donald G. Dutton, *The Psychology of Genocide, Massacres, and Extreme Violence: Why "Normal" People Come to Commit Atrocities* (Westport, CT/London: Praeger, 2007), 67.

103. Theweleit, *Male Fantasies*, Vol. 2, 144.

104. Ibid.

105. Ibid., 145.

106. Ibid., 146.

107. Ibid., 150.

108. Ibid.

109. Ibid., 154.

110. Ibid., 155.

111. Ibid., 159.
112. Ibid., 160.
113. On the role of comradeship in its relation to mass violence see Thomas Kühne, *The Rise and Fall of Comradeship: Hitler's Soldiers, Male Bonding and Mass Violence in the Twentieth Century* (Cambridge, UK: Cambridge University Press, 2017).
114. Theweleit, *Male Fantasies*, Vol. 2, 162.
115. Ibid., 166.
116. Ibid., 166 and 176.
117. Stanley Milgram, *Obedience to Authority: An Experimental View* (New York: Harper Perennial, 2009), 1.
118. For a description of the experiment, see ibid., 3–6.
119. Ibid., 4.
120. Ibid.
121. Ibid., 5.
122. Ibid., 6.
123. Ibid., 9. In the case of Nazi Germany, the Posen speeches are an example of an official glorification of violent acts to achieve a higher aim related to Nazi ideology. On the speeches and Himmler's intents, see Gerald Fleming, *Hitler and the Final Solution* (Berkeley: University of California Press, 1984), 50–60. For a broader context and additional materials see Peter Longerich, *Der ungeschriebene Befehl: Hitler und der Weg zur "Endlösung"* (Munich: Piper, 2001); Bradley F. Smith and Agnes F. Peterson, eds., *Heinrich Himmler: Geheimreden 1933 bis 1945* (Frankfurt am Main: Propyläen, 1974).
124. Milgram, *Obedience*, 135.
125. Ibid., 135–140.
126. Ibid., 142.
127. Ibid., 144.
128. Ibid., 146.
129. Ibid., 147.
130. Ibid.
131. Christ, "Gewaltforschung," 13.
132. Stefan Kühl, "Gewaltmassen: Zum Zusammenhang von Gruppen, Menschenmassen und Gewalt," *Aus Politik und Zeitgeschichte* 67, 4 (2017): *Gewalt*, 22.
133. Ibid.
134. Ibid., 24.
135. James Lide, "Recently Declassified Records at the U.S. National Archives Relating to Japanese War Crimes," in *Researching Japanese War Crimes Records: Introductory Essays*, ed. Edward Drea et al. (Washington, D.C.: National Archives and Records Administration for the Nazi War Crimes and Japanese Imperial Government Records Interagency Working Group, 2006), 62, gives some examples of violence by Japanese soldiers against civilians in the last phase of the war.
136. Michael Bollig, Erwin Orywal, and Aparna Rao, eds., *Krieg und Kampf: Die Gewalt in unseren Köpfen* (Berlin: Dietrich Reimer Verlag, 1996), 10; Trutz von Trotha, "Gewalttätige Globalisierung, globalisierte Gewalt und Gewaltmarkt," in *Globalisierung der Gewalt: Weltweite Solidarität angesichts neuer Fronten globaler (Un-)*

Sicherheit, ed. Matthias Kiefer and Johannes Müller (Stuttgart: Kohlhammer, 2005), 2.

137. Metz, *Geschichte der Gewalt*, 27.

138. Erwin Orywal, "Krieg und Frieden in den Wissenschaften," in *Krieg und Kampf: Die Gewalt in unseren Köpfen*, ed. Michael Bollig, Erwin Orywal, and Aparna Rao (Berlin: Dietrich Reimer Verlag, 1996), 18.

139. Metz, *Geschichte der Gewalt*, 299, 307.

140. Lindenberger and Lüdtke, "Einleitung," 7.

141. Sönke Neitzel and Harald Welzer, *Soldiers: German POWs on Fighting, Killing, and Dying* (New York: Vintage Books, 2013), ix.

142. Ibid., 44.

143. Ibid.

144. Ibid.

145. Ibid.

146. Ibid., 45.

147. Ibid., 49.

148. Ibid., 50.

149. Ibid., 52.

150. Ibid., 53.

151. Ibid.

152. Ibid., 64. For the hunting aspect see in broader detail, ibid., 65–69.

153. Ibid., 76.

154. Ibid., 89.

155. Ibid.

156. Thomas Kühne, *Belonging and Genocide: Hitler's Community, 1918–1945* (New Haven, CT/London: Yale University Press, 2010), 95.

157. Ibid., 96.

158. Ibid., 120.

159. Omer Bartov, "Introduction," in *The Holocaust: Origins, Implementation, Aftermath*, ed. Omer Bartov (London/New York: Routledge, 2000), 5.

160. Ibid., 7.

161. Ibid.

162. Ibid., 11.

163. Richard Bessel, *Political Violence and the Rise of Nazism: The Storm Troopers in Eastern Germany 1925–1934* (New Haven, CT/London: Yale University Press, 1984), 49.

164. Annette Abel, "Die verschleiernde Sprache der NS-Täter in Selbstzeugnissen und Ermittlungsakten: Mein Großvater als Offizier in der Waffen-SS," in *Nationalsozialistische Täterschaften: Nachwirkungen in Gesellschaft und Familie* (Reihe Neuengammer Kolloquien 6), ed. Oliver von Wrochem (Berlin: Metropol, 2016), 1.

165. Arendt, *Über das Böse*, 18.

166. Ibid., 28.

167. Ibid., 42.

168. Ibid., 52.

169. Ibid., 75.

Notes

170. John W. Dower, *Japan in War and Peace: Selected Essays* (New York: New Press, 1993), 2. The subsequent analysis follows Dower's arguments in this work and in *War without Mercy*.

171. Dower, *Japan*, 258.

172. Ibid., 260.

173. Ibid., 266, 268.

174. Japanese description of the POWs after Bataan, cited in ibid., 275.

175. Dower, *War without Mercy*, 9.

176. Ibid., 11.

177. Ibid., 43–44.

Chapter Two

1. Kasahara Tokushi, "Remembering the Nanking Massacre," in *Nanking 1937: Memory and Healing*, ed. Fei Fei Li, Robert Sabella, and David Liu (Armonk, NY/London: M. E. Sharpe, 2002), 75.

2. Noam Scheindlin, "Ignored Tragedy: The Moment before Tears Would Well Up," *Chinese American Forum* 29, 2 (2013), 22.

3. Kitamura Minoru, *The Politics of Nanjing: An Impartial Investigation* (Latham: University Press of America, 2007), 2. Kitamura's book was criticized for its interpretative and favorable use of specific source materials to lower the number of victims. It may not be considered a total denial of the events, but an attempt to attain a more favorable victimology from a Japanese perspective. For a critical evaluation, see Bob Tadashi Wakabayashi, "Kōkatsu na in'yō wo sareta rei toshite," *Shūkan Kinyōbi* August 2, 2002, 68–69.

4. "Announcement of the 1999 International Student Conference: Memories of Nanking (Nanjing): Toward a Global Consensus," Washington University St. Louis, MO (8–13 November 1999), *Chinese American Forum* 15, 3 (2000), 44.

5. Zhu Wenqi, "On the Tokyo Trial and Nanjing Massacre," *Zhengfa Luntan* (Tribune of Political Science and Law) 5 (2007), 122–136, Review by Li Hongying, in *Chinese Journal of International Law* 7, 2 (2008), 571.

6. David Askew, "New Research on the Nanjing Incident," December 31, 2004. Accessed October 10, 2017. http://china.usc.edu/new-research-nanjing-incident

7. Masahiro Yamamoto, *Nanking: Anatomy of an Atrocity* (Westport, CT: Praeger, 2000), 1.

8. Ibid., 5.

9. Ibid., 6.

10. Ibid., 6–7. My emphasis.

11. Ibid., 4.

12. Wakabayashi, "The Nanking 100-Man Killing Contest," 145.

13. Minoru, *The Politics of Nanjing*.

14. For critical reviews of Iris Chang's book, see Joshua A. Fogel, *Journal of Asian Studies* 57, 3 (1998), 818–220 and Mark Eykholt, *China International Review* 6, 1 (1999), 70–73.

15. Vera Schwarcz, "The 'Black Milk' of Historical Consciousness: Thinking about the Nanking Massacre in Light of Jewish Memory," in *Nanking 1937: Memory and Healing*, ed. Fei Fei Li, Robert Sabella, and David Liu (Armonk, NY/London: M. E. Sharpe, 2002), 183–204; Daqing Yang, "The Challengers of the Nanking Massacre: Reflections on Historical Inquiry," in *The Nanjing Massacre in History and Historiography*, ed. Joshua A. Fogel (Berkeley: University of California Press, 2000), 133–179.

16. Roger B. Jeans, "Victims or Victimizers? Museums, Textbooks, and the War Debate in Contemporary Japan," *The Journal of Military History* 69 (2005), 150.

17. For a detailed analysis of the Chinese historiography of the Rape of Nanjing, see Mark Eykholt, "Aggression, Victimization, and Chinese Historiography of the Nanjing Massacre," in *The Nanjing Massacre in History and Historiography*, ed. Joshua A. Fogel (Berkeley: University of California Press, 2000), 11–70.

18. Michael Berry, "Cinematic Representations of the Rape of Nanking," *East Asia* (2001), 85.

19. Yuki Miyamoto, "The Ethics of Commemoration: Religion and Politics in Nanking, Hiroshima, and Yasukuni," *Journal of the American Academy of Religion* 80, 1 (2012), 36–43.

20. Ibid., 43.

21. Ibid., 45.

22. Ibid.

23. Berry, "Cinematic Representations," 86.

24. "Never Forget," *Beijing Review*, March 6, 2014, 1.

25. "Massacre Heritage," *Beijing Review*, June 19, 2014, 4.

26. For films about the Rape of Nanjing, see Peter Furtado, "Nanking on Screen," *History Today* (2008), 7. An example of a novel related to the events is Meira Chand, *A Choice of Evils* (London: Weidenfeld & Nicolson, 1996).

27. Hann-Shuin Yew, "The Rape of Nanking: A Quest for Peace," *Chinese American Forum* 22, 3 (2007), 5.

28. Ruby Tsao, "Reflections: Why Did the Massacre Happen?," *Chinese American Forum* 30, 1 (2014), 29–30.

29. Yew, "The Rape of Nanking," 5.

30. Ian Buruma, "The Nanking Massacre as a Historical Symbol," in *Nanking 1937: Memory and Healing*, ed. Fei Fei Li, Robert Sabella, and David Liu (Armonk, NY/London: M. E. Sharpe, 2002), 4.

31. Ibid., 8.

32. Honda Katsuichi, *The Nanjing Massacre: A Japanese Journalist Confronts Japan's National Shame* (Armonk, NY/London: M. E. Sharpe, 1999), xxv.

33. Jeans, "Victims or Victimizers?" 149.

34. Kitamura, *The Politics of Nanjing*, 4–8 provides a more detailed explanation.

35. Higashinakano Shudo, *The Nanking Massacre: Fact Versus Fiction, a Historian's Quest for the Truth* (Tokyo: Sekai Shuppan, 2006), review by Bob Tadashi Wakabayashi, *Pacific Affairs* 79, 3 (2006), 526–527; Yamamoto, *Nanking*, 1–2.

36. Honda Katsuichi, *Chūgoku no tabi* (Tokyo: Asahi Shinbunsha, 1972). For Honda's role within the discourse about the historical debate and for English translations of his works, see Honda, *The Nanjing Massacre*.

37. Suzuki Akira, *Nanjing dai-gyakusatsu no maboroshi* (Tokyo: Bungei Shunjūsha, 1973).

38. Tanaka Masaaki, *Nankin gyakusatsu no kyokō: Matsui taishō no nikki o megutte* (Tokyo: Nihon Kyobunsha, 1984).

39. T. R. Reid, "Japan Marks Day of Defeat by Facing Up to the Truth," *International Herald Tribune*, August 15, 1994, 5; Kerry Smith, "The Showa Hall: Memorializing Japan's War at Home," *Public Historian* 24, 4 (2002), 35.

40. Jeans, "Victims or Victimizers?" 152 and 157.

41. Ibid., 193.

42. Ibid., 183–193.

43. Ibid., 193. For a discussion of the controversy, see Elizabeth Anne Dutridge-Corp, "Reconciling the Past: H.R. 121 and the Japanese Textbook Controversy" (MA thesis, Bowling Green State University, Bowling Green, OH, 2009).

44. Buruma, "The Nanking Massacre," 3–4.

45. Tsao, "Reflections," 27; Yew, "The Rape of Nanking," 4.

46. Fujiwara Akira, "The Nanking Atrocity: An Interpretive Overview," in *The Nanking Atrocity, 1937–38. Complicating the Picture*, ed. Bob Tadashi Wakabayashi (New York: Berghahn Books, 2008), 52.

47. David Askew, "Part of the Numbers Issue: Demography and Civilian Victims," in *The Nanking Atrocity, 1937–38. Complicating the Picture*, ed. Bob Tadashi Wakabayashi (New York: Berghahn Books, 2008), 96 and 112. On Nanjing's growth between 1927 and 1937, see Municipality of Nanking, *Nanking's Development, 1927–1937: Report on the Activities of the Municipality of Nanking* (Shanghai: Mercury Press, 1937). For the American influence on urban planning during this period, see Jeffrey W. Cody, "American Planning in Republican China," *Planning Perspectives* 11 (1996), 339–377.

48. Yamamoto, *Nanking*, 282.

49. Takashi Yoshida, "A Battle over History: The Nanjing Massacre in Japan," in *The Nanjing Massacre in History and Historiography*, ed. Joshua A. Fogel (Berkeley: University of California Press, 2000), 70–132.

50. For a survey and discussion of these arguments, see Takashi Yoshida, "Wartime Accounts of the Nanking Atrocity," in *The Nanking Atrocity, 1937–38. Complicating the Picture*, ed. Bob Tadashi Wakabayashi (New York: Berghahn Books, 2008), 248–249.

51. Kitamura, *The Politics of Nanjing*, 14–15 discusses available sources.

52. Shi Young and James Yin, *The Rape of Nanking: An Undeniable History in Photographs*, second expanded edition (Chicago/San Francisco: Innovative Publishing Group, 1997).

53. Peipei Qiu with Su Zhiliang and Chen Lifei, *Chinese Comfort Women: Testimonies from Imperial Japan's Sex Slaves* (Oxford/New York: Oxford University Press, 2013). For a survey on further Chinese accounts, see Yoshida, "Wartime Accounts," 249–254.

54. Documents of the Nanking Safety Zone, May 9, 1939, in David Nelson Sutton Papers, Box 7, Folder 27, Virginia Historical Society, Richmond, VA.

55. *Record of Middle China Operation*, Chapter 1: From Incident Outbreak until Nanjing Capture, The National Institute for Defense Studies, Ministry of Defense,

Army Records, Shina (China), The China Incident (Second Sino-Japanese War), Shanghai, Nanjing, C11111991300.

56. Amano Saburo, "Letters from a Reserve Officer Conscripted to Nanking," in *The Nanking Atrocity, 1937–38: Complicating the Picture*, ed. Bob Tadashi Wakabayashi (New York: Berghahn Books, 2008), 188–191; Kimura Kuninori, "Nankin kōryakusen 'Nakajima dai 16 shidanchō nikki,'" *Zōkan Rekishi to Jimbutsu* (1984), 252–271; Yoshida, "Wartime Accounts," 260.

57. Buruma, "The Nanking Massacre," 3.

58. Lu Yan, "Nanjing Massacre as Transnational Event and Global Icon," *Harvard Asia Pacific Review* 9, 2 (2008), 69.

59. Fujiwara, "The Nanking Atrocity," 31.

60. Ibid.

61. Ibid., 33.

62. Wakabayashi, "The Nanking 100-Man Killing Contest Debate, 1971–1975," 117–118 and 142.

63. "The Painful Memory," *Beijing Review*, May 28, 2009, 18.

64. Fujiwara, "The Nanking Atrocity," 43–50.

65. Yan, "Nanjing Massacre," 67.

66. Ibid.

67. Sheehan, *Kontinent der Gewalt*, 670.

68. Yan, "Nanjing Massacre," 67.

69. David Askew, "Westerners in Occupied Nanking: December 1937 to February 1938," in *The Nanking Atrocity, 1937–38. Complicating the Picture*, ed. Bob Tadashi Wakabayashi (New York: Berghahn Books, 2008), 227–229.

70. Suping Lu, *They Were in Nanjing: The Nanjing Massacre Witnessed by American and British Nationals* (Hong Kong: Hong Kong University Press, 2004), 283–285 lists the 51 Western foreigners who were active in the city during the Nanjing Massacre.

71. Ibid., 286–287.

72. Cited in Suping Lu, ed. *A Mission under Duress: The Nanjing Massacre and Post-Massacre Social Conditions Documented by American Diplomats* (Lanham, MD: University Press of America, 2010), 3.

73. Suping Lu, ed. *A Dark Page in History: The Nanjing Massacre and Post-Massacre Social Conditions Recorded in British Diplomatic Dispatches, Admiralty Documents, and U.S. Naval Intelligence Reports* (Lanham, MD: University Press of America, 2012), 18.

74. Ibid., 20.

75. Sun Jiang, "The Unbearable Heaviness of Memory: Nanjing to Tao Baojin and His Descendants," *Chinese Studies in History* 47, 1 (2013), 57.

76. Cited in ibid., 57–58.

77. Ying-Ying Chang, "Reflections on the Nanking Massacre: After 70 Years of Denial: In Memory of Our Daughter Iris Chang," *Harvard Asia Pacific Review* 9, 2 (2008), 76.

78. Hua-ling Hu and Zhang Lian-hong, eds., *The Undaunted Women of Nanking: The Wartime Diaries of Minnie Vautrin and Tsen Shui-Fang* (Carbondale: Southern Illinois University Press, 2010), 37.

Notes

79. Ibid.

80. Chang, "Reflections," 76. For a more detailed description of Minnie Vautrin's life and role during the Nanjing Massacre, see Hua-Ling Hu, *American Goddess at the Rape of Nanking: The Courage of Minnie Vautrin* (Carbondale: Southern Illinois University Press, 2000).

81. Hu, *The Undaunted Women*, 38.

82. Ibid., 40.

83. Ibid., 43.

84. Minnie Vautrin, *Terror in Minnie Vautrin's Nanjing: Diaries and Correspondence, 1937–38*, ed. Suping Lu (Urbana/Chicago: University of Illinois Press, 2008), 87.

85. Ibid., 89.

86. Andrew Carroll, "An American Missionary Describes 'Beastly' Atrocities in Nanking," *World War II* (July/August 2012), 25.

87. Ibid.

88. Ibid., 27.

89. Ibid.

90. Ibid.

91. Timothy Brook, ed. *Documents on the Rape of Nanking* (Ann Arbor: The University of Michigan Press, 1999), 207–254.

92. Ibid., 214.

93. Ibid.

94. "Letter Dr. Robert Wilson to His Family," January 28, 1938, Archives of the United Board for Christian Higher Education in Asia, Record Group No. 11, Box 229 Folder 3875: "College Files: University of Nanking: Correspondence: Wilson, Robert 1937." Accessed through The Nanking Massacre Archival Project, Yale Divinity Library, NMP0017, 1.

95. Ibid.

96. Ibid., 2.

97. Ibid.

98. Zhang Kaiyuan, ed. *Eyewitnesses to Massacre: American Missionaries Bear Witness to Japanese Atrocities in Nanjing* (Armonk, NY/ London: M. E. Sharpe, 2001), 4.

99. Ibid.

100. Qinna Shen, "Revisiting the Wound of a Nation: The 'Good Nazi' John Rabe and the Nanking Massacre," *Seminar* 47, 5 (2011), 661.

101. John Rabe, *Der gute Deutsche von Nanking*, ed. Erwin Wickert (Munich: Pantheon, 2008), 18–19.

102. Shen, "Revisiting the Wound of a Nation," 664.

103. Ibid., 669.

104. John Rabe, *The Good Man of Nanking: The Diaries of John Rabe* (New York: Vintage, 2007).

105. Takashi Yoshida, *The Making of the "Rape of Nanking": History and Memory in Japan, China, and the United States* (Oxford/New York: Oxford University Press, 2006), 4.

106. Ibid.

107. To name just one important example of Japanese research that also deals with the sources from a Japanese perspective, see Hora Tomio, *Nankin jiken* (Tokyo: Shin Jinbutsu Oraisha, 1972).

108. Richard Falk, "Redressing Grievances: Assessing the Nanking Massacre," in *Nanking 1937: Memory and Healing*, ed. Fei Fei Li, Robert Sabella, and David Liu (Armonk, NY/ London: M. E. Sharpe, 2002), 11.

109. Yew, "The Rape of Nanking," 3.

110. Kasahara, "Remembering the Nanking Massacre," 76; Lee En-Han, "The Nanking Massacre Reassessed: A Study of the Sino-Japanese Controversy over the Factual Number of Massacred Victims," in *Nanking 1937: Memory and Healing*, ed. Fei Fei Li, Robert Sabella, and David Liu (Armonk, NY/ London: M. E. Sharpe, 2002), 49.

111. "The Painful Memory," *Beijing Review*, May 28, 2009, 19.

112. Sun Zhaiwei, "Causes of the Nanking Massacre," in *Nanking 1937: Memory and Healing*, ed. Fei Li, Robert Sabella, and David Liu (Armonk, NY/ London: M. E. Sharpe, 2002), 37.

113. Kasahara, "Remembering the Nanking Massacre," 76.

114. Lee, "The Nanking Massacre Reassessed," 50.

115. Kasahara, "Remembering the Nanking Massacre," 76.

116. Kitamura, *The Politics of Nanjing*, 1.

117. Sun, "Causes of the Nanking Massacre," 44.

118. Kasahara, "Remembering the Nanking Massacre," 77.

119. Ibid., 80.

120. Ibid., 78.

121. Sun, "Causes of the Nanking Massacre," 39.

122. Lee, "The Nanking Massacre Reassessed," 50.

123. Yoshida, *The Making of the "Rape of Nanking,"* 5.

124. Ng, "The Great Denial," 34.

Chapter Three

1. Jonathan Gottschall, "Explaining Wartime Rape," *The Journal of Sex Research* 41, 2 (2004), 133.

2. Fiona E. Raitt and M. Suzanne Zeedyk, "Rape Trauma Syndrome: Its Corroborative and Educational Roles," *Journal of Law and Society* 24, 4 (1997), 559.

3. Cited in Irina Anderson and Kathy Doherty, *Accounting for Rape: Psychology, Feminism and Discourse Analysis in the Study of Sexual Violence* (London/New York: Routledge, 2008), 18.

4. Noreen Connell and Cassandra Wilson, *Rape: The First Sourcebook for Women* (New York: New American Library, 1974), 126.

5. Rochelle Semmel Albin, "Psychological Studies of Rape," *Signs* 3, 2 (1977), 423–424. For a discussion of Freud, psychoanalysis, and women, see Jean B. Miller, ed. *Psychoanalysis and Women: Contributions to New Theory and Therapy*

Notes

(New York: Brunner/Mazel, 1973). On Freud's views, see Sigmund Freud, "Some Psychical Consequences of the Anatomical Distinction Sexes," in *Gender and Envy*, ed. Nancy Burke (London/New York: Routledge, 1998), 19–26.

6. Albin, "Psychological Studies of Rape," 427.

7. For an example of such views, see R. J. McCaldon, "Rape," *Canadian Journal of Corrections* 9 (1967), 37–59.

8. Albin, "Psychological Studies of Rape," 425.

9. The author is aware that "comfort women" is a euphemism to describe female sex slaves of the Japanese army and navy. However, it will be employed due to its common usage in the field.

10. Raitt and Zeedyk, "Rape Trauma Syndrome," 557.

11. Susan B. Bond and Donald L. Mosher, "Guided Imagery of Rape: Fantasy, Reality, and the Willing Victim Myth," *The Journal of Sex Research* 22, 2 (1986), 162.

12. Ibid., 163.

13. Ibid.

14. Albin, "Psychological Studies of Rape," 423.

15. Raitt and Zeedyk, "Rape Trauma Syndrome," 552.

16. David J. Giacopassi and Karen R. Wilkinson, "Rape and the Devalued Victim," *Law and Human Behavior* 9, 4 (1985), 369.

17. Martha Burt and R. Estep, "Who Is Victim? Definitional Problems in Sexual Victimization," *Victimology* 6 (1981), 15–28.

18. Rosalind Coward, "Sexual Violence and Sexuality," *Feminist Review* 11 (1982), 9.

19. Susan Estrich, "Rape," *The Yale Law Journal* 95, 6 (1986), 1089 discusses this interrelationship for the United States.

20. Frederick Schauer, "Causation Theory and the Causes of Sexual Violence," *American Bar Foundation Research Journal* 12, 4 (1987), 741.

21. Ibid., 742.

22. Giacopassi and Wilkinson, "Rape and the Devalued Victim," 368.

23. Ibid.

24. Coward, "Sexual Violence and Sexuality," 9.

25. Albin, "Psychological Studies of Rape," 425. For the related study, see Harold Lindner, "The Blacky Pictures Test: A Study of Sexual Offenders and Sexual Offenders," *Journal of Projective Techniques* 17 (1953), 79–84.

26. Emanuel F. Hammer and Bernard C. Glueck, Jr. "Psychodynamic Patterns in Sex Offenders: A Four-Factor Theory," *Psychiatric Quarterly* 31 (1957), 325–345; Gerald R. Pascal and Frederick I. Herzberg, "The Detection of Deviant Sexual from Performance on the Rorschach Test," *Journal of Projective Techniques* 16 (1952), 366–375.

27. Albin, "Psychological Studies of Rape," 426.

28. Gloria Cowan and Robin R. Campbell, "Rape Causal Attitudes among Adolescents," *The Journal of Sex Research* 32, 2 (1995), 145.

29. Gottschall, "Explaining Wartime Rape," 129.

30. Ibid.

31. For some case studies, see Anne Llewellyn Barstow, ed. *War's Dirty Secret: Rape, Prostitution, and Other Crimes against Women* (Cleveland, OH: The Pilgrim Press, 2000); Nicole A. Dombrowski, ed. *Women and War in the Twentieth Century: Enlisted with or without Consent* (New York: Garland, 1999); Alexandra Stiglmayer, ed. *Mass Rape: The War Against Women in Bosnia-Herzegovina* (Lincoln: University of Nebraska Press, 1994).

32. Gottschall, "Explaining Wartime Rape," 130.

33. Ibid., 131.

34. Ruth Siefert, "War and Rape: A Preliminary Analysis," in *Mass Rape: The War against Women in Bosnia-Herzegovina*, ed. Alexandra Stiglmayer (Lincoln: University of Nebraska Press, 1994), 55.

35. Gottschall, "Explaining Wartime Rape," 131.

36. Stanley Rosenman, "The Spawning Grounds of the Japanese Rapists of Nanking," *Journal of Psychohistory* 28 (2000), 2–23.

37. For some studies on the interrelationship between war and rape, see Dara Kay Cohen, *Rape During Civil War* (Ithaca, NY: Cornell University Press, 2016); Miriam Gebhardt, *Crimes Unspoken: The Rape of German Women at the End of the Second World War* (London: Polity, 2017); Nicola Henry, *War and Rape: Law, Memory and Justice* (London/New York: Routledge, 2011); Carol Rittner and John K. Roth, eds., *Rape: Weapon of War and Genocide* (St. Paul, MN: Paragon House, 2012); Sara Sharatt, *Gender, Shame and Sexual Violence: The Voices of Witnesses and Court Members at War Crimes Tribunals* (Oxon/New York: Ashgate, 2011); Gina Marie Weaver, *Ideologies of Forgetting: Rape in the Vietnam War* (Albany, NY: SUNY Press, 2010).

38. Gottschall, "Explaining Wartime Rape," 131.

39. Debra B. Bergoffen, *Contesting the Politics of Genocidal Rape: Affirming the Dignity of the Vulnerable Body* (London/New York: Routledge, 2013); Adam Jones, ed. *Gendercide and Genocide* (Nashville: Vanderbilt University Press, 2004); Usta Kaitesi, *Genocidal Gender and Sexual Violence: The Legacy of the ICTR, Rwanda's Ordinary Courts and Gacaca Courts* (Cambridge, UK: Intersentia, 2014).

40. Alexandra Stiglmayer, "The Rapes in Bosnia-Herzegovina," in *Mass Rape: The War against Women in Bosnia-Herzegovina*, ed. Alexandra Stiglmayer (Lincoln: University of Nebraska Press, 1994), 82–169.

41. Benita Moolman, "The Reproduction of an 'Ideal' Masculinity through Gang Rape on the Cape Flats: Understanding Some Issues and Challenges for Effective Redress," *Agenda: Empowering Women for Gender Equity* 60 (2004): *Contemporary Activism?*, 110.

42. For a discussion of these perspectives with a special focus on sexual violence in India and Pakistan after their independence from Britain, see Veena Das, "Sexual Violence, Discursive Formations and the State," *Economic and Political Weekly* 31, 35/37 (1996), 2411.

43. Klaus Theweleit, *Male Fantasies*, Vol. 1: *Women, Floods, Bodies, History* (Minneapolis: University of Minnesota Press, 1987), 348.

44. Ibid., 346.

45. Gottschall, "Explaining Wartime Rape," 133.
46. Ibid.
47. Ruth Seifert, "The Second Front: The Logic of Sexual Violence in Wars," *Women's Studies International Forum* 19, 1/2 (1996), 36.
48. Gottschall, "Explaining Wartime Rape," 133.
49. For a further discussion, see Randy Thornhill and Craig T. Palmer, *Rape: A Natural History of Biological Bases of Sexual Coercion* (Cambridge, MA: MIT Press, 2000), 167–178.
50. Gottschall, "Explaining Wartime Rape," 133–134.
51. Tsun-Yin Luo, "'Marrying My Rapist?!': The Cultural Trauma among Chinese Rape Survivors," *Gender and Society* 14, 4 (2000), 582.
52. Anne Wolbert Burgess and Lynda Lytle Holmstrom, "Rape Trauma Syndrome," *American Journal of Psychiatry* 131, 9 (1974), 981–986.
53. Raitt and Zeedyk, "Rape Trauma Syndrome," 555.
54. Ibid.
55. On these issues, see Martha R. Burt and Bonnie L. Katz, "Dimensions of Recovery from Rape: Focus on Growth Outcomes," *Journal of Interpersonal Violence* 2, 1 (1987), 57–81; Patricia A. Resick, "The Psychological Impact of Rape," *Journal of Interpersonal Violence* 8, 2 (1993), 223–255; Gail Steketee and Edna B. Foa, "Rape Victims: Post-Traumatic Stress Responses and Their Treatment: A Review of the Literature," *Journal of Anxiety Disorders* 1, 1 (1987), 69–86.
56. Albin, "Psychological Studies of Rape," 431.
57. Larry May and Robert Strikwerda, "Men in Groups: Collective Responsibility for Rape," *Hypatia* 9, 2 (1994): *Feminism and Peace*, 135.
58. Catherine A. MacKinnon, "Turning Rape into Pornography: Postmodern Genocide," *Ms.* (1993), 30.
59. May and Strikwerda, "Men in Groups," 135.
60. Ibid., 136.
61. Ibid., 137.
62. Randy Thornhill and Nancy Wilmsen Thornhill, "The Evolutionary Psychology of Men's Coercive Sexuality," *Behavioral and Brain Sciences* 15, 2 (1992), 366.
63. Sam Keen, *Fire in the Belly* (New York: Bantam Books, 1991), 47.
64. May and Strikwerda, "Men in Groups," 145.
65. Gottschall, "Explaining Wartime Rape," 132.
66. For an analysis of such considerations in the case of the German army during World War II, see Frank Jacob, "Von der Schande zur Überlebensstrategie—Unterfränkische Perspektiven auf die Prostitution, 1933–1945," in *Prostitution: A Companion of Mankind*, ed. Frank Jacob (Frankfurt am Main: Peter Lang, 2016), 271–290.
67. Luo, "Marrying My Rapist," 583.
68. Ibid.

Chapter Four

1. Margaret D. Stetz and Bonnie B. C. Oh, "Introduction," in *Legacies of the Comfort Women of World War II*, ed. Margaret D. Stetz and Bonnie B. C. Oh (Armonk, NY/London: M. E. Sharpe, 2001), xi.

2. For a detailed analysis of these "Politics of Representation," see Chunghee Sarah Soh, "Prostitutes versus Sex Slaves: The Politics of Representing the 'Comfort Women'," in *Legacies of the Comfort Women of World War II*, ed. Margaret D. Stetz and Bonnie B. C. Oh (Armonk, NY/London: M. E. Sharpe, 2001), 69–87.

3. Yuki Tanaka, *Japan's Comfort Women: Sexual Slavery and Prostitution during World War II and the US Occupation* (London/New York: Routledge, 2002), 1.

4. Ibid.

5. Kazuko Watanabe, "Trafficking in Women's Bodies, Then and Now: The Issue of Military 'Comfort Women'," *Women's Studies Quarterly* 27, 1/2 (1999): *Teaching about Violence against Women*, 19.

6. Mina Chang, "The Politics of an Apology: Japan and Resolving the 'Comfort Women' Issue," *Harvard International Review* 31, 3 (2009), 35. The German leadership, especially Heinrich Himmler (1900–1945) and his SS, also tried to control wartime prostitution during the Second World War to prevent the spread of venereal diseases within the army. For a detailed discussion of that issue, see Frank Jacob, "Von der Schande zur Überlebensstrategie."

7. George Hicks, *The Comfort Women: Japan's Brutal Regime of Enforced Prostitution in the Second World War* (New York/London: Norton, 1995).

8. Watanabe, "Trafficking in Women's Bodies," 20. See also Kazuko Watanabe, "Militarism, Colonialism and Trafficking of Women: Military 'Comfort Women' Forced into Sexual Labor by Japanese Soldiers," *Bulletin of Concerned Asian Scholars* 26, 4 (1994), 3–16.

9. C. Sarah Soh, *The Comfort Women: Sexual Violence and Postcolonial Memory in Korea and Japan* (Chicago/London: The University of Chicago Press, 2008), 1.

10. Pyong Gap Min, "Korean 'Comfort Women': The Intersection of Colonial Power, Gender, and Class," *Gender and Society* 17, 6 (2003), 939.

11. Soh, *The Comfort Women*, 107.

12. Ibid., 108.

13. Ibid., 1–2.

14. Yoshimi Yoshiaki, Nishino Rumiko, and Hayashi Hirofumi, *Koko made wakatta! Nihongun "ianfu" seido* (Kyoto: Kamogawa Shuppan, 2007), 50–51.

15. Hayashi Yōko, "Issues Surrounding the Wartime 'Comfort Women,'" *Review of Japanese Culture and Society* 11/12 (1999–2000): *Violence in the Modern World*, 56.

16. Bart van Poelgeest, Report of a Study of Dutch Government Documents on the Forced Prostitution of Dutch Women in the Dutch East Indies during the Japanese Occupation, Unofficial Translation, January 24, 1994. Accessed November 20, 2017. http://www.awf.or.jp/pdf/0205.pdf. For a detailed discussion about the military brothels in the Dutch East Indies, see Yuki Tanaka, "'Comfort Women'

in the Dutch East Indies," in *Legacies of the Comfort Women of World War II*, ed. Margaret D. Stetz and Bonnie B. C. Oh (Armonk, NY/London: M. E. Sharpe, 2001), 42–68.

17. Soh, *The Comfort Women*, 21.
18. Ibid., 23.
19. Yang, "Documentary Evidence," 43.
20. Watanabe, "Trafficking in Women's Bodies," 24.
21. Hayashi, "Issues," 56.
22. Yang, "Documentary Evidence," 44.
23. Hayashi, "Disputes in Japan," 126.
24. Tanaka, *Japan's Comfort Women*, 8.
25. For an English translation of this important work, see Yoshimi Yoshiaki, *Comfort Women: Sexual Slavery in the Japanese Military during World War II* (New York: Columbia University Press, 2000).
26. Yoshiaki Yoshimi, *Jūgun ianfu* (Tokyo: Iwanami Shoten, 1995), 160–163.
27. Watanabe, "Trafficking in Women's Bodies," 21.
28. Yoshimi and Hirofumo, eds., *Nihongun ianfu*.
29. Hayashi, "Disputes in Japan," 128.
30. Hayashi Hirofumi, "Nihon no Haigaiteki Nashonarizumu wa Naze Taito shitaka," in *Kesareta Sabaki: NHK Bangumi Kaihen to Seiji Kainyu Jiken,* ed. VAWW-NET Japan (Tokyo: Gaifusha, 2005), 160–186. For a broad analysis of the conflicts about war memory in Japan, see Kamila Szczepanska, *The Politics of War Memory in Japan: Progressive Civil Society Groups and Contestation of Memory of the Asia-Pacific War* (London/New York: Routledge, 2014).
31. Yang, "Documentary Evidence," 39. One source that discusses the issue of Japanese soldiers raping civilians in war zones is Ogawa Sekijirō, *Aru gun hōmukan no nikki* (Tokyo: Misuzu shobō, 2000).
32. Kurahashi Masanao, *Jūgun ianfu mondai no rekishiteki kenkyū: Baishunfugata to seiteki doreigata* (Tokyo: Kyōei Shobō, 1994), 52–54.
33. Suzuki Yūko, *Jūgun ianfu, naisen kekkon* (Tokyo: Miraisha, 1992), 52. For a detailed discussion of Japan's engagement in Siberia, see Paul E. Dunscomb, *Japan's Siberian Intervention, 1918–1922* (Lanham, MD: Lexington Books, 2012).
34. Tanaka, *Japan's Comfort Women*, 10–11; Watanabe, "Trafficking in Women's Bodies," 21.
35. Tanaka, *Japan's Comfort Women*, 11.
36. Chang, "The Politics of an Apology," 35.
37. Hayashi, "Issues," 55.
38. Suzuki Yūko, *Chōsenjin jūgun ianfu: Shōgen Shōwa shi no danmen* (Tokyo: Iwanami Shoten, 1991), 53.
39. Min, "Korean 'Comfort Women,'" 110.
40. Hayashi, "Issues," 55–56. See also Suzuki, *Chōsenjin jūgun ianfu*, 20.
41. Hayashi, "Issues," 56.
42. Soh, *The Comfort Women*, 132. Yoshimi Yoshiaki, ed. *Jūgun ianfu shiryō-shū* (Tokyo: Ōtsuki shoten, 1992), 183–185.
43. Tanaka, *Japan's Comfort Women*, 9.

44. Inaba Masao, ed. *Okamura Yasuji Taishō shiryō*, Vol. 1 (Tokyo: Hara Shobō, 1970), 302.
45. Tanaka, *Japan's Comfort Women*, 11.
46. Ibid., 11–19.
47. Ibid., 12–13.
48. Ibid., 14–15.
49. Ibid., 15.
50. Soh, *The Comfort Women*, 114.
51. Ibid., 116.
52. Tanaka, *Japan's Comfort Women*, 25–26.
53. Ibid., 27.
54. Ibid.
55. Soh, *The Comfort Women*, 117, and more detailed 120–132; Tanaka, *Japan's Comfort Women*, 18–19.
56. Ibid., 19.
57. Soh, *The Comfort Women*, 117.
58. Ibid., 141; Tanaka, *Japan's Comfort Women*, 54.
59. Soh, *The Comfort Women*, 133–135.
60. Ibid., 140.
61. Tanaka, *Japan's Comfort Women*, 30.
62. Soh, *The Comfort Women*, 140–142; Tanaka, *Japan's Comfort Women*, 24 and 29.
63. Ibid., 28.
64. Ibid., 29.
65. Ibid., 31.
66. Korean Research Institute for Jungshindae, *Halmeoni, gunwianbu ka muyeyo?* (Seoul: Hankyoreh Shinmun, 2000), 30.
67. Tanaka, *Japan's Comfort Women*, 22.
68. Watanabe, "Trafficking in Women's Bodies," 23.
69. Mizobe Kazuto, ed. *Doku san ni: Mō hitotsu sensō* (N.p., 1983), 58, cited in ibid., 22.
70. The subsequent analysis follows Soh and Tanaka, if not explicitly mentioned otherwise.
71. For a detailed study of these changes, see Dennis L. McNamara, *Trade and Transformation in Korea, 1876–1945* (Boulder, CO: Westview Press, 1998).
72. Tanaka, *Japan's Comfort Women*, 35.
73. Ibid., 36.
74. Ibid., 38.
75. Soh, *The Comfort Women*, 2.
76. Ibid., 3.
77. Ibid., 4.
78. Ibid., 7.
79. Ibid., 9.
80. Ibid., 10.
81. Ibid., 15.

Notes

82. Ibid., 17. Min, "Korean 'Comfort Women,'" 951 argues that 59 percent of the women and girls who provided testimonies were drawn into the system by such false promises.

83. Soh, *The Comfort Women*, 80.

84. Tanaka, *Japan's Comfort Women*, 45. Pyong Gap Min argues that the Korean women were treated even more violently because they were considered the colonized people of the Japanese. Min, "Korean 'Comfort Women,'" 939.

85. Qiu, *Chinese Comfort Women*, provides numerous testimonies that describe the horrors Chinese women and girls endured during the war period.

86. Tanaka, *Japan's Comfort Women*, 46–47.

87. Ibid., 47.

88. Ibid., 49.

89. Hayashi, "Issues," 59–63; Myrna Elizabeth P. Borromeo, "Media for Justice and Healing: The Case of Philippine Comfort Women Survivors," *Review of Women's Studies* 20, 1–2 (2010), 87–122.

90. Her testimony is cited in Soh, *The Comfort Women*, 82–83.

91. Ibid., 83.

92. Ibid.

93. Ibid., 86–87.

94. Ibid., 86.

95. Ibid., 87.

96. Ibid., 88–90.

97. Ibid., 89.

98. Ibid., 91–92.

99. Ibid., 91.

100. This number is an estimate based on a week with six "working days" and 30 rapes a day.

101. Min, "Korean 'Comfort Women,'" 944.

102. Chang, "The Politics of an Apology," 34; Hayashi, "Issues," 54.

103. Ibid.

104. Chunghee Sarah Soh, "The Korean 'Comfort Women': Movement for Redress," *Asian Survey* 36, 12 (1996), 1229. The large number of testimonies in Korean Council, *Gangjero kkeulryeogan chosunin gunwianbudeul*, 5 vols. (Seoul, Pulbit: 1997–2001), supports the idea that the victims experienced a twofold trauma: that of the physical body and that of the mind, especially in the face of Korean postwar society.

105. Keith Howard, *True Stories of the Korean Comfort Women* (London/New York: Cassell, 1995), 18.

106. Min, "Korean 'Comfort Women,'" 952.

107. Nishino Rumiko, *Jūgun ianfu: Moto heishitachi no shōgen* (Tokyo: Akashi shoten, 1991), 42–43.

108. Watanabe, "Trafficking in Women's Bodies," 20.

109. Hayashi, "Issues," 54.

110. Min, "Korean 'Comfort Women,'" 941.

111. Tanaka, *Japan's Comfort Women*, 51–52.

112. Fukuchi Hiroaki, *Okinawa-sen no Onna-tachi: Chōsen-jin, Jūgun ianfu* (Naha, Japan: Kaifū-sha, 1992), 73, cited in ibid., 52.
113. Ibid.
114. Howard, *True Stories*, 45.
115. Tanaka, *Japan's Comfort Women*, 52–53.
116. Howard, *True Stories*, 85.
117. Ibid., 36.
118. Tanaka, *Japan's Comfort Women*, 58–59.
119. Borromeo, "Media for Justice and Healing," 88. For some of these accounts, see Firipin "Jūgun Ianfu" Hoshō Seikyū Saiban, ed. *Firipin no Nihongun "ianfu": Seiteki bōryoku no higaishatachi* (Tokyo: Akashi Shoten, 1995).
120. Maria Rosa Henson, *Comfort Woman: A Filipina's Story of Prostitution and Slavery under the Japanese Military* (Lanham, MD: Rowman & Littlefield, 1999), 35.
121. Ibid., 36.
122. Ibid.
123. Ibid.
124. Ibid., 37.
125. Ibid.
126. Ibid., 39.
127. Ibid., 40.
128. Ibid.
129. Ibid., 42.
130. Tanaka, *Japan's Comfort Women*, 21.
131. Ibid., 3.
132. Ibid., 5.
133. Ibid., 4.
134. Ibid.
135. Soh, *The Comfort Women*, 93–96.
136. Min, "Korean 'Comfort Women,'" 951.
137. Ibid., 105–106.
138. Soh, "The Korean 'Comfort Women,'" 1230.
139. Chang, "The Politics of an Apology," 35.
140. Min, "Korean 'Comfort Women,'" 941.
141. Watanabe, "Trafficking in Women's Bodies," 24.
142. Min, "Korean 'Comfort Women,'" 950.
143. Chang, "The Politics of an Apology," 36.
144. Watanabe, "Trafficking in Women's Bodies," 25. See also Chang, "The Politics of an Apology," 34 and Soh, "The Korean 'Comfort Women,'" 1233.
145. Alice Y. Chai, "Asian-Pacific Feminist Coalition Politics: The Chongsindae/Jugunianfu ('Comfort Women') Movement," *Korean Studies* 17 (1993), 67–91.
146. Margaret D. Stetz, "Teaching 'Comfort Women' Issues in Women's Studies Courses," *The Radical Teacher* 66 (2003), 17.
147. Min, "Korean 'Comfort Women,'" 950.
148. Dolgopol, "Women's Voices," 128.

149. Yang, "Documentary Evidence," 40. One report of a Dutch victim who explicitly rejects the term "comfort woman" but wants to be called a rape victim is Jeanne O'Herne, "Reipu sareta onna no sakebi," *Fukuin senkyō* 5 (1993), 18–39.

150. Allied Translator and Interpreter Section, Supreme Command for the Allied Powers, "Amenities in the Japanese Armed Forces," Research Report 120, Nov. 15, 1945, 9–20, Formerly Security-Classified Intelligence Reference Publications ("P" File) Received from U.S. Military Attachés, Military and Civilian Agencies of the United States, Foreign Governments and Other Sources, 1940–1945, NA, RG 165, Records of the War Department General and Special Staffs, entry 79, box 342. The document and its contents are discussed in Drea, "Introduction," 15.

151. Tanaka, *Japan's Comfort Women*, 85.

152. Ibid., 87–90.

153. Ibid., 87. See also Chang, "The Politics of an Apology," 36.

154. An early account by a former "comfort woman" is Pak Kyeong-Sik, *Chōsenjin kyōsei renkō no kiroku* (Tokyo: Mirai-sha, 1965).

155. Hayashi, "Issues," 57.

156. Ibid. and Min, "Korean 'Comfort Women,'" 939.

157. Shogo Suzuki, "The Competition to Attain Justice for Past Wrongs: The 'Comfort Women' Issue in Taiwan," *Pacific Affairs* 84, 2 (2011), 224.

158. Min, "Korean 'Comfort Women,'" 946.

159. Suzuki, "The Competition," 224.

160. Soh, "The Korean 'Comfort Women,'" 1235.

161. Chang, "The Politics of an Apology," 37.

162. Hayashi, "Disputes," 129.

Chapter Five

1. Kevin Murphy, "'To Sympathize and Exploit': Filipinos, Americans, and the Bataan Death March," *The Journal of American-East Asian Relations* 18, 3–4 (2011), 295.

2. Gregory J. Urwin, *Victory in Defeat: The Wake Island Defenders in Captivity, 1941–1945* (Annapolis, MD: Naval Institute Press, 2010), 335. See also U.S. Government Printing Office, Study of Former Prisoners of War: A Study Prepared by the Veterans Administration Submitted to the Committee on Veterans' Affairs, United States Senate, June 3, 1980, 33.

3. Murphy, "'To Sympathize and Exploit,'" 296.

4. Ibid.

5. Ibid., 297.

6. Ibid.

7. Ibid.

8. Paul Ashton, *And Somebody Gives a Damn* (Santa Barbara, CA: Ashton, 1990), 159.

9. Anthony Czerwien, *POW: Tears That Never Dry* (Monroe, NY: Library Research Associates, 1994), 33; Manny Lawton, *Some Survived* (Chapel Hill, NC: Algonquin, 1984), 21–22; Lester I. Tenney, *My Hitch in Hell: The Bataan Death March* (Washington, D.C.: Brassey's, 1995), 45.

10. For a collection of survivors' accounts, see Donald Knox, *Death March: The Survivors of Bataan* (New York: Harcourt, 1981).

11. Robert Levering, *Horror Trek: A True Story of Bataan—The Death March and Three and One Half Years in Japanese Prison Camps* (Dayton, OH: Horstman, 1948), cited in Kevin C. Murphy, *Inside the Bataan Death March: Defeat, Travail and Memory* (Jefferson, NC: McFarland, 2014), 138.

12. Richard M. Gordon, *Horyo: Memoirs of an American POW* (St. Paul, MN: Paragon, 1999), 102.

13. Robert S. LaForte, Ronald E. Marcello, and Richard L. Himmel, eds., *With Only the Will to Live: Accounts of Americans in Japanese Prison Camps, 1941–1945* (Wilmington, DE: Scholarly Resources, 1994), 80.

14. Fidel Ongpauco, *They Refused to Die: True Stories about World War II Heroes in the Philippines, 1941–1945* (Gatineau, Quebec: Lévesque, 1982), 136.

15. Stanley L. Falk, *Bataan: The March of Death* (Norwalk, CT: Easton Press, 1989), 102–112.

16. Dominic J. Caraccilo, ed., *Surviving Bataan and Beyond: Colonel Irvin Alexander's Odyssey as a Japanese Prisoner of War* (Mechanicsburg, PA: Stackpole, 1999), 43.

17. Murphy, "'To Sympathize and Exploit,'" 308.

18. William T. Garner, *A Study in Valor: The Faith of a Bataan Death March Survivor* (Silverton, ID: Mapletree, 2010), 61–62.

19. Cited in Murphy, "'To Sympathize and Exploit,'" 309.

20. Ibid., 312.

21. Ibid., 313 and 316.

22. Falk, *Bataan*, 159.

23. Ricardo T. José, "War and Violence, History and Memory: The Philippine Experience of the Second World War," *Asian Journal of Social Science* 29, 3 (2001): *Special Focus: Contestations of Memory in Southeast Asia*, 457.

24. Ibid.

25. Ibid., 458.

26. Ibid., 467.

27. Ibid., 464.

28. Kevin Blackburn, "War Memory and Nation-Building in South East Asia," *South East Asia Research* 18, 1 (2010), 7.

29. Ibid., 10.

30. Ibid.

31. Ibid., 11.

32. For a detailed discussion of the SCAP policies in Japan, see Jacob, "MacArthur's Legacy," 207–227.

33. Blackburn, "War Memory and Nation-Building," 12.

34. Murphy, "'To Sympathize and Exploit,'" 303.

35. Catherine Porter, "New Light on the Fall of the Philippines," *Pacific Affairs* 27, 4 (1954), 372.

36. Ibid.

37. Benjamin Appel, *We Were There at the Battle for Bataan* (New York: Grosset & Dunlap, 1957), 5.

38. Duane Schultz, *Hero of Bataan: The Story of General Jonathan M. Wainwright* (New York: St. Martin's Press, 1981), 2.

39. Ibid.

40. Porter, "New Light," 374.

41. Louis Morton, "Bataan Diary of Major Achille C. Tisdelle," *Military Affairs* 11, 3 (1947), 133.

42. Ibid., 130.

43. Porter, "New Light," 374–375.

44. James Russell Harris, "The Harrodsburg Tankers: Bataan, Prison, and the Bonds of Community," *The Register of the Kentucky Historical Society* 86, 3 (1988), 232.

45. Ibid., 246.

46. Murphy, "'To Sympathize and Exploit,'" 318.

47. Lt. Col. Wm. E. Dyess, *The Dyess Story: The Eye-Witness Account of the Death March from Bataan and the Narrative of Experiences in Japanese Prison Camps and of Eventual Escape*, ed., with a biographical introduction by Charles Leavelle (New York: G. P. Putnam's Sons, 1944).

48. Murphy, "'To Sympathize and Exploit,'" 298.

49. Dyess, *The Dyess Story*, 9.

50. Ibid., 12.

51. Ibid., 17.

52. Ibid.

53. Harris, "The Harrodsburg Tankers," 251.

54. Dyess, *The Dyess Story*, 20.

55. Ibid., 61.

56. Ibid., 68.

57. Ibid., 69.

58. Ibid.

59. Ibid., 69–70.

60. Ibid., 70.

61. Ibid.

62. Ibid., 71.

63. Ibid.

64. Ibid., 77.

65. Ibid.

66. Ibid.

67. Ibid., 79.

68. Ibid., 82.

69. Gene Boyt, *Bataan: A Survivor's Story* (Norman: University of Oklahoma Press, 2004), 124.

70. Ibid., 125.
71. Ibid., 127.
72. Ibid., 128.
73. Ibid.
74. Dyess, *The Dyess Story*, 83.
75. Boyt, *Bataan*, 129.
76. Ibid., 130.
77. Ibid., 131.
78. Ibid., 133.
79. Ibid., 135.
80. Ibid., 132.
81. Ibid.
82. Dyess, *The Dyess Story*, 84.
83. Ibid., 85.
84. Ibid., 85–86.
85. Michael Norman and Elizabeth M. Norman, *Tears in the Darkness* (New York: Picador, 2010), 182.
86. Dyess, *The Dyess Story*, 86.
87. Ibid., 90.
88. Ibid.
89. Ibid., 91.
90. Ibid., 94.
91. Harris, "The Harrodsburg Tankers," 255.
92. Boyt, *Bataan*, xxvii.
93. Ibid., 129.

Chapter Six

1. Ka'tzetnik 135633, *House of Dolls* (London: Muller, Blond & White, 1956).
2. Gregory J. Urwin, "Foreword," in Gene Boyt, *Bataan: A Survivor's Story* (Norman: University of Oklahoma Press, 2004), xii.
3. Ibid.
4. *The New York Times*, January 29, 1944, cited in ibid., xiii.
5. Ibid., xiv.
6. Ibid., xviii.
7. Ibid.
8. Higashinakano Shudo, *The Nanking Massacre: Fact Versus Fiction—A Historian's Quest for the Truth* (Tokyo: Sekai Shuppan, 2006), ii–iii.
9. Van Waterford, *Prisoners of the Japanese in World War II: Statistical History, Personal Narratives and Memorials Concerning POWs in Camps and on Hellships, Civilian Internees, Asian Slave Laborers and Others Captured in the Pacific Theater* (Jefferson, NC: McFarland, 1994), 1.
10. Roy Bulcock, *Of Death but Once* (Melbourne, Australia: F. W. Cheshire, 1947), 167.

11. Waterford, *Prisoners of the Japanese*, 2.
12. Harris, "The Harrodsburg Tankers," 255.
13. John R. Bumgarner, *Parade of the Dead: A U.S. Army Physician's Memoir of Imprisonment by the Japanese, 1942–1945* (Jefferson, NC: McFarland, 1995), 78.
14. Ibid.
15. Ibid., 79.
16. Ibid., 81.
17. John Henry Poncio and Marlin Young, *Girocho: A GI's Story of Bataan and Beyond* (Baton Rouge: Louisiana State University Press, 2003), 109.
18. Bumgarner, *Parade of the Dead*, 83.
19. Ibid.
20. Ibid., 84.
21. Boyt, *Bataan*, 139.
22. Ibid.
23. Ibid., 142.
24. Dyess, *The Dyess Story*, 99.
25. Boyt, *Bataan*, 142–143.
26. Ibid., 146.
27. Ibid.
28. Ibid., 147.
29. Dyess, *The Dyess Story*, 101. A further description of the lives and deaths of POWs at Camp O'Donnell follows Dyess's report.
30. Ibid., 103.
31. Ibid., 106.
32. Ibid., 107.
33. Poncio and Young, *Girocho*, 109.
34. Ibid.
35. Bumgarner, *Parade of the Dead*, 84.
36. Ibid., 87–88.
37. Poncio and Young, *Girocho*, 110.
38. Bumgarner, *Parade of the Dead*, 88.
39. Ibid., 89.
40. Ibid.
41. Harris, "The Harrodsburg Tankers," 258.
42. Bumgarner, *Parade of the Dead*, 91.
43. Ibid., 92.
44. Ibid., 96.
45. Ibid., 97.
46. Ibid., 98.
47. Ibid.
48. Ibid., 101.
49. Ibid.
50. Ibid., 102.
51. Ibid., 103.
52. Ibid.

53. Ibid.
54. Ibid., 109.
55. Poncio and Young, *Girocho*, 117.
56. Bumgarner, *Parade of the Dead*, 105.
57. Robert S. LaForte, Ronald E. Marcello, and Richard L. Himmel, eds., *With Only the Will to Live: Accounts of Americans in Japanese Prison Camps, 1941–1945* (Wilmington, DE: SR Books, 1994), 62.
58. Poncio and Young, *Girocho*, 111.
59. Ibid., 112.
60. Ibid.
61. Ibid., 116.
62. Bumgarner, *Parade of the Dead*, 114.
63. Ibid., 118.
64. Ibid., 119.
65. Gavan Daws, *Prisoners of the Japanese: POWS of World War II in the Pacific* (New York: William Morrow and Company, 1994), 260.
66. Bumgarner, *Parade of the Dead*, 117.
67. Ibid., 120.
68. Ibid., 121.
69. Ibid., 122.
70. Harris, "The Harrodsburg Tankers," 262.
71. For a detailed list and related British archival materials, see https://www.forces-war-records.co.uk/prisoners-of-war-of-the-japanese-1939-1945. Accessed September 30, 2017.
72. Daws, *Prisoners of the Japanese*, 283.
73. Ibid., 284.
74. Ibid.
75. Harris, "The Harrodsburg Tankers," 261.
76. Peter B. Marshall, *1368 Days: An American POW in WWII Japan*, ed. Cynthia Marshall Hopkins (Eugene, OR: Luminate Press, 2017), 57.
77. Donald T. Giles, Jr. *Captive of the Rising Sun: The POW Memoirs of Rear Admiral Donald T. Giles, USN* (Annapolis, MD: Naval Institute Press, 1994), 73.
78. Marshall, *1368 Days*, 60.
79. Ibid., 61.
80. Giles, *Captive of the Rising Sun*, 73–75.
81. Ibid., 77.
82. Ibid., 78.
83. Ibid., 82.
84. Ibid., 86–88.
85. Ibid., 83.
86. Ibid., 84.
87. Sir Harold Atcherley, *Prisoner of Japan: A Personal War Diary, Singapore, Siam and Burma, 1941–1945* (Cirencester, UK: Memoirs Publishing, 2012), ix.
88. Ibid., xii.

Notes

89. Ibid., xii–xiii.
90. Daws, *Prisoners of the Japanese*, 184.
91. Ibid.
92. For an American account, see H. Robert Charles, *Last Man Out—Surviving the Burma-Thailand Death Railway: A Memoir* (St. Paul, MN: Zenith Press, 2006).
93. The colonel had to stand trial in Singapore in 1946. Australia, Military Jurisdiction, *Prosecutor v. Yoshitada Nagatomo et al.*, National Archives Kew, London, A-0471 No. 81655. When the role of orders was discussed and to what end orders were responsible for the actions tried by the court, the defending counsel called "the attention of the witness to the fact that he can refuse to answer that question," whereas the prosecutor simply remarked: "If the witness [Branch Commander Yanagida] contends that the answer to that question may incriminate him, well I cannot press the question. It seems remarkable that he says he was only carrying out orders and by doing that it incriminates him" (ibid., 139).
94. Cited in Daws, *Prisoners of the Japanese*, 185.
95. Atcherley, *Prisoner of Japan*, xiv.
96. Ibid.
97. Ibid., xv.
98. Ibid., xvi–xviii.
99. Ibid., xix–xx. Atcherley, like Primo Levi, also felt guilty for having survived while so many had not: "This euphoria [of being free again] was, however, tempered by a feeling of guilt that one had survived when so many thousands had died" (ibid., xx).
100. Ibid., 93.
101. Ibid., 102.
102. Ibid., 106.
103. Ibid., 107.
104. Ibid., 109.
105. Ibid., 107.
106. Ibid., 110.
107. Ibid., 120.
108. Ibid., 135.
109. Daws, *Prisoners of the Japanese*, 191.
110. Ibid., 192.
111. Ibid., 195.
112. Ibid., 219.
113. Ibid.
114. Ibid.
115. Ibid.
116. Ibid., 221.
117. Ibid.
118. Ibid., 222.
119. Ibid., 223.
120. Ibid., 247.

121. Atcherley, *Prisoner of Japan*, ix.
122. Daws, *Prisoners of the Japanese*, 268.
123. Ibid., 273.
124. Ibid., 275.
125. Ibid., 276.
126. Ibid., 284.
127. Harris, "The Harrodsburg Tankers," 257.
128. Poncio and Young, *Girocho*, 119–120.
129. Waterford, *Prisoners of the Japanese*, 22.
130. Daws, *Prisoners of the Japanese*, 254.
131. Ibid., 255.
132. Waterford, *Prisoners of the Japanese*, 21.
133. Ibid., 23.
134. Ibid., 38.
135. Ibid., 39.
136. Ibid.
137. Daws, *Prisoners of the Japanese*, 258–259.

Chapter Seven

1. Mark Felton, *The Devil's Doctors: Japanese Human Experiments on Allied Prisoners of War* (Barnsley, UK: Pen & Sword, 2012), 2.
2. Daqing Yang, "Documentary Evidence and the Studies of Japanese War Crimes: An Interim Assessment," in *Researching Japanese War Crimes Records: Introductory Essays*, ed. Edward Drea et al. (Washington, D.C.: National Archives and Records Administration for the Nazi War Crimes and Japanese Imperial Government Records Interagency Working Group, 2006), 36.
3. Felton, *The Devil's Doctors*, 5.
4. Cited in Daniel Barenblatt, *A Plague upon Humanity: The Hidden History of Japan's Biological Warfare Program* (New York: Harper, 2005), xviii–xix.
5. For testimonies of former members of Unit 1644, see Mizutani Naoko, "Moto 1644 butai'in no shōgen," *Sensō sekinin kenkyū* 10 (1995), 56–65.
6. Yang, "Documentary Evidence," 38–39 cites Chinese works on Japan's chemical warfare program, of which *Zuie di "731" "100": Qin-Hua Rijun xijun budui dang'an ziliao xuan bian* (Shenyang: Liaoning minzu chubanshe, 1995) and Sha Dongxun, *Jie kai "8604" zhi mi: Qin Hua Rijun zai Yue mimi jinxing xijunzhan dapuguang* (Guangzhou: Huacheng chubanshe, 1995) are of interest.
7. Felton, *The Devil's Doctors*, 2.
8. Ibid., 3.
9. Tsuneishi Keiichi, *Kieta saikinsen butai: Kantogun Dai 731-butai* (Tokyo: Kaimeisha, 1981) and Tsuneishi Keiichi and Asano Tomizo, *Saikinsen butai to jiketsushita futari no igakusha* (Tokyo: Shinchōsha, 1982) provide a detailed analysis of the overlaps between the experiments and medical publications during the Second World War.

10. For an English version, see Yamada Otozō, *Materials on the Trial of Former Servicemen of the Japanese Army, Charged with Manufacturing and Employing Bacteriological Weapons* (Moscow: Foreign Languages Publishing House, 1950).

11. Yang, "Documentary Evidence," 35. For a detailed discussion of the "American cover-up," see Sheldon Harris, *Factories of Death: Japanese Biological Warfare, 1932–1945, and the American Cover-up*, revised edition (New York: Routledge, 2002 [1994]).

12. Yang, "Documentary Evidence," 34.

13. Daniel Barenblatt, *A Plague upon Humanity: The Hidden History of Japan's Biological Warfare Program* (New York: Harper, 2005), 22.

14. Hal Gold, *Unit 731 Testimony* (Tokyo: Tuttle, 1997), 96.

15. Ibid., 115. Also see ibid., 96–101 for a discussion of the continuities of Japanese medical careers after the war.

16. Barenblatt, *A Plague upon Humanity*, xxiii.

17. Ibid.

18. For a detailed discussion of Ishii's role during the program's establishment and in Unit 731 specifically, see Aoki Fukiko, *731—Ishii Shirō to saikinsen butai no yami wo abaku* (Tokyo: Asahi Shinbunsha, 2008).

19. Yang, "Documentary Evidence," 37.

20. Edward Drea, "Introduction," in *Researching Japanese War Crimes Records: Introductory Essays*, ed. Edward Drea et al. (Washington, D.C.: National Archives and Records Administration for the Nazi War Crimes and Japanese Imperial Government Records Interagency Working Group, 2006), 17.

21. John W. Powell, "Japan's Germ Warfare: The U.S. Cover-up of a War Crime," *Bulletin of Concerned Asian Scholars* 12, 4 (1980), 2–17.

22. Tsuneishi Keiichi, ed. *Hyōteki Ishii: 731 butai to Beigun chōhō katsudō* (Tokyo: Ōtsuki shoten, 1984).

23. For a survey of research between the early 1980s and early 2000s, see Kondo Shōji, "731 butai o meguru chōsa kenkyū no genjō," *Sensō sekinin kenkyū* 46 (2004), 38–43. For a recent discussion of the interrelationship between the Second World War and Japanese science, see Tsuneishi Keiichi, "731 butai: Sensō to gakujutsu wo kangaeru genten toshite," *Kagaku* 86, 10 (2016), 1044–1048. For sources related to Unit 731, see Tanaka Akira and Matsumura Takao, eds., *731 butai sakusei shiryō* (Tokyo: Fuji Shuppan 1991).

24. Barenblatt, *A Plague upon Humanity*, xviii.

25. Ibid., xxii.

26. Felton, *The Devil's Doctors*, 6.

27. Barenblatt, *A Plague upon Humanity*, 1.

28. Gold, *Unit 731*, 23.

29. Barenblatt, *A Plague upon Humanity*, 64–65.

30. Ibid., 2.

31. Gold, *Unit 731*, 29.

32. Barenblatt, *A Plague upon Humanity*, 3.

33. Ibid.

34. Ibid., 4.

35. Ibid., 4–5.
36. Ibid., 7.
37. Ibid., 7–8.
38. Ibid., 8.
39. *Materials on the Trial of Former Servicemen*, 295.
40. Barenblatt, *A Plague upon Humanity*, 15–16.
41. On Heydrich, see Robert Gerwath, *Hitler's Hangman: The Life of Heydrich* (New Haven, CT: Yale University Press, 2011).
42. Barenblatt, *A Plague upon Humanity*, 20.
43. Ibid., 22.
44. Gold, *Unit 731*, 48.
45. Ibid., 48–59.
46. Ibid., 32–48.
47. Ibid., 70–85. The plague was particularly interesting, because "armies that want to use disease as a military weapon want something that acts fast and is fatal" ibid., 74.
48. Ibid., 59.
49. Ibid., 60.
50. Barenblatt, *A Plague upon Humanity*, 38–48.
51. Ibid., 72–77.
52. Ibid., 23.
53. Ibid., 27. See also Yang, "Documentary Evidence," 39.
54. Barenblatt, *A Plague upon Humanity*, xviii.
55. Ibid., xix–xx.
56. Gold, *Unit 731*, 31.
57. Cited in Barenblatt, *A Plague upon Humanity*, 29.
58. Ibid.
59. Cited in ibid., 45.
60. Ibid., 50.
61. Ibid.
62. Cited in ibid., 51.
63. Ibid., 55.
64. Ibid., 60.
65. Gold, *Unit 731*, 181.
66. Barenblatt, *A Plague upon Humanity*, 30.
67. Ibid., 30–41.
68. For a detailed analysis, see Bernd C. Wagner, *IG Auschwitz: Zwangsarbeit und Vernichtung von Häftlingen des Lagers Monowitz 1941–1945* (Munich: K. G. Saur, 2000).
69. Barenblatt, *A Plague upon Humanity*, 69.
70. Ibid.
71. Ibid., xxi.
72. Ibid., 43–44.
73. Gold, *Unit 731*, 171.
74. Ibid., 178.

75. Barenblatt, *A Plague upon Humanity*, 44.
76. Ibid., 45.
77. Ibid., 46.
78. Ibid.
79. Yoshimura Hisato, "Tōshō ni tsuite" (1941), in *731 butai sakusei shiryō*, ed. Tanaka Akira and Matsumura Takao (Tokyo: Fuji Shuppan 1991), 225–288.
80. For a discussion about the self-determination of the doctors involved, see Tsuchiya Takashi, "Self Determination by Imperial Japanese Doctors: Did They Freely Decide to Perform Deadly Experiments?" Paper presented at UNESCO-Kumamoto University Bioethics Roundtable 2007, "Perspectives on Self-Determination," Kumamoto, Japan, December 16, 2007. Accessed October 15, 2017. http://www.lit.osaka-cu.ac.jp/user/tsuchiya/gyoseki/presentation/UNESCOkumamoto07.html
81. Gold, *Unit 731*, 182.
82. Ibid., 187.
83. Barenblatt, *A Plague upon Humanity*, 13.
84. Gold, *Unit 731*, 222.
85. Ibid., 139–143.

Conclusion

1. Hannah Arendt, *Denktagebuch, 1950–1973*, Vol. 1, ed. Ursula Ludz and Ingeborg Nordmann, second edition (Munich/Zurich: Piper, 2003), 3.
2. Ibid., 4.
3. Ibid., 69.

Works Cited

Abel, Annette. "Die verschleiernde Sprache der NS-Täter in Selbstzeugnissen und Ermittlungsakten: Mein Großvater als Offizier in der Waffen-SS." In *Nationalsozialistische Täterschaften: Nachwirkungen in Gesellschaft und Familie* (Reihe Neuengammer Kolloquien 6), ed. Oliver von Wrochem, 433–48. Berlin: Metropol, 2016.

Albin, Rochelle Semmel. "Psychological Studies of Rape." *Signs* 3, 2 (1977): 423–35.

Allied Translator and Interpreter Section, Supreme Command for the Allied Powers. "Amenities in the Japanese Armed Forces," Research Report 120, Nov. 15, 1945, 9–20, Formerly Security-Classified Intelligence Reference Publications ("P" File) Received from U.S. Military Attachés, Military and Civilian Agencies of the United States, Foreign Governments and Other Sources, 1940–1945, NA, RG 165, Records of the War Department General and Special Staffs, entry 79, box 342.

Amano Saburo. "Letters from a Reserve Officer Conscripted to Nanking." In *The Nanking Atrocity, 1937–38: Complicating the Picture*, ed. Bob Tadashi Wakabayashi, 181–95. New York: Berghahn Books, 2008.

Anderson, Irina and Kathy Doherty. *Accounting for Rape: Psychology, Feminism and Discourse Analysis in the Study of Sexual Violence*. London/New York: Routledge, 2008.

"Announcement of the 1999 International Student Conference: Memories of Nanking (Nanjing): Toward a Global Consensus." Washington University, St. Louis, MO (November 8–13, 1999), *Chinese American Forum* 15, 3 (2000): 44.

Aoki Fukiko. *731—Ishii Shirō to saikinsen butai no yami wo abaku*. Tokyo: Asahi Shinbunsha, 2008.

Appel, Benjamin. *We Were There at the Battle for Bataan*. New York: Grosset & Dunlap, 1957.

Arendt, Hannah. *On Violence*. New York: Houghton Mifflin Harcourt Publishing, 1970.

Arendt, Hannah. *Eichmann in Jerusalem: A Report on the Banality of Evil.* New York: Penguin, 1978.

Arendt, Hannah. *Eichmann in Jerusalem: A Report on the Banality of Evil.* New York: Penguin 1997 [1963].

Arendt, Hannah. *Denktagebuch, 1950–1973*, Vol. 1, ed. Ursula Ludz and Ingeborg Nordmann, 2nd edition. Munich/Zurich: Piper, 2003.

Arendt, Hannah. *Über das Böse: Eine Vorlesung zu Fragen der Ethik*, 4th edition. Munich/Zurich: Piper, 2010 [2007].

Arendt, Hannah. *Macht und Gewalt*, 20th edition. Munich/Zurich: Piper, 2011 [1970].

Ashton, Paul. *And Somebody Gives a Damn.* Santa Barbara, CA: Ashton, 1990.

Askew, David. "New Research on the Nanjing Incident." December 31, 2004. Accessed October 10, 2017. http://china.usc.edu/new-research-nanjing-incident

Askew, David. "Part of the Numbers Issue: Demography and Civilian Victims." In *The Nanking Atrocity, 1937–38: Complicating the Picture*, ed. Bob Tadashi Wakabayashi, 86–114. New York: Berghahn Books, 2008.

Askew, David. "Westerners in Occupied Nanking: December 1937 to February 1938." In *The Nanking Atrocity, 1937–38. Complicating the Picture*, ed. Bob Tadashi Wakabayashi, 227–47. New York: Berghahn Books, 2008.

Atcherley, Sir Harold. *Prisoner of Japan: A Personal War Diary, Singapore, Siam and Burma, 1941–1945.* Cirencester, UK: Memoirs Publishing, 2012.

Baberowski, Jörg and Gabriele Metzler, eds. *Gewalträume: Soziale Ordnungen im Ausnahmezustand.* Frankfurt am Main, Germany: Campus, 2012.

Bajohr, Frank. "Neuere Täterforschung." In *Nationalsozialistische Täterschaften: Nachwirkungen in Gesellschaft und Familie* (Reihe Neuengammer Kolloquien 6), ed. Oliver von Wrochem, 19–31. Berlin: Metropol, 2016.

Barenblatt, Daniel. *A Plague upon Humanity: The Hidden History of Japan's Biological Warfare Program.* New York: Harper, 2005.

Bar-On, Dan. *Legacy of Silence: Encounters with Children of the Third Reich.* Cambridge, MA: Harvard University Press, 1989.

Barstow, Anne Llewellyn, ed. *War's Dirty Secret: Rape, Prostitution, and Other Crimes against Women.* Cleveland: The Pilgrim Press, 2000.

Bartov, Omer. "Introduction." In *The Holocaust: Origins, Implementation, Aftermath*, ed. Omer Bartov, 1–18. London/New York: Routledge, 2000.

Bauman, Zygmunt. "Alte und neue Gewalt." *Journal für Konflikt- und Gewaltforschung* 2 (2000): 28–42.

Bergoffen, Debra B. *Contesting the Politics of Genocidal Rape: Affirming the Dignity of the Vulnerable Body.* London/New York: Routledge, 2013.

Berry, Michael. "Cinematic Representations of the Rape of Nanking." *East Asia* 19, 4 (2001): 85–108.

Bessel, Richard. *Political Violence and the Rise of Nazism: The Storm Troopers in Eastern Germany 1925–1934.* New Haven, CT/London: Yale University Press, 1984.

Bessho Yoshimi. "The Logic of Apologizing for War Crimes 'as a Japanese.'" *Review of Japanese Culture and Society* 11/12 (1999–2000): *Violence in the Modern World:* 32–42.

Bessmann, Alyn and Jeanette Touissant. "Weibliche und männliche Täterschaft im Familiengedächtnis: Überlegungen zu Geschlecht als Kategorie der Auseinandersetzung mit NS-Verbrechen." In *Nationalsozialistische Täterschaften: Nachwirkungen in Gesellschaft und Familie* (Reihe Neuengammer Kolloquien 6), ed. Oliver von Wrochem, 232–36. Berlin: Metropol, 2016.

Betts, Paul and Christian Wiese. "Introduction." In *Years of Persecution, Years of Extermination: Saul Friedländer and the Future of Holocaust Studies*, ed. Christian Wiese and Paul Betts, 1–20. London/New York: Continuum, 2010.

Bjorklund, David F. and Patricia H. Hawley. "Aggression Grows Up: Looking through an Evolutionary Developmental Lens to Understand the Causes and Consequences of Human Aggression." In *The Evolution of Violence*, ed. Todd K. Shackelford and Ranald D. Hansen, 159–86. New York: Springer, 2014.

Blackburn, Kevin. "War Memory and Nation-Building in South East Asia." *South East Asia Research* 18, 1 (2010): 5–31.

Bollig, Michael, Erwin Orywal, and Aparna Rao, eds. *Krieg und Kampf: Die Gewalt in unseren Köpfen.* Berlin: Dietrich Reimer Verlag, 1996.

Bond, Susan B. and Donald L. Mosher. "Guided Imagery of Rape: Fantasy, Reality, and the Willing Victim Myth." *The Journal of Sex Research* 22, 2 (1986): 162–83.

Borromeo, Myrna Elizabeth P. "Media for Justice and Healing: The Case of Philippine Comfort Women Survivors." *Review of Women's Studies* 20, 1–2 (2010): 87–122.

Boyt, Gene. *Bataan: A Survivor's Story.* Norman: University of Oklahoma Press, 2004.

Bradsher, Greg. "The Exploitation of Captured and Seized Japanese Records Relating to War Crimes, 1942–1945." In *Researching Japanese War Crimes Records: Introductory Essays*, ed. Edward Drea et al., 151–68. Washington, D.C.: National Archives and Records Administration for the Nazi War Crimes and Japanese Imperial Government Records Interagency Working Group, 2006.

Brieskorn, Norbert S. J. "Grausamkeit—Gewalt—Macht." In *Globalisierung der Gewalt: Weltweite Solidarität angesichts neuer Fronten globaler (Un-)Sicherheit*, ed. Matthias Kiefer and Johannes Müller, 71–98. Stuttgart: Verlag W. Kohlhammer, 2005.

Brook, Timothy, ed. *Documents on the Rape of Nanking.* Ann Arbor: The University of Michigan Press, 1999.

Brown, Seyom. *The Causes and Prevention of War*, 2nd edition. New York: St. Martin's Press, 1994.

Browning, Christopher R. *Ordinary Men: Reserve Police Battalion 101 and the Final Solution in Poland*, new edition. New York: Harper Perennial, 2017.

Bulcock, Roy. *Of Death but Once*. Melbourne, Australia: F. W. Cheshire, 1947.
Bumgarner, John R. *Parade of the Dead: A U.S. Army Physician's Memoir of Imprisonment by the Japanese, 1942–1945*. Jefferson, NC: McFarland, 1995.
Burgess, Anne Wolbert and Lynda Lytle Holmstrom. "Rape Trauma Syndrome." *American Journal of Psychiatry* 131, 9 (1974): 981–86.
Burt, Martha R. and Bonnie L. Katz. "Dimensions of Recovery from Rape: Focus on Growth Outcomes." *Journal of Interpersonal Violence* 2, 1 (1987): 57–81.
Buruma, Ian. "The Nanking Massacre as a Historical Symbol." In *Nanking 1937: Memory and Healing*, ed. Fei Fei Li, Robert Sabella, and David Liu, 3–9. Armonk, NY/London: M. E. Sharpe, 2002.
Buruma, Ian. *The Wages of Guilt: Memories of War in Germany and Japan*, new edition. New York: New York Review of Books, 2015.
Buss, David M. and Joshua D. Duntley. "Intimate Partner Violence in Evolutionary Perspective." In *The Evolution of Violence*, ed. Todd K. Shackelford and Ranald D. Hansen, 1–21. New York: Springer, 2014.
Caraccilo, Dominic J., ed. *Surviving Bataan and Beyond: Colonel Irvin Alexander's Odyssey as a Japanese Prisoner of War*. Mechanicsburg, PA: Stackpole, 1999.
Carroll, Andrew. "An American Missionary Describes 'Beastly' Atrocities in Nanking." *World War II* 27, 2 (2012): 25–27.
Chai, Alice Y. "Asian-Pacific Feminist Coalition Politics: The Chongsindae/Jugunianfu ('Comfort Women') Movement." *Korean Studies* 17 (1993): 67–91.
Chand, Meira. *A Choice of Evils*. London: Weidenfeld & Nicolson, 1996.
Chang, Iris. *The Rape of Nanking: The Forgotten Holocaust of World War II*. New York: Basic Books, 2011 [1997].
Chang, Mina. "The Politics of an Apology: Japan and Resolving the 'Comfort Women' Issue." *Harvard International Review* 31, 3 (2009): 34–7.
Chang, Ying-Ying. "Reflections on the Nanking Massacre: After 70 Years of Denial: In Memory of Our Daughter Iris Chang." *Harvard Asia Pacific Review* 9, 2 (2008): 75–8.
Charles, H. Robert. *Last Man Out—Surviving the Burma-Thailand Death Railway: A Memoir*. St. Paul, MN: Zenith Press, 2006.
Christ, Michaela. "Gewaltforschung: Ein Überblick." *Aus Politik und Zeitgeschichte* 67, 4 (2017): *Gewalt:* 9–15.
Chūgoku kikansha rengokai. *Sankō*. Tokyo: Kōbunsha, 1957.
Clauss, Bärbel, Katja Koblitz, and Detlef Richter, eds. *Kriegsansichten—Friedensansichten. Vom Umgang mit Konflikten in Theorie und Realität*. Münster, Germany: LIT Verlag, 1993.
Cody, Jeffrey W. "American Planning in Republican China." *Planning Perspectives* 11 (1996): 339–77.
Cohen, Dara Kay. *Rape during Civil War*. Ithaca, NY: Cornell University Press, 2016.
Connaughon, Richard, John Pimlott, and Duncan Anderson. *Battle for Manila*. Novato, CA: Presidio Press, 1995.
Connell, Noreen and Cassandra Wilson. *Rape: The First Sourcebook for Women*. New York: New American Library, 1974.

Cornelißen, Christoph, Lutz Klinkhammer, and Wolfgang Schwentker, eds. *Erinnerungskulturen: Deutschland, Italien und Japan seit 1945*. Frankfurt am Main, Germany: Fischer, 2003.

Cowan, Gloria and Robin R. Campbell. "Rape Causal Attitudes among Adolescents." *The Journal of Sex Research* 32, 2 (1995): 145–53.

Coward, Rosalind. "Sexual Violence and Sexuality." *Feminist Review* 11 (1982): 9–22.

Czerwien, Anthony. *POW: Tears That Never Dry*. Monroe, NY: Library Research Associates, 1994.

Das, Veena. "Sexual Violence, Discursive Formations and the State." *Economic and Political Weekly* 31, 35/37 (1996): 2411–13, 2415–18, and 2420–23.

Daws, Gavan. *Prisoners of the Japanese: POWS of World War II in the Pacific*. New York: William Morrow and Company, 1994.

Documents of the Nanking Safety Zone, May 9, 1939. In David Nelson Sutton Papers, Box 7, Folder 27, Virginia Historical Society, Richmond, VA.

Dolgopol, Ustinia. "Women's Voices, Women's Pain." *Human Rights Quarterly* 17, 1 (1995): 127–54.

Dombrowski, Nicole A. ed. *Women and War in the Twentieth Century: Enlisted with or without Consent*. New York: Garland, 1999.

Dower, John W. *Japan in War and Peace: Selected Essays*. New York: New Press, 1993.

Dower, John W. *War without Mercy: Race and Power in the Pacific War*, 7th edition. New York: Pantheon Books, 1993.

Drea, Edward. "Introduction." In *Researching Japanese War Crimes Records: Introductory Essays*, ed. Edward Drea et al., 3–20. Washington, D.C.: National Archives and Records Administration for the Nazi War Crimes and Japanese Imperial Government Records Interagency Working Group, 2006.

Dülffer, Jost. *Im Zeichen der Gewalt: Frieden und Krieg im 19. und 20. Jahrhundert*. Cologne/Weimar/Vienna: Böhlau Verlag, 2003.

Dunscomb, Paul E. *Japan's Siberian Intervention, 1918–1922*. Lanham, MD: Lexington Books, 2012.

Dutridge-Corp, Elizabeth Anne. "Reconciling the Past: H.R. 121 and the Japanese Textbook Controversy." M. A. thesis, Bowling Green State University, Bowling Green, OH, 2009.

Dutton, Donald G. *The Psychology of Genocide, Massacres, and Extreme Violence: Why "Normal" People Come to Commit Atrocities*. Westport, CT/London: Praeger, 2007.

Dyess, Lt. Col. William. E. *The Dyess Story: The Eye-Witness Account of the Death March from Battan and the Narrative of Experiences in Japanese Prison Camps and of Eventual Escape*, ed., with a biographical introduction by Charles Leavelle. New York: G. P. Putnam's Sons, 1944.

Erstein, Kali, Cheryl Lindsey Seelhoff, Angie Manzano, and Karla Mantilla. "JAPAN: Comfort Women Demand Justice." *Off Our Backs* 36, 4 (2006): 3.

Escoda y Minguez, Jose Ma. Bonifacio. *Warsaw of Asia: The Rape of Manila.* Quezon City, Philippines: Giraffe Books, 2000.

Estrich, Susan. "Rape." *The Yale Law Journal* 95, 6 (1986): 1087–184.

Eykholt, Mark. "Aggression, Victimization, and Chinese Historiography of the Nanjing Massacre." In *The Nanjing Massacre in History and Historiography*, ed. Joshua A. Fogel, 11–70. Berkeley: University of California Press, 2000.

Falk, Richard. "Redressing Grievances: Assessing the Nanking Massacre." In *Nanking 1937: Memory and Healing*, ed. Fei Fei Li, Robert Sabella, and David Liu, 10–32. Armonk, NY/ London: M. E. Sharpe, 2002.

Falk, Stanley L. *Bataan: The March of Death.* Norwalk, CT: Easton Press, 1989.

Felton, Mark. *The Devil's Doctors: Japanese Human Experiments on Allied Prisoners of War.* Barnsley, UK: Pen & Sword, 2012.

Fink, Udo. "Der Krieg und seine Regeln." In *Kriegsgreuel: Die Entgrenzung der Gewalt in kriegerischen Konflikten vom Mittelalter bis ins 20. Jahrhundert*, ed. Daniel Hohrath and Daniel Neitzel, 39–56. Paderborn, Germany: Ferdinand Schöningh, 2008.

Firipin "Jūgun Ianfu" Hoshō Seikyū Saiban, ed. *Firipin no Nihongun "ianfu": Seiteki bōryoku no higaishatachi.* Tokyo: Akashi Shoten, 1995.

Fleming, Gerald. *Hitler and the Final Solution.* Berkeley: University of California Press, 1984.

Fogel, Joshua A. *The Nanjing Massacre in History and Historiography.* Berkeley: University of California Press, 2000.

Freud, Sigmund. "Some Psychical Consequences of the Anatomical Distinction Sexes." In *Gender and Envy*, ed. Nancy Burke, 19–26. London/New York: Routledge, 1998.

Friedel, Anne-Sophie. "Editorial." *Aus Politik und Zeitgeschichte* 67, 4 (2017): *Gewalt:* 3.

Friedländer, Saul. *The Years of Extermination: Nazi Germany and the Jews, 1939–1945.* London: Harper Collins, 2007.

Fujiwara Akira. "The Nanking Atrocity: An Interpretive Overview." In *The Nanking Atrocity, 1937–38. Complicating the Picture*, ed. Bob Tadashi Wakabayashi, 29–54. New York: Berghahn Books, 2008.

Fukuchi Hiroaki. *Okinawa-sen no Onna-tachi: Chōsen-jin, Jūgun ianfu.* Naha, Japan: Kaifū-sha, 1992.

Furtado, Peter. "Nanking on Screen." *History Today* (2008): 7.

Galtung, Johan. "Gewalt, Frieden und Friedensforschung." In *Kritische Friedensforschung*, ed. Dieter Senghaas, 55–104. Frankfurt am Main, Germany: Surhkamp, 1971.

Garner, William T. *A Study in Valor: The Faith of a Bataan Death March Survivor.* Silverton, ID: Mapletree, 2010.

Gebhardt, Miriam. *Crimes Unspoken: The Rape of German Women at the End of the Second World War.* London: Polity, 2017.

Gerlach, Christian. *Extremely Violent Societies: Mass Violence in the Twentieth-Century World.* Cambridge, UK: Cambridge University Press, 2010.

Geyer, Michael. "Eine Kriegsgeschichte, die vom Tod spricht." In *Physische Gewalt: Studien zur Geschichte der Neuzeit*, ed. Thomas Lindenberger and Alf Lüdtke, 136–61. Frankfurt am Main, Germany: Suhrkamp, 1995.

Giacopassi, David J. and Karen R. Wilkinson. "Rape and the Devalued Victim." *Law and Human Behavior* 9, 4 (1985): 367–83.

Giles, Donald T., Jr. *Captive of the Rising Sun: The POW Memoirs of Rear Admiral Donald T. Giles, USN*. Annapolis, MD: Naval Institute Press, 1994.

Gold, Hal. *Unit 731 Testimony*. Tokyo: Tuttle, 1997.

Goldhagen, Daniel J. *Hitler's Willing Executioners: Ordinary Germans and the Holocaust*. New York: Vintage Books, 1997.

Gordon, Richard M. *Horyo: Memoirs of an American POW*. St. Paul, MN: Paragon, 1999.

Gottschall, Jonathan. "Explaining Wartime Rape." *The Journal of Sex Research* 41, 2 (2004): 129–36.

Gouri, Haim. *Facing the Glass Booth: The Jerusalem Trial of Adolf Eichmann*. Detroit: Wayne State University Press, 2004.

Gross, Raphael and Werner Renz, eds. *Der Frankfurter Auschwitz Prozess (1963–1965): Kommentierte Quellenedition*, 2 Vols. Frankfurt am Main, Germany/ New York: Campus, 2013.

Grosse, Christiane. *Der Eichmann-Prozess zwischen Recht und Politik*. Frankfurt am Main, Germany: Peter Lang, 1995.

Habermas, Jürgen. *Eine Art Schadensabwicklung*. Frankfurt am Main, Germany: Suhrkamp, 1987.

Hammer, Emanuel F. and Bernard C. Glueck, Jr. "Psychodynamic Patterns in Sex Offenders: A Four-Factor Theory." *Psychiatric Quarterly* 31 (1957): 325–45.

Hanyok, Robert. "Wartime COMINT Records in the National Archives about Japanese War Crimes in the Asia and Pacific Theaters, 1978–1997." In *Researching Japanese War Crimes Records: Introductory Essays*, ed. Edward Drea et al., 111–50. Washington, D.C.: National Archives and Records Administration for the Nazi War Crimes and Japanese Imperial Government Records Interagency Working Group, 2006.

Harris, James Russell. "The Harrodsburg Tankers: Bataan, Prison, and the Bonds of Community." *The Register of the Kentucky Historical Society* 86, 3 (1988): 230–77.

Harris, Sheldon. *Factories of Death: Japanese Biological Warfare, 1932–1945, and the American Cover-up*, revised edition. New York: Routledge, 2002 [1994].

Hata Ikuhiko. "From Consideration to Contempt: The Changing Nature of Japanese Military and Popular Perceptions of Prisoners of War through the Ages." In *Prisoners of War and Their Captors in World War II*, ed. Bob Moore and Kent Fedorowich, 253–76. Washington, D.C.: Berg, 1996.

Häussler, Matthias. "Grausamkeit und Kolonialismus. Zur Dynamik von Grausamkeit." In *On cruelty, Sur la cruauté, Über Grausamkeit*, ed. Jakob Rösel and Trutz von Trotha, 511–37. Cologne: Rüdiger Köppe Verlag, 2011.

Hayashi Hirofumi. "Disputes in Japan over the Japanese Military 'Comfort Women' System and Its Perception in History." *The Annals of the American Academy of Political and Social Science* 617 (2008): *The Politics of History in Comparative Perspective:* 123–32.

Hayashi Hirofumi. "Nihon no haigaiteki nashonarizumu wa naze taito shitaka." In *Kesareta sabaki: NHK bangumi kaihen to Seiji Kainyu Jiken,* ed. VAWW-NET Japan, 160–86. Tokyo: Gaifusha, 2005.

Hayashi Yōko. "Issues Surrounding the Wartime 'Comfort Women.'" *Review of Japanese Culture and Society* 11/12 (1999–2000): *Violence in the Modern World:* 54–65.

Helbing, Jürg. "The Tactical Use of Cruelty in Tribal Warfare." In *On Cruely, Sur la cruauté, Über Grausamkeit,* ed. Jakob Rösel and Trutz von Trotha, 149–73. Cologne, Germany: Rüdiger Köppe Verlag, 2011.

Henry, Nicola. *War and Rape: Law, Memory and Justice.* London/New York: Routledge, 2011.

Henson, Maria Rosa. *Comfort Woman: A Filipina's Story of Prostitution and Slavery under the Japanese Military.* Lanham, MD: Rowman & Littlefield, 1999.

Hicks, George. *The Comfort Women: Japan's Brutal Regime of Enforced Prostitution in the Second World War.* New York/London: Norton, 1995.

Higashinakano Shudo. *The Nanking Massacre: Fact versus Fiction—A Historian's Quest for the Truth.* Tokyo: Sekai Shuppan, 2006.

Higashinakano Shudo. The Nanking Massacre: Fact versus Fiction, A Historian's Quest for the Truth (Tokyo: Sekai Shuppan, 2006), Review by Bob Tadashi Wakabayashi, *Pacific Affairs* 79, 3 (2006): 526–27.

Hinton, Alexander L. *Man or Monster? The Trial of a Khmer Rouge Torturer.* Durham, NC/London: Duke University Press, 2016.

Hofmeister, Heimo. *Der Wille zum Krieg oder die Ohnmacht der Politik: Ein philosophisch-politischer Traktat.* Göttingen, Germany: Vandenhoeck & Rupprecht, 2001.

Hohrath, Daniel and Daniel Neitzel. "Entfesselter Kampf oder gezähmte Kriegführung? Gedanken zur regelwidrigen Gewalt im Krieg." In *Kriegsgreuel: Die Entgrenzung der Gewalt in kriegerischen Konflikten vom Mittelalter bis ins 20. Jahrhundert,* ed. Daniel Hohrath and Daniel Neitzel, 9–37. Paderborn, Germany: Ferdinand Schöningh, 2008.

Honda Katsuichi. *Chūgoku no tabi.* Tokyo: Asahi Shinbunsha, 1972.

Honda Katsuichi. *The Nanjing Massacre: A Japanese Journalist Confronts Japan's National Shame,* ed. Frank Gibney, transl. Karen Sandness. Armonk, NY: M. E. Sharpe, 1999.

Honda Katsuichi. *Sensō o okosareru gawa no ronri.* Tokyo: Gendai Shiryō Sentā Shuppankai, 1972.

Hora Tomio. *Nankin jiken.* Tokyo: Shin Jinbutsu Oraisha, 1972.

Howard, Keith, ed. *True Stories of the Korean Comfort Women.* London/New York: Cassell, 1995.

Hu, Hua-Ling. *American Goddess at the Rape of Nanking: The Courage of Minnie Vautrin.* Carbondale: Southern Illinois University Press, 2000.

Hu, Hua-ling and Zhang Lian-hong, eds. *The Undaunted Women of Nanking: The Wartime Diaries of Minnie Vautrin and Tsen Shui-Fang.* Carbondale: Southern Illinois University Press, 2010.
Imbusch, Peter. *Moderne und Gewalt: Zivilisationstheoretische Perspektiven auf das 20. Jahrhundert.* Wiesbaden, Germany: VS Verlag für Sozialwissenschaften, 2005.
Inaba Masao, ed. *Okamura Yasuji Taishō shiryō*, Vol. 1. Tokyo: Hara Shobō, 1970.
Jacob, Frank. 2013. "A Crossroad on the Way to Destruction: The Impossibility of the Madagascar Plan and the Destruction of the European Jews." Accessed October 10, 2017. http://www.academia.edu/7438779/A_Crossroad_on _the_Way_to_Destruction_The_Impossibility_of_the_Madagascar_Plan _and_the_Destruction_of_the_European_Jews
Jacob, Frank. "MacArthur's Legacy: Japan and the Early Years of the Cold War." In *Peripheries of the Cold War*, ed. Frank Jacob, 207–27. Würzburg, Germany: Königshausen & Neumann, 2015.
Jacob, Frank. "Von der Schande zur Überlebensstrategie—Unterfränkische Perspektiven auf die Prostitution, 1933–1945." In *Prostitution: A Companion of Mankind*, ed. Frank Jacob, 271–90. Frankfurt am Main, Germany: Peter Lang, 2016.
Jacob, Frank. "Banzai! And the Others Die—Collective Violence in the Rape of Nanking." In *Global Lynching and Collective Violence*, Vol. 1: *Asia, Africa, and the Middle East*, ed. Michael J. Pfeifer, 78–102. Urbana: University of Illinois Press, 2017.
Jeans, Roger B. "Victims or Victimizers? Museums, Textbooks, and the War Debate in Contemporary Japan." *The Journal of Military History* 69 (2005): 149–95.
Jiang, Sun. "The Unbearable Heaviness of Memory: Nanjing to Tao Baojin and His Descendants." *Chinese Studies in History* 47, 1 (2013): 53–70.
Jones, Adam, ed. *Gendercide and Genocide*. Nashville: Vanderbilt University Press, 2004.
José, Ricardo T. "War and Violence, History and Memory: The Philippine Experience of the Second World War." *Asian Journal of Social Science* 29, 3 (2001): *Special Focus: Contestations of Memory in Southeast Asia:* 457–70.
Kaitesi, Usta. *Genocidal Gender and Sexual Violence: The Legacy of the ICTR, Rwanda's Ordinary Courts and Gacaca Courts.* Cambridge, UK: Intersentia, 2014.
Kasahara Tokushi. "Remembering the Nanking Massacre." In *Nanking 1937: Memory and Healing*, ed. Fei Fei Li, Robert Sabella, and David Liu, 75–94. Armonk, NY/London: M. E. Sharpe, 2002.
Katz, Jack. "Criminal's Passions and the Progressive's Dilemma." In *America at Century's End*, ed. Alan Wolfe, 396–417. Berkeley/Los Angeles/Oxford: University of California Press, 1991.
Katz, Jack. "From How to Why. On Luminous Description and Causal Inference in Ethnography (Part 1)." *Ethnography* 4 (2001): 443–73.
Ka'tzetnik 135633. *House of Dolls*. London: Muller, Blond & White, 1956.
Keegan, John. *Die Kultur des Krieges*. Berlin: Rowohlt Verlag, 1995.

Keeley, Lawrence H. "War before Civilization—15 Years On." In *The Evolution of Violence*, ed. Todd K. Shackelford and Ranald D. Hansen, 23–31. New York: Springer, 2014.

Keen, Sam. *Fire in the Belly*. New York: Bantam Books, 1991.

Kimura Kuninori. "Nankin kōryakusen 'Nakajima dai 16 shidanchō nikki'." *Zōkan Rekishi to Jimbutsu* (1984): 252–71.

Kitamura Minoru. *The Politics of Nanjing: An Impartial Investigation*. Latham, MD: University Press of America, 2007.

Klatetzki, Thomas. "Cruel Identities." In *On cruely, Sur la cruauté, Über Grausamkeit*, ed. Jakob Rösel and Trutz von Trotha, 189–210. Cologne: Rüdiger Köppe Verlag, 2011.

Klute, Georg. "Kleinkrieg und Raum." In *Begegnungen und Auseinandersetzungen: Festschrift für Trutz von Trotha*, ed. Katharina Inhetveen and Georg Klute Rüdiger, 283–303. Cologne: Koppe Verlag, 2009.

Knöbl, Wolfgang. "Gewalt erklären?" *Aus Politik und Zeitgeschichte* 67, 4 (2017): *Gewalt:* 4–8.

Knox, Donald. *Death March: The Survivors of Bataan*. New York: Harcourt, 1981.

Koloma Beck, Teresa. "(Staats-)Gewalt und moderne Gesellschaft: Der Mythos vom Verschwinden der Gewalt." *Aus Politik und Zeitgeschichte* 67, 4 (2017): *Gewalt:* 16–21.

Kondo Shōji. "731 butai o meguru chōsa kenkyū no genjō." *Sensō sekinin kenkyū* 46 (2004): 38–43.

Korean Council. *Gangjero kkeulryeogan chosunin gunwianbudeul*, 5 vols. Seoul, Pulbit: 1997–2001.

Korean Research Institute for Jungshindae, *Halmeoni, gunwianbu ka muyeyo?* Seoul: Hankyeore Shinmunsa, 2000.

Kovály, Heda and Erazim V Kohák. *The Victors and the Vanquished*. New York: Horizon Press, 1973.

Kramer, Alan. "Mass Killing and Genocide from 1914 to 1945: Attempting a Comparative Analysis." In *Years of Persecution, Years of Extermination: Saul Friedländer and the Future of Holocaust Studies*, ed. Christian Wiese and Paul Betts, 213–32. London/New York: Continuum, 2010.

Kühl, Stefan. "Gewaltmassen: Zum Zusammenhang von Gruppen, Menschenmassen und Gewalt." *Aus Politik und Zeitgeschichte* 67, 4 (2017): *Gewalt:* 22–26.

Kühne, Thomas. *Belonging and Genocide: Hitler's Community, 1918–1945*. New Haven, CT/London: Yale University Press, 2010.

Kühne, Thomas. "Dämonisierung, Viktimisierung, Diversifizierung: Bilder von nationalsozialistischen Gewalttätern in Gesellschaft und Forschung seit 1945." In *Nationalsozialistische Täterschaften: Nachwirkungen in Gesellschaft und Familie* (Reihe Neuengammer Kolloquien 6), ed. Oliver von Wrochem, 32–55. Berlin: Metropol, 2016.

Kühne, Thomas. *The Rise and Fall of Comradeship: Hitler's Soldiers, Male Bonding and Mass Violence in the Twentieth Century*. Cambridge, MA: Cambridge University Press, 2017.

Kurahashi Masanao. *Jūgun ianfu mondai no rekishiteki kenkyū: Baishunfugata to seiteki doreigata*. Tokyo: Kyōei Shobō, 1994.

Kurbjuweit, Dirk. "Der Wandelt der Vergangenheit." *Der Spiegel* 7 (2014). Accessed September 25, 2017. http://www.spiegel.de/spiegel/print/d-124956878.html

Kuß, Susanne. *Deutsches Militär auf kolonialen Kriegsschauplätzen: Eskalation von Gewalt zu Beginn des 20. Jahrhunderts*. Berlin: Ch. Links Verlag, 2010.

LaForte, Robert S., Ronald E. Marcello, and Richard L. Himmel, eds. *With Only the Will to Live: Accounts of Americans in Japanese Prison Camps, 1941–1945*. Wilmington, DE: Scholarly Resources, 1994.

Langer, Lawrence. "Redefining Heroic Behavior: The Impromptu Self and the Holocaust Experience." In *The Holocaust: Origins, Implementation, Aftermath*, ed. Omer Bartov, 235–50. London/New York: Routledge, 2000.

Lawton, Manny. *Some Survived*. Chapel Hill, NC: Algonquin, 1984.

LeBlanc, Steven A. "Warfare in Human Nature." In *The Evolution of Violence*, ed. Todd K. Shackelford and Ranald D. Hansen, 73–97. New York: Springer, 2014.

Lee En-Han. "The Nanking Massacre Reassessed: A Study of the Sino-Japanese Controversy over the Factual Number of Massacred Victims." In *Nanking 1937: Memory and Healing*, ed. Fei Fei Li, Robert Sabella, and David Liu, 47–74. Armonk, NY/London: M. E. Sharpe, 2002.

"Letter Dr. Robert Wilson to His Family," January 28, 1938, Archives of the United Board for Christian Higher Education in Asia, Record Group No. 11, Box 229 Folder 3875: "College Files: University of Nanking: Correspondence: Wilson, Robert 1937." Accessed through The Nanking Massacre Archival Project, Yale Divinity Library, NMP0017.

Levering, Robert. *Horror Trek: A True Story of Bataan—The Death March and Three and One Half Years in Japanese Prison Camps*. Dayton, OH: Horstman, 1948.

Levi, Primo. *The Drowned and the Saved*. New York: Vintage International, 1988.

Levi, Primo. "Grey Zone." In *The Holocaust: Origins, Implementation, Aftermath*, ed. Omer Bartov, 251–72. London/New York: Routledge, 2000.

Li, Enhan. *Ribenjun zhanzheng baoxing zhi yanju*. Taipei: Taiwan shangwu chubanshe, 1994.

Lide, James. "Recently Declassified Records at the U.S. National Archives Relating to Japanese War Crimes." In *Researching Japanese War Crimes Records: Introductory Essays*, ed. Edward Drea et al., 57–78. Washington, D.C.: National Archives and Records Administration for the Nazi War Crimes and Japanese Imperial Government Records Interagency Working Group, 2006.

Lindenberger, Thomas and Alf Lüdtke. "Einleitung: Physische Gewalt—eine Kontinuität der Moderne." In *Physische Gewalt: Studien zur Geschichte der Neuzeit*, ed. Thomas Lindenberger and Alf Lüdtke, 7–38. Frankfurt am Main, Germany: Suhrkamp, 1995.

Lindner, Harold. "The Blacky Pictures Test: A Study of Sexual Offenders and Sexual Offenders." *Journal of Projective Techniques* 17 (1953): 79–84.

Lipstadt, Deborah E. *The Eichmann Trial*. New York: Schocken, 2011.
Longerich, Peter. *Der ungeschriebene Befehl: Hitler und der Weg zur "Endlösung."* Munich/Zurich: Piper, 2001.
Longerich, Peter. *"Davon haben wir nichts gewusst!" Die Deutschen und die Judenverfolgung 1933–1945*. Munich, Germany: Pantheon, 2007.
Lu, Suping, ed. *A Mission under Duress: The Nanjing Massacre and Post-Massacre Social Conditions Documented by American Diplomats*. Lanham, MD: University Press of America, 2010.
Lu, Suping, ed. *A Dark Page in History: The Nanjing Massacre and Post-Massacre Social Conditions Recorded in British Diplomatic Dispatches, Admiralty Documents, and U.S. Naval Intelligence Reports*. Lanham, MD: University Press of America, 2012.
Luo, Tsun-Yin. "'Marrying My Rapist?!': The Cultural Trauma among Chinese Rape Survivors." *Gender and Society* 14, 4 (2000): 581–97.
MacKinnon, Catherine A. "Turning Rape into Pornography: Postmodern Genocide." In: *Mass Rape: The War Against Women in Bosnia-Herzegovina*, ed. Alexandra Stiglmayer, 73–81. Lincoln: University of Nebraska Press, 1994.
Magilow, Daniel H. and Lisa Silverman. *Holocaust Representations in History: An Introduction*. London: Bloomsbury, 2015.
Mailänder, Elissa. "Unsere Mütter, unsere Großmütter: Erforschung und Repräsentation weiblicher NS-Täterschaft in Wissenschaft und Gesellschaft." In *Nationalsozialistische Täterschaften: Nachwirkungen in Gesellschaft und Familie* (Reihe Neuengammer Kolloquien 6), ed. Oliver von Wrochem, 83–101. Berlin: Metropol, 2016.
Marshall, Peter B. *1368 Days: An American POW in WWII Japan*, ed. Cynthia Marshall Hopkins. Eugene, OR: Luminate Press, 2017.
"Massacre Heritage." *Beijing Review,* June 19, 2014: 4.
May, Larry and Robert Strikwerda. "Men in Groups: Collective Responsibility for Rape." *Hypatia* 9, 2 (1994): *Feminism and Peace*: 134–51.
McCaldon, R. J. "Rape." *Canadian Journal of Corrections* 9 (1967): 37–59.
McCormack, Gavan and Hank Nelson, eds. *The Burma-Thailand Railway: Memory and History*. St. Leonards, Australia: Allen & Unwin, 1993.
McNamara, Dennis L. *Trade and Transformation in Korea, 1876–1945*. Boulder, CO: Westview Press, 1998.
Melber, Takuma. *Zwischen Kollaboration und Widerstand: Die japanische Besatzung in Malaya und Singapur (1942–1945)*. Frankfurt am Main, Germany: Campus, 2017.
Messerschmidt, Astrid. "Selbstbilder zwischen Unschuld und Verantwortung: Beziehungen zu Täterschaft in Bildungskontexten." In *Nationalsozialistische Täterschaften: Nachwirkungen in Gesellschaft und Familie* (Reihe Neuengammer Kolloquien 6), ed. Oliver von Wrochem, 115–33. Berlin: Metropol, 2016.
Metz, Karl Heinz. *Geschichte der Gewalt: Krieg—Revolution—Terror*. Darmstadt, Germany: Wissenschaftliche Buchgesellschaft, 2010.

Milgram, Stanley. *Obedience to Authority: An Experimental View*. New York: Harper Perennial, 2009.

Miller, Jean B., ed. *Psychoanalysis and Women: Contributions to New Theory and Therapy*. New York: Brunner/Mazel, 1973.

Min, Pyong Gap. "Korean 'Comfort Women': The Intersection of Colonial Power, Gender, and Class." *Gender and Society* 17, 6 (2003): 938–57.

Miyamoto Yuki. "The Ethics of Commemoration: Religion and Politics in Nanking, Hiroshima, and Yasukuni." *Journal of the American Academy of Religion* 80, 1 (2012): 34–63.

Mizobe Kazuto, ed. *Doku san ni: Mō hitotsu sensō*. N.p., 1983.

Mizutani Naoko. "Moto 1644 butai'in no shōgen." *Sensō sekinin kenkyū* 10 (1995): 56–65.

Moebius, Stephan and Angelika Wetterer. "Symbolische Gewalt." *Österreichische Zeitschrift für Soziologie* 4 (2011): 1–10.

Moolman, Benita. "The Reproduction of an 'Ideal' Masculinity through Gang Rape on the Cape Flats: Understanding Some Issues and Challenges for Effective Redress." *Agenda: Empowering Women for Gender Equity* 60 (2004): *Contemporary Activism?*: 109–124.

Morton, Louis. "Bataan Diary of Major Achille C. Tisdelle." *Military Affairs* 11, 3 (1947): 130–48.

Mummendey, Amélie. "Macht—Konflikt—Gewalt: Eine sozialpsychologische Betrachtung von Individuen und Gruppen." In *Krieg, Konflikt, Kommunikation: Der Traum von einer friedlichen Welt*, ed. Gerold Mikula and Manfred Prisching, 31–46. Vienna, Austria: Passagen Verlag, 1991.

Municipality of Nanking. *Nanking's Development, 1927–1937: Report on the Activities of the Municipality of Nanking*. Shanghai, China: Mercury Press, 1937.

Munn, Samson. "Post-Genocide and Related Dialogue: What Dan Bar-On Began." In *Nationalsozialistische Täterschaften: Nachwirkungen in Gesellschaft und Familie* (Reihe Neuengammer Kolloquien 6), ed. Oliver von Wrochem, 257–77. Berlin: Metropol, 2016.

Murphy, Kevin C. "'To Sympathize and Exploit': Filipinos, Americans, and the Bataan Death March." *The Journal of American-East Asian Relations* 18, 3–4 (2011): 295–319.

Murphy, Kevin C. *Inside the Bataan Death March: Defeat, Travail and Memory*. Jefferson, NC: McFarland, 2014.

Nakagaki Hideo. "Nankin jiken no shinsō." *Defense* 31, 1 (2012): 232–57.

"Nankin jiken kōkoku kyohi ha Chūnichi shinbun no jisatsu da." *Monthly Will* 91 (2012): 104–12.

"'Nankin Jiken' no kyokō ha kantan ni setsumei dekiru." *Monthly Will* 89 (2012): 76–81.

"'Nankin Jiken' shōko shashin ha subete decchiage." *Monthly Will* 89 (2012): 82–9.

Navarrete, Carlos David and Melissa M. McDonald. "Sexual Selection and the Psychology of Intergroup Conflict." In *The Evolution of Violence*, ed. Todd K. Shackelford and Ranald D. Hansen, 99–116. New York: Springer, 2014.

Nedelmann, Birgitta. "Gewaltsoziologie am Scheideweg: Die Auseinandersetzung in der gegenwärtigen und Wege der künftigen Gewaltforschung." In *Soziologie der Gewalt, Kölner Zeitschrift für Soziologie und Sozialpsychologie*, Sonderheft 37 (1997), ed. Trutz von Trotha, 59–85. Opladen, Germany: Westdeutscher Verlag, 1997.

Neitzel, Sönke and Harald Welzer. *Soldiers: German POWs on Fighting, Killing, and Dying.* New York: Vintage Books, 2013.

"Never Forget." *Beijing Review*, March 6, 2014.

Ng, Kevin. "The Great Denial: How Japan's Policies Regarding Its Actions during WWII Are Denying Both Its Own People and the World of Moral Betterment, Social Progress and Political Integration." *Chinese American Forum* 23, 3 (2008): 33–6.

Nishino Rumiko. *Jūgun ianfu: Moto heishitachi no shōgen.* Tokyo: Akashi shoten, 1991.

Norman, Michael and Elizabeth M. Norman. *Tears in the Darkness.* New York: Picador, 2010.

Ogawa Sekijirō. *Aru gun hōmukan no nikki.* Tokyo: Misuzu shobō, 2000.

O'Herne, Jeanne. "Reipu sareta onna no sakebi." *Fukuin senkyō* 5 (1993): 18–39.

Ongpauco, Fidel. *They Refused to Die: True Stories about World War II Heroes in the Philippines, 1941–1945.* Gatineau, Quebec: Lévesque, 1982.

Orywal, Erwin. "Krieg und Frieden in den Wissenschaften." In *Krieg und Kampf: Die Gewalt in unseren Köpfen*, ed. Michael Bollig, Erwin Orywal, and Aparna Rao, 13–43. Berlin: Dietrich Reimer Verlag, 1996.

"The Painful Memory." *Beijing Review*, May 28, 2009: 18–19.

Pak Kyeong-sik, *Chōsenjin kyōsei renkō no kiroku.* Tokyo: Mirai-sha, 1965.

Palmer, Craig T. "Human Rape: Adaptation or By-Product?" *The Journal of Sex Research* 28, 3 (1991): 365–86.

Pascal, Gerald R. and Frederick I. Herzberg. "The Detection of Deviant Sexual from Performance on the Rorschach Test." *Journal of Projective Techniques* 16 (1952): 366–75.

Paul, Gerhard. "'Dämonen'—'Schriebtischtäter'—'Pfadfinder': Die Wandlungen des Bildes von NS-Tätern in Gesellschaft und Wissenschaft am Beispiel von Eichmann und Höß." In *Nationalsozialistische Täterschaften: Nachwirkungen in Gesellschaft und Familie* (Reihe Neuengammer Kolloquien 6), ed. Oliver von Wrochem, 56–68. Berlin: Metropol, 2016.

Pinker, Steven. *Gewalt: Eine neue Geschichte der Menschheit.* Frankfurt am Main, Germany: Fischer, 2011.

Poncio, John Henry and Marlin Young. *Girocho: A GI's Story of Bataan and Beyond.* Baton Rouge: Louisiana State University Press, 2003.

Porter, Catherine. "New Light on the Fall of the Philippines." *Pacific Affairs* 27, 4 (1954): 370–77.

Powell, John W. "Japan's Germ Warfare: The U.S. Cover-up of a War Crime." *Bulletin of Concerned Asian Scholars* 12, 4 (1980): 2–17.

Prisching, Manfred. "Einleitung." In *Krieg, Konflikt, Kommunikation: Der Traum von einer friedlichen Welt*, ed. Gerold Mikula and Manfred Prisching, 11–16. Vienna, Austria: Passagen Verlag, 1991.

Qiu, Peipei with Su Zhiliang and Chen Lifei. *Chinese Comfort Women: Testimonies from Imperials Japan's Sex Slaves.* Oxford/New York: Oxford University Press, 2013.

Rabe, John. *The Good Man of Nanking: The Diaries of John Rabe.* New York: Vintage, 2007.

Rabe, John. *Der gute Deutsche von Nanking*, ed. Erwin Wickert. Munich, Germany: Pantheon, 2008.

Raitt, Fiona E. and M. Suzanne Zeedyk. "Rape Trauma Syndrome: Its Corroborative and Educational Roles." *Journal of Law and Society* 24, 4 (1997): 552–68.

Record of Middle China Operation, Chapter 1: From Incident Outbreak Until Nanjing Capture. The National Institute for Defense Studies, Ministry of Defense, Army Records, Shina (China), The China Incident (Second Sino-Japanese War), Shanghai, Nanjing, C11111991300.

Reemtsma, Jan Philipp. "Grußwort: Zur Eröffnung der Ausstellung über Fritz Bauer." *Einsicht* 12 (2014): 58–9.

Reid, T. R. "Japan Marks Day of Defeat by Facing Up to the Truth." *International Herald Tribune,* August 15, 1994: 5.

Resick, Patricia A. "The Psychological Impact of Rape." *Journal of Interpersonal Violence* 8, 2 (1993): 223–55.

Rieckenberg, Michael. "Auf dem Holzweg? Über Johan Galtungs Begriff der 'strukturellen Gewalt.'" *Zeithistorische Forschungen/Studies in Contemporary History* 5 (2008): 172–77.

Rittner, Carol and John K. Roth, eds. *Rape: Weapon of War and Genocide.* St. Paul, MN: Paragon House, 2012.

Röhl, John C. G. "Ordinary Germans as Hitler's Willing Executioners? The Goldhagen Controversy." In *Historical Controversies and Historians*, ed. William Lamont, 15–22. London: Routledge, 1998.

Rosenman, Stanely. "The Spawning Grounds of the Japanese Rapists of Nanking." *Journal of Psychohistory* 28 (2000): 2–23.

Rückerl, Adalbert. "Einleitung." In *NS-Prozesse: Nach 25 Jahren Strafverfolgung, Möglichkeiten—Grenzen—Ergebnisse*, ed. Adalbert Rückerl, 9–11. Karlsruhe, Germany: Verlag C. F. Müller, 1971.

Rückerl, Adalbert. "NS-Prozesse: Warum erst heute?—Warum noch heute?—Wie lange noch?" In *NS-Prozesse: Nach 25 Jahren Strafverfolgung, Möglichkeiten—Grenzen—Ergebnisse*, ed. Adalbert Rückerl, 13–34. Karlsruhe, Germany: Verlag C. F. Müller, 1971.

Russell of Liverpool, Lord [Edward Frederick Langley]. *The Knights of Bushido: A History of Japanese War Crimes During World War II.* Barnsley, UK: Frontline Books, 2013 [1958].

Sato, Gayle K. "Witnessing Atrocity through Autobiography: Wing Tek Lum's The Nanjing Massacre: Poems." *Inter-Asia Cultural Studies* 13, 2 (2012): 211–25.

Satoshi Hattori. "Dai-ichiji Sekaitaisen to Nihon rikugun no kindaika: Sono seika to genkai." *The Journal of International Security* 36, 3 (2008): 25–50.

Schauer, Frederick. "Causation Theory and the Causes of Sexual Violence." *American Bar Foundation Research Journal* 12, 4 (1987): 737–70.
Scheindlin, Noam. "Ignored Tragedy: The Moment Before Tears Would Well Up." *Chinese American Forum* 29, 2 (2013): 22–3.
Schimanski, Folke. "Zum Fortdauern nationalsozialistischer Ideologie in der Familie: Die Folgen von Täterschaft in der zweiten Generation." In *Nationalsozialistische Täterschaften: Nachwirkungen in Gesellschaft und Familie* (Reihe Neuengammer Kolloquien 6), ed. Oliver von Wrochem, 373–83. Berlin: Metropol, 2016.
Schlichte, Klaus. "Krieg und bewaffneter Konflikt als sozialer Raum." In *Kriege als (Über)Lebenswelten. Schattenglobalisierung, Kriegsökonomien und Inseln der Zivilität*, ed. Sabine Kurtenbach and Peter Lock, 184–99. Bonn, Germany: J. H. Dietz Verlag, 2004.
Schultz, Duane. *Hero of Bataan: The Story of General Jonathan M. Wainwright*. New York: St. Martin's Press, 1981.
Seifert, Ruth. "War and Rape: A Preliminary Analysis." In *Mass Rape: The War Against Women in Bosnia-Herzegovina*, ed. Alexandra Stiglmayer, 54–72. Lincoln: University of Nebraska Press, 1994.
Seifert, Ruth. "The Second Front: The Logic of Sexual Violence in Wars." *Women's Studies International Forum* 19, 1/2 (1996): 35–43.
Sellin, Volker. *Gewalt und Legitimität: Die europäische Monarchie im Zeitalter der Revolution*. Munich, Germany: Oldenbourg Verlag, 2011.
Sharatt, Sara. *Gender, Shame and Sexual Violence: The Voices of Witnesses and Court Members at War Crimes Tribunals*. Oxon, UK/New York: Ashgate, 2011.
Sheehan, James J. *Kontinent der Gewalt: Europas langer Weg zum Frieden*. Munich, Germany: C. H. Beck, 2008.
Shen, Qinna. "Revisiting the Wound of a Nation: The 'Good Nazi' John Rabe and the Nanking Massacre." *Seminar: A Journal of Germanic Studies* 47, 5 (2011): 661–80.
Smith, Bradley F. and Agnes F. Peterson, eds. *Heinrich Himmler: Geheimreden 1933 bis 1945*. Frankfurt am Main, Germany: Propyläen, 1974.
Smith, Kerry. "The Showa Hall: Memorializing Japan's War at Home." *Public Historian* 24, 4 (2002): 35.
Snyder, Timothy. *Bloodlands: Europa zwischen Hitler und Stalin*. Munich, Germany: C. H. Beck, 2011.
Sofsky, Wolfgang. "Gewaltzeit." In *Soziologie der Gewalt, Kölner Zeitschrift für Soziologie und Sozialpsychologie*, Sonderheft 37 (1997), ed. Trutz von Trotha, 102–21. Opladen, Germany: Westdeutscher Verlag, 1997.
Soh, Chunghee Sarah. "The Korean 'Comfort Women': Movement for Redress." *Asian Survey* 36, 12 (1996): 1226–40.
Soh, Chunghee Sarah. "Prostitutes versus Sex Slaves: The Politics of Representing the 'Comfort Women.'" In *Legacies of the Comfort Women of World War II*, ed. Margaret D. Stetz and Bonnie B. C. Oh, 69–87. Armonk, NY/London: M. E. Sharpe, 2001.

Soh, Chunghee Sarah. *The Comfort Women: Sexual Violence and Postcolonial Memory in Korea and Japan*. Chicago/London: The University of Chicago Press, 2008.
Steketee, Gail and Edna B. Foa. "Rape Victims: Post-Traumatic Stress Responses and Their Treatment: A Review of the Literature." *Journal of Anxiety Disorders* 1, 1 (1987): 69–86.
Stetz, Margaret D. and Bonnie B. C. Oh. "Introduction." In *Legacies of the Comfort Women of World War II*, ed. Margaret D. Stetz and Bonnie B. C. Oh, xi–xvi. Armonk, NY/London: M. E. Sharpe, 2001.
Stetz, Margaret D. and Bonnie B. C. Oh. "Teaching 'Comfort Women' Issues in Women's Studies Courses," *The Radical Teacher* 66 (2003): 17–21.
Stiglmayer, Alexandra, ed. *Mass Rape: The War against Women in Bosnia-Herzegovina*. Lincoln: University of Nebraska Press, 1994.
Stiglmayer, Alexandra. "The Rapes in Bosnia-Herzegovina." In *Mass Rape: The War against Women in Bosnia-Herzegovina*, ed. Alexandra Stiglmayer, 82–169. Lincoln: University of Nebraska Press, 1994.
Stobbe, Heinz-Günther. "Mitleid und Grausamkeit. Anthropologische Erwägungen in theologischer Perspektive." In *Begegnungen und Auseinandersetzungen. Festschrift für Trutz von Trotha*, ed. Katharina Inhetveen and Georg Rüdiger Klute, 377–92. Cologne, Germany: Koppe Verlag, 2009.
Sun Zhaiwei. "Causes of the Nanking Massacre." In *Nanking 1937: Memory and Healing*, ed. Fei Fei Li, Robert Sabella, and David Liu, 35–46. Armonk, NY/ London: M. E. Sharpe, 2002.
Suzuki Akira. *Nanjing dai-gyakusatsu no maboroshi*. Tokyo: Bungei Shunjūsha, 1973.
Suzuki Shogo. "The Competition to Attain Justice for Past Wrongs: The 'Comfort Women' Issue in Taiwan." *Pacific Affairs* 84, 2 (2011): 223–44.
Suzuki Yūko. *Chōsenjin jūgun ianfu: Shōgen Shōwa shi no danmen*. Tokyo: Iwanami Shoten, 1991.
Suzuki Yūko. *Jūgun ianfu, naisen kekkon*. Tokyo: Miraisha, 1992.
Szczepanska, Kamila. *The Politics of War Memory in Japan: Progressive Civil Society Groups and Contestation of Memory of the Asia-Pacific War*. London/ New York: Routledge, 2014.
Takashi Yoshida. *The Making of the "Rape of Nanking": History and Memory in Japan, China, and the United States*. Oxford/New York: Oxford University Press, 2006.
Tanaka Akira and Matsumura Takao, eds. *731 Butai sakusei shiryō*. Tokyo: Fuji Shobō, 1991.
Tanaka Hiromi. *Bei gikai toshokan shozo senryō sesshu kyū rikukaigun shiryō sōmokuroku*. Tokyo: Tōyō shorin, 1995.
Tanaka Hiroshi. *Chūgokujin kyōsei renkō shiryō*, 5 vols. Tokyo: Gendai shobō, 1995.
Tanaka Masaaki. *Nankin gyakusatsu no kyokō: Matsui taishō no nikki o megutte*. Tokyo: Nihon Kyobunsha, 1984.
Tanaka Yuki. "'Comfort Women' in the Dutch East Indies." In *Legacies of the Comfort Women of World War II*, ed. Margaret D. Stetz and Bonnie B. C. Oh, 42–68. Armonk, NY/London: M. E. Sharpe, 2001.

Tanaka Yuki. *Japan's Comfort Women: Sexual Slavery and Prostitution during World War II and the US Occupation*. London/New York: Routledge, 2002.

Tenney, Lester I. *My Hitch in Hell: The Bataan Death March*. Washington, D.C.: Brassey's, 1995.

Theweleit, Klaus. *Male Fantasies*, Vol. 1: *Women, Floods, Bodies, History*. Minneapolis: University of Minnesota Press, 1987.

Theweleit, Klaus. *Male Fantasies*, Vol. 2: *Male Bodies: Psychoanalyzing the White Terror*. Minneapolis: University of Minnesota Press, 1989.

Thornhill, Randy and Craig T. Palmer. *Rape: A Natural History of Biological Bases of Sexual Coercion*. Cambridge, MA: MIT Press, 2000.

Thornhill, Randy and Nancy Wilmsen Thornhill. "The Evolutionary Psychology of Men's Coercive Sexuality." *Behavioral and Brain Sciences* 15, 2 (1992): 363–75.

Trotha, Trutz von. "Zur Soziologie der Gewalt." In *Soziologie der Gewalt, Kölner Zeitschrift für Soziologie und*, Sonderheft 37 (1997), ed. Trutz von Trotha, 9–56. Opladen, Germany: Westdeutscher Verlag, 1997.

Trotha, Trutz von. "Gewalttätige Globalisierung, globalisierte Gewalt und Gewaltmarkt." In *Globalisierung der Gewalt: Weltweite Solidarität angesichts neuer Fronten globaler (Un-)Sicherheit*, ed. Matthias Kiefer and Johannes Müller, 1–26. Stuttgart, Germany: Kohlhammer, 2005.

Trotha, Trutz von. "Dispositionen der Grausamkeit: Über die anthropologischen Grundlagen grausamen Handelns." In *On Cruely, Sur la cruauté, Über Grausamkeit*, ed. Jakob Rösel and Trutz von Trotha, 122–46. Cologne, Germany: Rüdiger Köppe Verlag, 2011.

Trotha, Trutz von. "On Cruelty: Conceptual Considerations and the Summary of an Interdisciplinary Debate." In *On cruely, Sur la cruauté, Über Grausamkeit*, ed. Jakob Rösel and Trutz von Trotha, 1–67. Cologne, Germany: Rüdiger Köppe Verlag, 2011.

Tsao, Ruby. "Reflections: Why Did the Massacre Happen?" *Chinese American Forum* 30, 1 (2014): 27–30.

Tsuchiya Takashi. "Self Determination by Imperial Japanese Doctors: Did They Freely Decide to Perform Deadly Experiments?" Paper presented at UNESCO-Kumamoto University Bioethics Roundtable 2007, "Perspectives on Self-Determination," December 16, 2007. Accessed October 15, 2017. http://www.lit.osaka-cu.ac.jp/user/tsuchiya/gyoseki/presentation/UNESCOkumamoto07.html

Tsuneishi Keiichi. *Kieta saikinsen butai: Kantogun Dai 731-butai*. Tokyo: Kaimeisha, 1981.

Tsuneishi Keiichi, ed. *Hyōteki Ishii: 731 butai to Beigun chōhō katsudō*. Tokyo: Ōtsuki shoten, 1984.

Tsuneishi Keiichi. "731 butai: Sensō to gakujutsu wo kangaeru genten toshite." *Kagaku* 86, 10 (2016): 1044–48.

Tsuneishi Keiichi and Asano Tomizo. *Saikinsen butai to jiketsushita futari no igakusha*. Tokyo: Shinchōsha, 1982.

Urwin, Gregory J. "Foreword." In *Bataan: A Survivor's Story*, ed. Gene Boyt, xi–xxii. Norman: University of Oklahoma Press, 2004.

Urwin, Gregory J. *Victory in Defeat: The Wake Island Defenders in Captivity, 1941–1945*. Annapolis, MD: Naval Institute Press, 2010.

U.S. Government Printing Office, Study of Former Prisoners of War: A Study Prepared by the Veterans Administration Submitted to the Committee on Veterans' Affairs, United States Senate, June 3, 1980.

Vallacher, Robin R. and Christopher Brooks. "Adaption and Coherence: Evolutionary and Dynamical Perspectives on Human Violence." In *The Evolution of Violence*, ed. Todd K. Shackelford and Ranald D. Hansen, 187–209. New York: Springer, 2014.

Vautrin, Minnie. *Terror in Minnie Vautrin's Nanjing: Diaries and Correspondence, 1937–38*, ed. Suping Lu. Urbana/Chicago: University of Illinois Press, 2008.

Wagner, Bernd C. *IG Auschwitz: Zwangsarbeit und Vernichtung von Häftlingen des Lagers Monowitz 1941–1945*. Munich, Germany: K. G. Saur, 2000.

Wakabayashi, Bob Tadashi. "The Nanjing Massacre: Now You See It . . ." *Monumenta Nipponica* 56, 4 (2001): 521–44.

Wakabayashi, Bob Tadashi. "Kōkatsu na in'yō wo sareta rei toshite." *Shūkan Kinyōbi*, August 2, 2002: 68–69.

Wakabayashi, Bob Tadashi. "The Messiness of Historical Reality." In *The Nanking Atrocity, 1937–38: Complicating the Picture*, ed. Bob Tadashi Wakabayashi, 3–28. New York: Berghahn Books, 2008.

Wakabayashi, Bob Tadashi. "The Nanking 100-Man Killing Contest Debate, 1971–1975." In *The Nanking Atrocity, 1937–38: Complicating the Picture*, ed. Bob Tadashi Wakabayashi, 115–48. New York: Berghahn Books, 2008.

Watanabe Hisashi. "Nankin jiken no gyakusha wo saikō suru." *Chôkiren: Sensô no shinjitsu wo kataritsugu* 16 (2012): 85–103.

Watanabe Kazuko. "Militarism, Colonialism and Trafficking of Women: Military 'Comfort Women' Forced into Sexual Labor by Japanese Soldiers." *Bulletin of Concerned Asian Scholars* 26, 4 (1994): 3–16.

Watanabe Kazuko. "Trafficking in Women's Bodies, Then and Now: The Issue of Military 'Comfort Women'," *Women's Studies Quarterly* 27, 1/2 (1999): *Teaching about Violence against Women*: 19–31.

Waterford, Van. *Prisoners of the Japanese in World War II: Statistical History, Personal Narratives and Memorials Concerning POWs in Camps and on Hellships, Civilian Internees, Asian Slave Laborers and Others Captured in the Pacific Theater*. Jefferson, NC: McFarland, 1994.

Weaver, Gina Marie. *Ideologies of Forgetting: Rape in the Vietnam War*. Albany, NY: SUNY Press, 2010.

Welzer, Harald. *Täter: Wie aus ganz normalen Menschen Massenmörder werden*, 5th edition. Frankfurt am Main, Germany: Fischer, 2011.

Wildt, Michael. *Generation des Unbedingten: Das Führungskorps des Reichssicherheitshauptamtes*. Hamburg, Germany: Hamburger Edition, 2003.

Winter, Sebastian. "Lieber 'Kriegskind' als 'Täterkind'? Sozialpsychologische Überlegungen zur affektiven Funktion erinnerungskultureller Generationenkonstruktionen." In *Nationalsozialistische Täterschaften: Nachwirkungen in Gesellschaft und Familie* (Reihe Neuengammer Kolloquien 6), ed. Oliver von Wrochem, 102–12. Berlin: Metropol, 2016.

Winters, Peter Jochen. *Den Mördern ins Auge gesehen: Berichte eines jungen Journalisten vom Frankfurter Auschwitz-Prozess 1963–1965* (ZeitgeschichteN 14). Berlin: Metropol, 2015.

Wittes, Benjamin and Gabriella Blum. *The Future of Violence*. New York: Basic Books, 2015.

Wrochem, Oliver von. "Einleitung." In *Nationalsozialistische Täterschaften: Nachwirkungen in Gesellschaft und Familie* (Reihe Neuengammer Kolloquien 6), ed. Oliver von Wrochem, 9–16. Berlin: Metropol, 2016.

Yamada Otozō. *Materials on the Trial of Former Servicemen of the Japanese Army, Charged with Manufacturing and Employing Bacteriological Weapons*. Moscow: Foreign Languages Publishing House, 1950.

Yamamoto Masahiro. *Nanking: Anatomy of an Atrocity*. Westport, CT: Praeger, 2000.

Yan, Lu. "Nanjing Massacre as Transnational Event and Global Icon." *Harvard Asia Pacific Review* 9, 2 (2008): 67–70.

Yang, Daqing. "Convergence or Divergence? Recent Historical Writings on the Rape of Nanjing." *American Historical Review* 104, 3 (1999): 842–865.

Yang, Daqing. "Documentary Evidence and the Studies of Japanese War Crimes: An Interim Assessment." In *Researching Japanese War Crimes Records: Introductory Essays*, ed. Edward Drea et al., 21–56. Washington, D.C.: National Archives and Records Administration for the Nazi War Crimes and Japanese Imperial Government Records Interagency Working Group, 2006.

Yew, Hann-Shuin. "The Rape of Nanking: A Quest for Peace." *Chinese American Forum* 22, 3 (2007): 3–6.

Ying, Ding. "History in Japanese Eyes." *Beijing Review*, May 28, 2009: 18.

Yoshida Takashi. "A Battle over History: The Nanjing Massacre in Japan." In *The Nanjing Massacre in History and Historiography*, ed. Joshua A. Fogel, 70–132. Berkeley: University of California Press, 2000.

Yoshida Takashi. *The Making of the Rape of Nanking*. New York: Oxford University Press, 2006.

Yoshida Takashi. "Wartime Accounts of the Nanking Atrocity." In *The Nanking Atrocity, 1937–38. Complicating the Picture*, ed. Bob Tadashi Wakabayashi, 248–64. New York: Berghahn Books, 2008.

Yoshimi Yoshiaki, ed. *Jūgun ianfu shiryō-shū*. Tokyo: Ōtsuki shoten, 1992.

Yoshimi Yoshiaki. *Jūgun ianfu*. Tokyo: Iwanami Shoten, 1995.

Yoshimi Yoshiaki. *Comfort Women: Sexual Slavery in the Japanese Military During World War II*. New York: Columbia University Press, 2000.

Yoshimi Yoshiaki and Hayashi Hirofumi, eds. *Kyōdō kenkyū Nihongun ianfu*. Tokyo: Ōtsuki Shoten, 1995.

Yoshimi Yoshiaki, Nishino Rumiko, and Hayashi Hirofumi. *Koko made wakatta! Nihongun "ianfu" seido*. Kyoto, Japan: Kamogawa Shuppan, 2007.

Yoshimura Hisato. "Tōshō ni tsuite." (1941) In *731 butai sakusei shiryō*, ed. Tanaka Akira and Matsumura Takao, 225–88. Tokyo: Fuji Shuppan, 1991.

Young, Donald J. *The Fall of the Philippines: The Desperate Struggle against the Japanese Invasion, 1941–1942*. Jefferson, NC: McFarland, 2015.

Young, Shi, Margaret Stetz, and Bonnie Oh, eds. *Legacies of the Comfort Women of World War II*. Armonk, NY: M. E. Sharpe, 2001.

Young, Shi and James Yin. *The Rape of Nanking: An Undeniable History in Photographs*, second expanded edition. Chicago/San Francisco: Innovative Publishing Group, 1997.

Zhang Kaiyuan, ed. *Eyewitnesses to Massacre: American Missionaries Bear Witness to Japanese Atrocities in Nanjing*. Armonk, NY/London: M. E. Sharpe, 2001.

Zhu Wenqi. "On the Tokyo Trial and Nanjing Massacre." *Zhengfa Luntan* (Tribune of Political Science and Law) 5 (2007), 122–36, Review by Li Hongying, in *Chinese Journal of International Law* 7, 2 (2008), 571.

Index

Note: Page numbers followed by *t* indicate tables.

Abe Shinzo, 7
Acceptance of the past, 147
Agents provocateurs, 57
Albin, Rochelle Semmel, 56
American archives, 152 n.44
Anger, 145–146
Anti-Comintern Pact, 52
Apology. *See* Official apology
Appel, Benjamin, 98
Araki Sadao, 137
Arendt, Hannah, 12, 14, 25–27, 36, 147
Asaka Yasuhiko, 2
Asian Holocaust, 1. *See also* Rape of Nanjing
Asian-Pacific Feminist Coalition, 91
Asian Women's Fund, 71
Askew, David, 44
Assailants, 18. *See also* Perpetrators
Assault No. 1, 85
Atcherley, Harold, 123–127
Autotelic violence, 33–34

Bajohr, Frank, 26
Banality of evil, 25
Banality of violence, 35
Barbaric nature of Japanese militarism, 54

Barenblatt, Daniel, 134, 140, 142
Bartov, Omer, 35
Bataan Death March, 94–108;
  commemoration ceremonies, 97;
  defense and surrender, 98–99;
  delirium, 105; "Dyess Story," 99,
  100; dysentery, 105, 106; forms of
  victims' suffering, 100; insanity of
  POWs (soldiers who went mad),
  105; kindness of local population,
  96, 106; lack of water, 104; length
  of march, 97; map (Battles of
  Bataan and Corregidor), 95; reasons
  for actions of Japanese soldiers,
  107–108; space-time continuum,
  107, 108
Bates, Miner Searle, 51
Battle of Bataan (map), 95
Battle of Corregidor (map), 95
Battle of Manila, 5
Battlefield, 34
Bauman, Zygmunt, 15
Belief in a greater cause, 143–144, 147
Beriberi, 114, 127
Berry, Michael, 40
Bilibid Prison, 112
Biological determinism theory of wartime rape, 63

Biological warfare program, 132–144; acquiring more test subjects, 141; analogy to the Holocaust, 141–142; areas of experimentation, 138; burning of prisoners' bodies, 140, 141–142; civilian accomplices, 142, 143; classified documents, 135; dehumanization of victims/ dehumanizing effect on perpetrators, 141; deniers, 144; greater good of Japan, 143–144; group dynamics, 144; human guinea pigs, 132, 141; Ishii Shiro, 136–138, 142–143; lack of morals or ethics, 141; life expectancy of prisoners, 140; *maruta* (logs of wood), 139, 140; other chemical warfare units, 132; Pingfang facility, 139, 143; postwar complicity of Western allies, 134; space-time continuum, 140, 144; Unit 731, 132, 138; willful amnesia, 134
Biosocial theory of rape, 62–63
Black Sun: The Nanjing Massacre (film), 41
Bond, Susan B., 57
Bourdieu, Pierre, 157 n.40
Boyt, Gene, 103, 104, 106, 107, 112
Bridge on the River Kwai, The (film), 5, 123
British archival materials, 182 n.71
Brooks, Christopher, 14
Brothel system. *See* Comfort women system
Brutalization hypothesis, 33
Bumgarner, John R., 111, 112, 115, 116
Bureaucratization of killing, 25
Burgess, Anne Wolbert, 63
Burma-Siam (Burma-Thailand) Railway, 4, 5, 110, 123–128
Burning of prisoners' bodies, 140, 141–142

Burris, Charles W., 118
Buss, David M., 23

Camp Cabanatuan, 115–120
Camp O'Donnell, 112–114
Castration anxiety, 59
Centrist School, 42
Chai, Alice Y., 91
Chang, Iris, 1–3, 32, 40, 60, 70
Chang, Ying-Ying, 48–49
"Chaste"/ "unchaste" women, 58
Chemical warfare. *See* Biological warfare program
Chinese obsession of virginity, 66
"Chineseness" of victims, 66
Cholera Hill, 127
Civilian accomplices, 142, 143
Class B war criminals, 38
Collective violence, 24*t*
Collectivization through crime, 27
Colonial wars, 17, 22
Colonialism, 22
Comfort women system, 6–7, 67–93; age of prostitutes, 80; Allied prosecutors, 91–92; Asian-Pacific Feminist Coalition, 91; Chinese women and girls, 81–82; common soldiers, 89; condoms, 77, 86; crime against humanity, 88; deniers, 69, 78; dichotomy of comfort and rape, 85; Filipino redress movement, 97; four forms of victimization, 68, 86, 90; ideology of masculinity, 89; Korean redress movement, 70; Korean women and girls, 78–81, 90–91; local administrations, 69, 75; motives for establishing brothels, 65, 76; number of comfort stations, 74, 75; number of comfort women, 77; official apology, 71, 92; origins of the system, 72–75; pregnancy, 86; prices, 76; racist colonialism, 85; testimonies of comfort women,

82–88; ticket system, 76; treatment of women as military supplies, 77; types of military brothels, 75t; venereal disease (VD), 72–74, 76–77, 85; well-planned policy by top military leaders, 88; "wild" rape stations, 77; women subjected to torture, beating and stabbing, 85; Women's Voluntary Service Corps (WVSC), 92
Committee to Compile Materials on the Japanese Military's Nanjing Massacre, 40–41
Conciliation, 147
"Criminal's Passions and the Progressive's Dilemma" (Katz), 156 n.19
Cruelty, 16, 22
Cultural pathology theory of rape, 59, 60–61

Daws, Gavan, 120
Day of Valour, 97
Death March of Bataan. *See* Bataan Death March
Death Valley No. 1, 127
Deindividualization, 28
Demonizing image of perpetrators, 25
Deniers, 3, 27; biological warfare program, 144; comfort women system, 69, 78; prisoners of war (POWs), 110; Rape of Nanjing, 42, 44
De-Nur, Yehiel, 109
Destruction of compromising archival materials, 4
Dolgopol, Ustinia, 6
Don't Cry, Nanking (film), 41
Dower, John W., 9, 36, 37
Drea, Edward J., 3
Duntley, Joshua D., 23
Dyess, William E., 99–102, 104–106, 109, 113, 114
"Dyess Story," 99, 100
Dysentery, 105, 106, 116, 127

Eichmann, Adolf, 27
Enjoyment, 23
Epidemic Prevention and Water Purification Corps, 138
Epidemic Prevention and Water Supply Unit of the Kwangtung Army, 138
Extremely violent societies, 26

Factors affecting Japanese atrocities: anger, 145–146; Bataan Death March, 107–108; belief in a greater cause, 143–144, 147; group dynamics, 146; ideological preconditioning, 147; joy, 146; power, 146; prisoners of war (POWs), 130–131; Rape of Nanjing, 54–55
Farming project, 118–119
Felton, Mark, 132
Feminist theory of rape, 60
F-Force, 127, 128
Filipino redress movement, 97
Food-related hallucinations, 114
Formal apology. *See* Official apology
Forms of violence, 21, 23
Frankfurt Auschwitz Trials, 25
Friedländer, Saul, 2
Fujiwara Akira, 45

Galtung, Johan, 19
Gang rape, 64, 65
Gender, 23
Gendercide, 61
Geneva Convention, 19, 136
Genocidal rape, 61
Gerlach, Christian, 26
Giacopassi, David J., 58
Giles, Donald T., 121, 122
Glory, 19
Gold, Hal, 143
Goldhagen Controversy, 24, 158 n.72
Gordon, Richard M., 96
Gottschall, Jonathan, 56, 60, 62

Grandiosity, 35
Greater good of Japan, 143–144, 147
Group dynamics, 146; biological warfare program, 144; prisoners of war (POWs), 131; rape, 64
Group identities, 8
Guerilla warfare, 17

Habermas, Jürgen, 1
Harris, James Russel, 99
Hatoyama Ichiro, 3
Hayashi Hirofumi, 71
Hayashi Yoko, 84
Hell Ships, 5, 120–121
Henson, Maria Rosa Luna, 86–88, 97
Heydrich, Reinhard, 137
Hicks, George, 67
Hirohito, Emperor, 3, 135, 142
Hisao Tani, 38
Historikerstreit, 149 n.4
History of Violence (Metz), 15
History textbook controversy, 3
Holmstrom, Lynda Lytle, 63
Holocaust, 1, 24, 25, 149 n.4
Honda Katsuichi, 42
Honor, 19
Human guinea pigs, 132, 141
Human nature, 148
Human psyche, 32
Hunger (nutritional deficiencies), 114, 116, 117–118, 119, 126

Ianfu, 67
Ideological justification, 31
Ideological preconditioning, 147
Ideology of masculinity, 89
IG Farben, 142
Ikeda Hayato, 3
Illusion School, 42
Imbusch, Peter, 24
Individual violence, 24t
Inhumane nature of Japanese Army, 54
Institutionally determined practice of action, 26
International Convention for the Suppression of the Traffic in Women and Children, 71
Ishii Shiro, 135, 136–138, 142–143
Iwane Matsui, 38, 52

Japan Center for Research on War Responsibility, 5
Japanese feeling of superiority, 54, 62, 89
"Japanese History Textbook Controversy amid Post-War Sino-Japanese Relations, The," 151 n.25
Japanese soldiers, 36–37. *See also* Perpetrators
Japanese War Crimes during World War II, overview, 12
Japan's samurai culture, 107, 108
Jeans, Roger B., 40, 43
José, Ricardo T., 96
Joy, 146
Just war, 23

Kajiura Ginjiro, 134
Karasawa Tomio, 140
Kasahara Tokushi, 38, 54
Kato Norihiro, 7
Katz, Jack, 16
Keen, Sam, 65
Kenpeitai (military police corps), 130, 140
Kiichi Miyazawa, 71
Killing, 28, 34–35
Kim Hak-Sun, 86, 91
Kim Ok-Sil, 84
Kim Soo-Ja, 92
Kishi Nobusuke, 3
Knöbl, Wolfgang, 15
Koizumi Chikahiko, 137
Koloma Beck, Teresa, 20
Kondo Shoji, 135

Index

Korean Association of Pacific War Victims and Bereaved Families, 90
Korean redress movement, 70
Kovàly, Heda, 10
Kramer, Alan, 9
Kühne, Thomas, 25, 27, 35
Kunii Shigeru, 74
Kuss, Susanne, 17, 18
Kwangtung Army, 138

Langer, Lawrence, 9, 10
Last Rites for the dying, 117
Learned paradigms, 23
Leavelle, Charles, 100
LeBlanc, Steven A., 23
Lee Young-Ok, 91
Levi, Primo, 10, 11, 35, 129
Li Xiumei, 82
Lice and bedbugs, 113, 118, 121
"Little" perpetrators, 24, 35
Liu Mianhuan, 82
Luck, 129
Luo, Tsun-Yin, 66

MacArthur, Douglas, 3, 36, 97, 99, 135
MacKinnon, Catherine A., 64
Macro violence, 24t
Male-dominated Japanese society, 54
Manchuria (map), 68
Manchurian Incident, 72
Maps: Battles of Bataan and Corregidor, 95; Manchuria, 68; Pacific theater (1941–1945), 133
Marshall, Peter B., 121
Martial masculinity, 29
Maruta (logs of wood), 139, 140
Massacre in Nanjing (film), 41
Massacre School, 42
May, Larry, 64, 65
McCallum, James, 48, 49
McCoy, Melvyn H., 109
Mellnik, S. M., 109
Memories of cruelty and atrocity, 10

Metz, Karl Heinz, 15, 33
Micro violence, 24t
Milgram, Stanley, 30, 31
Military brothel system. *See* Comfort women system
Military culture, 9
Military training, 28
Min, Pyong Gap, 85, 91
Miyamoto Yuki, 41
Moolman, Benita, 61
Moral compass, 23, 35, 37
Moral no man's land, 35
Morality, 31
Morton, Louis, 99
Mosher, Donald L., 57
Motives, 16
Mukai Toshiaki, 45
Mummendey, Amélie, 26
Mun P'il-gi, 83
Murphy, Kevin, 94

Nagata Tetsuzan, 137
Nagatomo Yoshitada, 124
Nanjing Massacre, 1, 38. *See also* Rape of Nanjing
Nanjing Mausoleum, 2
Nanjing Memorial Hall, 40, 41
Nanjing Safety Zone, 46–49
Nanjing War Crimes Tribunal, 43
Nanking: Anatomy of an Atrocity (Yamamoto), 2, 39
National superiority, 54, 62, 89
Nedelmann, Birgitta, 21
Neitzel, Sönke, 33, 34
Ng, Kevin, 55
Nihon Tokoshu Kogyo, 142
Nishino Rumiko, 135
Noda Takeshi, 45

Obedience, 28, 30–31
Official apology: comfort women system, 6, 71, 92; crimes against humanity, 3
Okamura Yasuji, 72

Omnipotence, 35
Overkill phenomenon, 23

Pacific theater (map), 133
Pacific War, 69, 76
Pae Chok-kan, 81
Paranoid fears of nonexistent enemy, 23
Pathology theory of rape, 60–61
Perpetrator culture, 11
Perpetrators: abnormal as, 25; acclimatized to committing extreme forms of violence, 33; aspects to consider, 18; brutalization hypothesis, 33; cognitive factors, 25t; demonizing image of, 25; diverse images, 25; human beings who execute an act related to guilt, 27; Japaneseness, 37; killing, 28; low-rank, 24, 35; martial masculinity, 29; military training, 28; obedience, 28, 30–31; racial revenge, 37; racist perception, 36; situational factors, 25t; unexpected acts of humanity, 11; victims of bureaucratization of killing, 25
Pingfang facility, 139, 143
Pinker, Steven, 8
Poisonous gas. *See* Biological warfare program
Poncio, John Henry, 114, 118
Powell, John W., 135
Power, 22, 26, 146
Preconditioning, 147
Pressure cooker theory, 60
Prisoners of war (POWs), 5–6, 109–131; beriberi, 114, 127; Bilibid Prison, 112; Burma-Siam Railway, 110, 123–128; Camp Cabanatuan, 115–120; Camp O'Donnell, 112–114; death march (*see* Bataan Death March); deniers, 110; dysentery, 116, 127; factors affecting captor-captive relationships, 130; farming project, 118–119; F-Force, 127, 128; food-related hallucinations, 114; group dynamics, 131; Hell Ships, 120–121; hunger (nutritional deficiencies), 114, 116, 117–118, 119, 126; Japanese unpreparedness for so many prisoners, 120, 123; Kenpeitai (military police corps), 130; Last Rites for the dying, 117; lice and bedbugs, 113, 118, 121; luck, 129; Machiavellian plan to establish order by fear, 122; *New York Times* report (Jan/1944), 109; POW camps in Japan, 121–122; POW not viewed as honorable enemy, 114, 129; POW revenge on Japanese guards, 129; reasons for Japanese violence, 130–131; Rule of Ten, 113, 117; Seralang labor camp, 125, 126; space-time continuum, 119, 131; triangle of death, 119; volunteering for outside work security details, 119; Zentsuji Camp, 121–122; Zero Ward, 116
Prosecutor v. Yoshitada Nagatomo et al., 183 n.93
Prostitution, 65, 67. *See also* Comfort women system
Psychological reformation, 28
Pure evil, 12

Rabe, John, 52
Race war, 9
Racial revenge, 37
Racism, 76
Racist colonialism, 85
Racist ideologies, 28, 35
Racist perception, 36
Raitt, Fiona E., 56
Rape, 56–66; *agents provocateurs*, 57; biosocial theory, 62–63; "chaste"/"unchaste" women, 58;

"Chineseness" of victims, 66; cultural pathology theory, 60–61; defined, 57; feminist theory, 60; Freudian interpretation, 56; gang, 64, 65; genocidal rape/gendercide, 61; group dynamics, 64; national superiority, 62; omnipresence of rape in context of war, 60; power and domination, 57, 62, 63; pressure cooker theory, 60; rape trauma syndrome, 63; sex slavery, 65–66; strategic rape theory, 61–62; threat to military success as, 65; various sexualities of men and women alike, 64–65; venereal disease (VD), 65; youth of Japanese soldiers, 59

Rape of Nanjing, 38–55; basis of antipathy between China and Japan, 2; Centrist School, 42; Chang, Iris, 1–3, 40; class B war criminals, 38; Committee to Compile Materials, 40–41; deniers, 42, 44; documentary films, 41; Illusion School, 42; inhumane nature of Japanese Army, 54; Japanese feeling of superiority, 54; male-dominated Japanese society, 54; mass killings/sporadic killings, 53; Massacre School, 42; museums, 43; Nanjing Memorial Hall, 40, 41; Nanjing Safety Zone, 46–49; Nanjing War Crimes Tribunal, 43; nonhistorians, 42; number of victims, 44; overview, 38; reasons for use of excessive violence, 54–55; revenge, 54; sex slaves, 51; Shanghai incident, 45; textbook struggle, 43; what happened (events at Nanjing), 45–52; willful amnesia, 43

Rape of Nanking, The Forgotten Holocaust of World War II, The (Chang), 149 n.1

Rape trauma syndrome, 63
Red Swastika Society, 47
Remembering, 10
Research in War Responsibility, 5
Roman Empire, 19
Roosevelt, Franklin, 99, 109
Rosenblatt, Daniel, 143
Rule of Ten, 113, 117
Russian Revolution, 72
Russo-Japanese War, 6, 72, 80

Samurai culture, 107, 108
Sato, Gayle K., 1
Schauer, Frederick, 58
Schultz, Duane, 98
Second Sino-Japanese War, 2
Seifert, Ruth, 62
Self-defense, 16
Seralang labor camp, 125, 126
Sex slaves. *See* Comfort women system
Sexual violence, 58, 62. *See also* Rape
Shanghai Incident, 45, 73
Shigemitsu Mamoru, 3
Shinozuka Yoshio, 132, 141
Shit Creek, 127
Sino-Japanese War, 2, 69, 72
Social bonds, 29
Social norms, 15, 16
Sociopsychological group mechanisms, 26
Soh, Chunghee Sarah, 67–69, 74–76, 79, 84
Soldiers, 28–29. *See also* Perpetrators
Song Sin-Do, 84
Space-time continuum: anybody can be a perpetrator, 145; Bataan Death March, 107, 108; biological warfare program, 140, 144; comfort women system, 69, 90; female perpetrators, 27; legitimizing violence, 16, 19, 27; prisoners of war (POWs), 119, 131; rape of young women and girls, 69
Stetz, Margaret D., 91

Stiglmayer, Alexandra, 61
Strategic rape theory, 61–62
Strikwerda, Robert, 64, 65
Suzuki Akira, 43
Symbolic violence, 157 n.40

Takashi Yoshida, 52
Tanaka Masaaki, 43
Tanaka Yuki, 67, 72, 73–75, 77, 85, 89, 92
Tao Baojin, 48
Taylor, Preston, 117
Textbook dispute, 43, 70
Thai-Burma (Burma-Siam) railway, 4, 5, 110, 123–128
The why of Japanese atrocities. *See* Factors affecting Japanese atrocities
Theweleit, Klaus, 28, 29, 34, 62, 130
Three sparkles policy, 72
Togo Shigenori, 75
Tokyo War Crimes Tribunal, 3
Triangle of death, 119
Trotha, Trutz von, 8, 20–22
Tsuneishi Keiichi, 135

"Unchaste" women, 58
Unit 731, 132, 138. *See also* Biological warfare program.
Urwin, Gregory J., 110

Vallacher, Robin R., 14
Vautrin, Minnie, 48, 49
Venereal disease (VD), 65, 72–74, 76–77, 85
Victims' culture, 11
Violence: autotelic, 33–34; banality of, 35; cognitive factors, 25t; colonial wars, 17, 22; dynamic process as, 21; expression of specific human emotions, 16; form of historical experience, 14, 15, 33; form of social action, 15; forms of, 21, 23; gender, 23; hierarchy between perpetrators and victims, 20; individual vs. collective, 24t; initial mobilizers, 22; instrumental by its nature, 15; midwife of history, 14; modern society, 19–20; motives, 16; Nedelmann's five points, 21–22; overkill phenomenon, 23; paranoid fears of nonexistent enemy, 23; perpetrator memory, 33–36; power and, 26; *sine qua non* for victory, 35; situational factors, 25t; social act as, 21; social norms, 15, 16; sociology of cause, 20; space-time continuum, 16, 19; symbolic, 157 n.40; tool for one's own advantage, 14; war vs. peace, 34; WHO definition, 14. *See also* War

Wainwright, Jonathan Mayhew, IV, 98, 99
Wakabayashi, Bob Tadashi, 45
War: group identities, 8; memories of cruelty and atrocity, 10; moral no man's land, 35; morality, 31; noncombatants, 8; options available to people in general, 8; violence and, 34, 148. *See also* Violence
War crimes: political issue, 2; quarterly journal, 5; Soh's definition, 68–69; space-time continuum, 148
Wartime rape, 63. *See also* Rape
Watanabe Kazuko, 70
Waterford, Van, 110, 130
Welzer, Harald, 28, 33, 34
"Wild" rape stations, 77
Wilkinson, Karen R., 58
Willful amnesia, 43, 134
Willoughby, Charles A., 135
Wilson, Robert O., 50, 51
Women's Voluntary Service Corps (WVSC), 92
World War I, 6

Index

Yamamoto Masahiro, 2, 39, 40, 44
Yan, Lu, 45, 46
Yang, Daqing, 2
Yasukuni Shrine Museum, 3, 43
Yi Sang-Ok, 83
Yoshimi Yoshiaki, 71
Yoshimura Hisato, 143
Yoshio Shinozuka, 132, 141

Yoshio Tsuneyoshi, 112–113
Young, Marlin, 114, 118
Yun Jeong-Ok, 70
Yusasa Ken, 144

Zeedyk, M. Suzanne, 56
Zentsuji Camp, 121–122
Zero Ward, 116

About the Author

Frank Jacob is Professor of Global History (19th and 20th Centuries) at Nord University, Norway. He holds an MA in Modern History, Ancient History, and Japanese Studies (2010) from Würzburg University, Germany, and a PhD in Japanese Studies (2012) from Erlangen University, Germany. His research foci include Modern Japanese History, Global and Military History. Dr. Jacob is author or editor of more than 40 books and edits several journals, including Simon Fraser University Press's *Global Military Studies Review*. His latest monographs include *The Russo-Japanese-War and Its Shaping of the 20th Century* (Routledge, 2017) and *Gallipoli 1915/16: Britain's Most Terrible Defeat* (in German, Schöningh 2018). Among his (co)edited volumes are *Migration and the Crisis of the Modern Nation State?* (Vernon Press, 2018) and *Jewish Radicalisms: Historical Perspectives on a Phenomenon of Global Modernity* (DeGruyter, 2018). Jacob also published numerous source editions, including *George Kennan on the Spanish-American War: A Critical Edition of "Cuba and the Cubans"* (Palgrave, 2018) and the Kurt Eisner papers (10 volumes, 2016–2019). His current projects focus on Transatlantic Radicalism in the 20th Century and the Continuities and Discontinuities of Anti-Left State Violence in Japan (1868–1951).